DEPRESSION AND THE EROSION OF THE SELF IN LATE MODERNITY

DEPRESSION AND THE EROSION OF THE SELF IN LATE MODERNITY

The Lesson of Icarus

Barbara Dowds

Routledge
Taylor & Francis Group
LONDON AND NEW YORK

First published 2018
by Routledge
2 Park Square, Milton Park, Abingdon, Oxon OX14 4RN

and by Routledge
711 Third Avenue, New York, NY 10017

Routledge is an imprint of the Taylor & Francis Group, an informa business

British Library Cataloguing-in-Publication Data
A catalogue record for this book is available from the British Library

Library of Congress Cataloging-in-Publication Data
A catalog record has been requested for this book

ISBN: 978-1-78220-590-6 (pbk)

Typeset in Palatino
by V Publishing Solutions Pvt Ltd., Chennai, India

To the memoir writers and all who struggle with depression

It would be a poor result of all our anguish and our wrestling, if we won nothing but our old selves at the end of it—if we could return to the same blind loves, the same self-confident blame, … the same feeble sense of that Unknown towards which we have sent forth irrepressible cries in our loneliness.

George Eliot, *Adam Bede*

CONTENTS

PART II: THE SCIENCE OF DEPRESSION

PART III: A DEPRESSIVE SOCIETY? THE IMPACT ON THE SELF, RELATIONSHIPS, AND MEANING

ACKNOWLEDGEMENTS

Special thanks to Ted Dinan, Trish Morgan, and Paschal Preston for casting expert eyes over sections of the manuscript that are on the fringes of my own territory. In particular, Paschal and Trish's generosity and enthusiasm affirmed my confidence and gave me the energy to keep going with the long haul. I also want to thank former science colleagues Ann Burnell, Martin Downes, Christine Griffin, and Thecla Ryan for reading one of the chapters. I am grateful to my clients for all they continue to teach me, and to my friends and therapy colleagues Ger Byrne, Pauline Macey, Josephine Murphy, and Marjorie Travers for loving support. Also warm appreciation to Sean Rothery for his fellowship and coffees as we shared the progress of our respective manuscripts.

Most of all, as usual, I owe an enormous debt to Peter Labanyi: for particular help with the contents of Chapter Seven, for reading the entire manuscript multiple times, for access to the library of his mind, for his inspired discussions, suggestions, and corrections, and above all, for his Winnicottian mothering and mood regulation.

Finally I want to thank Rod Tweedy at Karnac for believing in this project, and for his continuing encouragement and support. And thanks also to Constance Govindin, Kate Pearce and the rest of the team at Karnac for all their help and assistance.

ABOUT THE AUTHOR

Barbara Dowds, B.A. Ph.D. MIAHIP MIACP SIACP SIAHIP, was educated at Trinity College Dublin (TCD) and had a previous career in science as a researcher at the University of California and TCD, and later as a senior lecturer in molecular genetics at Maynooth University. She completed her therapy training in 2002, and then began to work as a humanistic and integrative psychotherapist. Barbara taught on various psychotherapy trainings between 2003 and 2014, and was on the editorial board of *Eisteach* (the journal of the Irish Association for Counselling and Psychotherapy) for seven years. She is the author of numerous articles and of *Beyond the Frustrated Self* (Karnac, 2014). Barbara is currently in private practice as therapist and supervisor and presents postgraduate training workshops. For more information, see www.barbaradowds.net

INTRODUCTION

I was motivated to research and write this book because so much I read or hear about depression seems wrong, trivial, unhelpful, or unethical. It is wrong that something that is escalating so fast is put down to genetics or an imbalance of brain chemicals. It is trivial to focus therapy on symptoms, such as negative thinking, rather than the fundamental causes. It is unhelpful to put so much research funding into neuroscience, where the outcome is a detailed understanding of physiological mechanisms without any understanding of what it means to be a human being living in a particular society and time. It is unethical to condemn so many to drug dependence and the belief that they are defective, that the problem is theirs individually, rather than ours collectively. My aim is to explore the origins of depression and why the rate is increasing so rapidly (by twenty per cent per year according to Healthline—www.healthline.com). I began my inquiry by examining personal accounts of depressive breakdown for clues about possible childhood influences and adult triggers. I then moved on to search for socio-cultural changes that might make sense of what is an epidemic of depression, given that as many as one quarter of people in the developed world have a lifetime risk of suffering from it.

The lack of any biological marker or indeed of any simple cause of depression tells us that it is not a disease. Our genetic makeup changes slowly over thousands of years, so the current increase in depression cannot be ascribed to faulty genes. While the statistical rise may partly be due to greater reporting of the condition now that there are more effective treatments available, it must also be connected to changes in the way we are living. I have written this book to get people to wake up: living the way we increasingly are in the twenty-first century is endangering our psychic health. We are living in the best of times and the worst of times. Health, longevity, material well-being, and freedom of mobility and action are all unprecedented in the developed world. But our freedom is restricted to a limited range of things, many of which don't ultimately matter; and it is restricted to certain people, the poor or socially disenfranchised being excluded. Even for the privileged, there is a price to pay for our affluence and, like the obese on junk food diets who have vitamin deficiencies, we seem to be starving in the midst of plenty.

Depression may be experienced as intense sadness, or as numbness or emptiness, and it is usually accompanied by anxiety. It is a somewhat vague term that can refer to an ongoing minor experience of low mood or to suicidal misery. Deep depression manifests as a mood disturbance that equals or exceeds the diagnostic threshold for major depression. This is characterised by having five or more of the nine symptoms listed by DSM-5: depressed mood; loss of interest or pleasure; sleep disturbance; guilt; low energy; psychomotor changes; inability to concentrate; change in weight or appetite; self-harm or thoughts of death. Nevertheless, depression is a term that is applied to low mood that lasts from minutes to years, to the condition of a morose temperament or to a suicidal breakdown.

Subjectively there are vast differences in the depth and length of depressive episodes, but it appears that while the experience may vary enormously, the roots of shallow and deep depression are the same. There are common risk factors, and longitudinal studies show that low-grade depression is a precursor of deep depression (Rottenberg, 2014). Likewise, after recovery from the worst of deep depression, patients typically continue to experience periods of shallow depression. Patients with a clinical diagnosis of minor depression have the same kinds of symptoms as patients with major depression, but fewer of them; and the condition is persistent, with most people still experiencing some symptoms a year later. Alarmingly, the chances of developing major depression are five times greater if you already have minor depression (ibid.). For these reasons, this book does not distinguish between different degrees of depression.

The book opens with an analysis of twenty-one memoirs of depressive breakdown. The authors represent a subgroup of educated, ambitious, middle-class people who write as part of their professional lives and thus have the wherewithal to produce and publish a memoir. But while they are not therefore typical of the general population, it will become evident that not just the experiences but the underlying causes of their distress are representative of depression in our twenty-first century society. Recently I witnessed a distressing scene at a livestock market in a part of Romania where horses have not yet been replaced by tractors. A horse had been harnessed to a very large block of concrete to demonstrate its strength. The owner was whipping the horse, who frantically jumped and struggled but could not move the heavy weight. The man continued to beat the horse, refusing to accept that it was not strong enough for the job. In the same way have the memoir writers used the will to whip the embodied self. When we no longer have the strength, energy, or libido for a life task, when its goal is not authentically ours but imposed by pressure to perform, compete, and win, we give up and lie down: we become depressed.

What I am presenting here is a biopsychosocial model, which locates the origins of depression in interactions between childhood relationships, the social environment, and genetic vulnerability. Low mood has evolved as an adaptive response to conditions of helplessness, hopelessness, chronic stress, separation from or loss of a major attachment figure, indeed frustration of any of our fundamental needs. The variation in susceptibility to depression within a population can be partially attributed to genetic makeup, but only to a limited extent (heritability of thirty-seven per cent). Most of the roots lie in the childhood relationships that shape the formation of the self and determine our resilience to life's stressors, and in our adult socio-cultural conditions in the degree to which they generate or protect against stress, loss, and meaning. While it is impossible to prove causality in any simple way, one can build up evidence from many different angles and sources that weigh the probability. It is like showing that smoking increases your chances of getting lung cancer—there is not just one single piece of evidence. Some who smoke don't get cancer, but your chances are greatly increased if you do smoke. It will be clear on almost every page of the book that the division into chapters is artificial. It conceals the real and complex interactions between multiple internal and external influences from the distant or recent past. The division is merely a regrettable consequence of the need for linear presentation.

A major risk factor for depression is having a depressed mother, particularly in the early years, and we will see that in societies where the extended family or friends support the mother there is a lower incidence of postnatal depression. Anything that interferes with the maintenance of an attuned relationship between carer and child increases the child's risk for a range of emotional and developmental disorders. Such adverse circumstances include stressed caregivers, emotionally unavailable parents, or being reared in a crowded environment without attuned one-to-one care during the first two years of life. We will see that, alongside the rise in depression and anxiety, there are parallel increases in narcissism (i.e., deficient self-structure) and insecure attachment, especially the avoidant kind. My core argument is that we should view depression less as a mood disorder—which merely describes the symptoms—but more fundamentally as a disorder of the self. An empty, false, fragmented, or otherwise fragile self leaves us with an underlying depression that can be activated in later life by stress, loss, or even quite trivial setbacks.

The book explores the kinds of changes in society that may be impacting on our self-formation and relationships and that affect our sense of life as being meaningful—changes that leave us vulnerable to depression. I criticise our current society not just because I don't like many aspects of it, but, as I argue with the help of theories of human needs, because our most fundamental psychosocial needs are no longer being adequately met. Human beings cannot flourish without close, supportive relationships; without authenticity, stability, meaning, and a wider context for their lives; without contact with the earth; and without an understanding of what is going on around them. We cannot thrive when our sense of self is increasingly shrinking: from the connected self to the individualised self to the postmodern sense of self that is little more than a wilful ego masking an inner void.

Technology and a maximising ethos of productivity have disenchanted, de-souled the world and its inhabitants and reframed them as resources to be exploited. We are living in an atomised society that has been taken over by the toxic values of competitive individualism, where trusting, co-operative communities have been replaced by anxious monads in an endlessly mutating and inhospitable world. We instrumentalise both ourselves and others: instead of inhabiting the authentic self, young people increasingly perform a persona for the benefit of the ego and the audience, and simultaneously try to eliminate the competition. A population of narcissists, for whom a belief in entitlement far exceeds any sense of personal responsibility, exacerbates individualism and aggression—even hatred—in the public sphere, and adds to the erosion of the social matrix. Our culture is both impinging and abandoning (try ringing a help-line), at the same time too much (speed, stimulus, change, pressure) and too little (meaning, holding, support, boundaries, control over our own lives). We no longer know where power resides, but we suspect that actually nobody is in charge and that the system is out of control, in a chaotic state. Late modernity fosters vulnerability to depression because of the increasingly adverse conditions for raising infants, and at the same time provides adult triggers for depression in the shape of endemic stress and loss. Like Icarus, our late-capitalist society is flying too close to the sun. Increasing numbers of people who are compelled to buy into its ideology are crashing to the ground. Depression is the collapse of the individual with an over-reaching ego that rejects all authority (from the deeper self) other than its own will-driven impulses. Such an ego-focused identity may be free, but it is a negative freedom: from both containment and nourishment, from connection and therefore meaning.

It is beyond the scope of this book to compare different cultures and their experience of depression, and the reader is referred to other sources such as Eshun and Gurung (2009). Overall we can say that culture influences the awareness of symptoms, the meaning people attribute to their suffering as well as the treatments they may find useful and acceptable. Thus, depression is always embedded in a particular socio-cultural context, which may be a contributory or a protective factor. Low mood equips us to respond appropriately to our social and material environments and is therefore saturated with meaning. We ignore the messages of depression at our peril.

An important and relevant work was published just too late to influence and focus my book. *The Political Self: Understanding the Social Context for Mental Illness* argues that psyche and society are interpenetrated. Highlighted in particular is the prevalence of left hemisphere-mediated dissociation and dehumanisation of others under late capitalism.

Coming from quite different starting points from my own argument, the editor nevertheless reaches similar conclusions, while ending with an inspiring flourish (Tweedy, 2017). Symptoms (such as depression) "—the displayed symbols of our broken world—are … both indicators of sickness and also latent signs of life". Tweedy argues for a two-fold response: not just therapy taking note of social reality, but also "putting the psyche back in the world" (p. lii) and thereby de-dissociating and revitalising the public sphere.

PART I

THE SELF: EXPERIENCE AND DEVELOPMENT

CHAPTER ONE

The experience of depressive breakdown: the role of loss and rejection

Empirical research into depression provides data on demographics—how different population groups and locations fare in the depression stakes. It indicates possible causes of depression in generalised terms—childhood abuse, significant life events, etc. However, none of these statistics convey either the experience of depression or the sheer complexity of a life and how many possible causes interact to generate clinical depression. While the statistics may show that a certain percentage of those who have a major depressive episode go on to have second, third, and more relapses, they fail to reveal the systemic and relational aetiology and the dynamic process of a life punctuated by depressive illness. Thus, there is a real benefit in examining the first-hand descriptions of individual lives: what we lose in scale and rigour, we gain in concreteness, depth, and complexity, and we can generate fruitful hypotheses that might guide future population research.

In this section, I analyse twenty one memoirs of depressive breakdown, among which two (Jamison, Merritt) or possibly three (Wurtzel received varying diagnoses) of the authors suffer from bipolar disorder, and the remainder from unipolar depression. The writers comprise fourteen women and seven men, the same ratio in which depression occurs in the population at large. They include two poets, three fiction writers, two non-fiction writers, eight journalists (in a perilous profession), one biologist, three psychologists, one psychiatrist, and one actor. I have included one fictionalised account—Sylvia Plath's *The Bell Jar*—amongst them because it is so closely based on the author's own experience of depression and early suicide attempt. Depression amongst the poor and indigent does not benefit from this first-hand description, though Andrew Solomon (2014) has provided space for their voices in his book *The Noonday Demon*. Inevitably I am constrained by the narrative choices and level of self-awareness of the memoir writers: in particular, some tell us a great deal about childhood experiences, others very little.

I will attempt to categorise the memoirs according to my understanding of likely causes of the depression. I will leave the question of genetics aside in this section (but return to it in Chapter Six) and restrict myself to environmental causes, whether originating in childhood, familial, or societal culture, or current lifestyle causes. Any simple notion that depression is caused by an unhappy childhood where the individual suffers rejection, abuse, or neglect is confounded by some of these accounts. Some of these writers record happy, stable childhoods (e.g., McEvoy, Rice-Oxley, and Jamison), while several others had happy home lives but were unpopular at school. Some were much loved, but perhaps overprotected (e.g., Kelly), while others were rejected by a parent, had a depressed and/or anxious parent, an unstable childhood, or lived in a psychologically unhealthy culture (of guilt or lies, for example).

While I have categorised the memoirists according to one major factor contributing to their depression, most could have—and some have—been located under several different headings, showing how multifactorial the condition is. The various causative factors also interact with each other in complex ways. In addition to possible genetic vulnerability, depression usually has distal causes in childhood upbringing that result in a fragile sense of self (next chapter and later) and/or insecure relationships (this chapter and later). Proximal initiating events in adulthood, such as stress or loss, may then provoke an apparently mystifying slide into depression. At the same time, childhood primary causes and adulthood secondary triggers are not independent of each other. Loss in adulthood is far more likely to induce depression if it restimulates insecurity from the past. A stressful lifestyle in adulthood is often a defence against an empty sense of self or poor self-esteem, and cannot therefore be separated from the childhood origins of depression. The challenge for each individual is to make sense of what the depression is telling her and what needs to be attended to in therapy or in her manner of living.

Amongst the memoir writers who had other family members who suffered from depression, almost all of them attributed the family pattern to genetic propensity. This shows how the genetic/medical model has infiltrated the general population as well as the physicians and therapists with whom they come into contact. In reality, as we will see in Chapter Six, there is no way for the individual to know whether familial similarity originates in inherited susceptibility or in upbringing or other environmental patterns shared by the family members.

Depression as a result of loss or separation anxiety

Loss of major attachment figures

One theory of depression centres on our innate need for attachment to parents in childhood and the effect of the loss or absence of that secure base in generating grief and panic (see Chapter Five). It doesn't take a great leap to envisage depression and anxiety as more long-term versions of grief and panic. Indeed, while focusing on grief, Wolpert (1999) has suggested that depression is a "malignant" version of the normal response of sadness, analogous to cancer being a malignant form of normal cell division. The loss of an attachment figure such as a spouse, partner, or parent may provoke depression. But so too can other losses—of physical health, home, career, religious faith, or anything that we cathect and love that is of defining importance for our identity or security or that shapes the world as we know it. A world that is changing too rapidly will bring ongoing loss, which can contribute to depression, though more likely as a low-level, chronic condition.

We are more vulnerable to loss if we have not internalised a childhood experience of secure attachment. Such insecurely attached children are likely to carry that attachment pattern into adulthood: by not having a spouse or partner or by forming a physically or emotionally distant, unreliable, entangled, or abusive relationship. Insecure attachment can be generated by permanent or temporary loss (death, hospitalisation, etc.) of a parent in childhood, but it is more frequently driven by the inability of the parents to "read" the child in an empathic and attuned manner. A sensitively attuned parent consistently intuits and responds appropriately to the child's needs, with the result that the child feels safe and valued, learns to be aware of and respect his own feelings and needs, and to develop emotional intelligence towards himself and others. In the absence of this attunement, a child is emotionally abandoned, which generates both anxiety and depression. Emotionally or physically abandoned children may suffer severe separation anxiety which can continue into adult life. "No one told me that grief felt so much like fear," observed C. S. Lewis (2013, p. 1), reflecting the insecurity that accompanies loss of an attachment figure.

Bereavement that is not grieved plays a role in the aetiology of depression, as was the case for Sylvia Plath and her alter ego Esther Greenwood (childhood loss of her father), William Styron (whose mother died when he was thirteen), and Linda Gask whose father died just as her career in medicine was beginning. Styron—significantly given his failure to mourn—writes at arms-length in the third person about "the young person [who] … carries within himself … an insufferable burden of which rage and guilt, and not only dammed-up sorrow, are a part, and become the potential seeds of self-destruction" (1992, pp. 79–80). Lewis Wolpert (1999) was convinced that his depression was triggered by his new heart drug. His wife believed that it was linked with his planned trip to South Africa where his father had been murdered some years before, but Wolpert doesn't tell us enough about his feelings for us to know whether this was another case of unprocessed grief or horror (though the exclusion of these details is surely significant). Elizabeth Wurtzel's father disappeared for a few years during her adolescence, leaving his family of origin with instructions not to tell her of his whereabouts. This was both more and less cruel than a death: less in being reversible, more in the rejection explicit in his behaviour. The only way to recover from a loss, however many years have passed, is to grieve; only then can the individual move on.

Sally Brampton was a successful journalist, novelist, and magazine editor, including launch editor of *Elle Magazine*, who in her early fifties slid into three years of catastrophic depression. This included two suicide attempts, developing alcohol dependency, and three stays in psychiatric wards. The immediate triggers for her depression were a succession of losses: the (amicable) breakup of her marriage with the loss of home as well as husband; the loss of a job in which she did not fit; as well as falling in love with a man who reciprocated but was not available because of family responsibilities. She was physically unwell and lost a close friend (Paula Yates) to suicide as she sank deeper into depression. She tried two psychoanalysts but didn't like them or their approach and didn't continue with either. Three months passed before she was admitted to hospital with severe clinical depression. Her adult losses replicated her childhood experience of being repeatedly plucked from home as she followed her father to his latest work posting. As she says, "In all these losses, I had lost myself" (2008, p. 64).

Brampton's parents did not speak the language of emotions, so she learned to be stoic, without wants or needs—in other words, to abandon herself. Superficially she engaged with others, but she hid how she was really feeling. She noted: "my natural default setting is to shut down and hide … Yet every time I manage to answer the phone, make a call or seek out the company of friends, I am amazed at the way that my mood can lift" (ibid., p. 123). While she loved and felt loved by her parents, she didn't feel seen or understood. Developmentally, love is not enough for self-formation if mirroring, understanding, and attunement are lacking, as we will see in later chapters. Her mother probably suffered from dysthymia, a condition that has fewer or less serious symptoms than major depression, but which lasts longer. Sally realised in adulthood that her father almost certainly had undiagnosed Asperger's syndrome: he couldn't understand or empathise with body language or the more subtle emotions, interpret social cues, or grasp implied meanings. Thus Brampton's feelings were not recognised or addressed, and she learned to ignore and override them herself. It is not surprising that all three children (Brampton and her two brothers) of the family developed depression. There is a strong pattern of depression in Brampton's family: her mother, two brothers, and—since her book was published—a major depressive episode in her seventeen-year-old daughter. This could be due to either common genetic and/or environmental/upbringing factors.

The trigger experience for Andrew Solomon's first depressive breakdown was his much-loved mother's death, after a two-year battle with cancer when he was twenty-seven. Once there was no hope left for recovery she killed herself, having previously ordered the drugs with the help of her husband and sons. Solomon describes her suicide as the "cataclysm" of his life (2014, p. 268) despite admiring her for it and believing in what she did. After her death, he felt great sorrow and anger, but was not yet "crazy". He started psychoanalysis, and the following year he fell in love with a woman, but after a tumultuous two years they broke up by mutual agreement. When, a few months later, his analyst announced her plan to retire, he felt "devastatingly lonely and entirely betrayed" (ibid., p. 45), despite the fact that he had been considering ending the therapy anyway. These losses along with his coming out as a gay man (following the publication of his first novel with its overtly gay content) appear to have been the triggers that initiated his breakdown.

In reflecting on the sadness of his depression, Solomon speaks about the loss of past joy and love. He finds this loss harder to process than past pain. This he can leave in the past, but past joy is experienced as current loss: "The worst of depression lies in a present moment that cannot escape the past it idealizes" (ibid., p. 99). One could interpret this as an inability to live intensely in the present. Holding on to the past may block or compensate for the present, but one could alternatively argue that letting go of what is most precious in the past impoverishes the present. As Proust proclaimed wistfully: "the true paradises are the paradises that we have lost" (1992, p. 222).

Grief and bereavement

Freud (1917e) viewed melancholia as a consequence of inner conflicts between love and hatred for the deceased, which block the healthy process of grieving. Self-reproach on account of these unconscious feelings of hostility—repression of anger—was thought to generate depression. Karl Abraham and Melanie Klein both believed that internalisation of the loved one and conflict of emotions were intrinsic to all forms of mourning because our relations to others begin in ambivalence (Leader, 2009). Klein argued that once children move beyond the splitting defence, they see that the individual who has bad attributes also has good ones. This realisation is followed by a phase of sorrow and concern during which we attempt to make amends for our earlier aggression. This is the depressive position, and it must be re-entered again and again with every loss we suffer. If such early struggles have not been dealt with, depression is more likely to develop.

Loss may be followed by depression when the work of mourning is blocked. In Anita Brookner's novel *Latecomers* (1989), a Jewish boy Fibich is sent to England at the age of seven to escape the Nazis. His parents do not survive the death camps, and his last memory is of being torn from them at the train station and his mother fainting into his father's arms. He lives with anxiety and depression all his life: to make Brookner's favourite distinction, he is not viable, not compared to his robust and valiant friend Hartmann who vigorously repudiates the value of looking back on his very similar fate. Fibich is irresistibly drawn back into his past, but at the same time can remember virtually nothing of his childhood. It is only when, in his sixties, he *feels* the grief of separating from his parents and his burning regret that he didn't get off the train, that he can begin to inhabit the present, and the future in the shape of his son. In the very different responses of the friends to similar circumstances, we can see the role of temperament and earlier childhood experience in the kind of defensive stance adopted.

The grief from bereavement can feel just like depression. Within a six-month period, Tracy Thompson's father died and she also lost a long-term and a short-term boyfriend. "The grief I felt … was exacerbated by the extent to which I had depended on these men for my self-worth" (1995, p. 72). As she says perceptively: "That winter, grief made its acquaintance with depression, its near neighbor" (ibid., p. 73). Likewise, when Wolpert's wife died he felt as if his depression was starting again, but his daughter reassured him that he was confusing normal mourning with depression (1999). However, Rottenberg (2014) has argued persuasively that the two are indistinguishable except in the way society responds to them. While depression often remains a stigmatised secret, the healing of grief is supported by culturally based rituals and practical and emotional support. Likewise Keedwell (2008) notes that depression and grief overlap in terms of triggers as well as subjective experience and duration, and we will see in Chapter Five that low mood may offer a selective advantage to young animals undergoing the distress of separation from the mother.

Other losses

Loss of faith

In Bergman's grief-saturated film *Winter Light* and in some of the memoirs, loss of faith contributes to depression. Stephanie Merritt, for example, grew up in a family that were committed members of a conservative, charismatic, Christian church, which formed the centre of their social lives. At university she gave up attending church and had to cope with the disappointment of her parents and others in the church as well as with "a kind of severance that would not be easily mended" (Merritt, 2009, p. 73) because the loss simultaneously encompassed family, community, and a whole worldview and sense of meaning. She chose reason over faith, but at the time "had no sense of the cost involved" (ibid., p. 110). The depression returned the summer she graduated, when she felt expelled from the place where she had belonged, and had broken up with her boyfriend; she had no job, no future, no money, and nowhere to live. Her perception of the distance from her family generated by her departure from the church also meant she could not go home. While hanging round Cambridge in the months following, she slid into "anomie" (ibid., p. 78), often unable to get out of bed or see people, and cancelling job interviews. Though Merritt suffered an earlier depression before losing her faith, the two experiences have remained inseparable for her and she felt intensely pressurised to fit everything into this short and finite life now that there was no eternal hereafter.

After a brief four-year vocation Michael Harding, aged thirty-two, left the Catholic priesthood for the woman who became his wife, but he remained highly conflicted about the role of religion in his life. He became aware that "the priesthood embodied my depression. It was the glove. The wrap-around numb bodysuit that I put on to isolate myself from ordinary life" (Harding, 2013, p. 47). He still wanted to have the kudos of being a priest without losing the woman he loved, and felt guilty for forgetting "the ecstasy to be found in solitude and prayer" (ibid., p. 78). He calls his religious faith "magical thinking", a belief that a "benign deity" (ibid., p. 118) was intervening on his behalf to smooth and bless his path in life.

In his late fifties Harding suffered from depression linked to physical illness and a mid-life crisis. "In the months that followed, my usual melancholy transformed into a swamp of sorrow, an ocean of grief …" (ibid., p. 168). While he lay in bed for the four months of the worst of his depression, Harding's wife tended him and gave him the "time to mourn and to cry for all the lives that I had never lived. Before I let them go" (p. 188). He contemplated the role that faith played in his life and realised that it was fear that kept him clinging to religion, and at the heart of that "the fear of death that lies at the root of all depression" (p. 280). And he notes: "whether it's in society or in an individual, whether it is gradually over years or suddenly in trauma, the ebbing away of religious belief causes sorrow and loneliness, melancholy and depression" (p. 161). The book ends when he realises that he has "returned once more to a place of true belonging … When we abandon all our beliefs and dogmas that are spun in fear and when we release ourselves from anxiety and surrender to the mothering that the earth can do and the healing that time can offer" (p. 310). But while the beauty and transcendence that can be gained from the natural world may comfort, they cannot heal the original attachment wound or the shaming that formed the early origins of Harding's depression. The role of religious faith in protecting against depression is discussed further in Chapter Ten.

Loss of home

Any loss that affects our security or identity will cause sadness, fear, and a draining away of meaning. These include loss of home, as is the case for many stone-age tribes who lose their entire ecosystem, homeland, and village, the people often ending up in urban poverty, abusing alcohol in a vain attempt to ease the pain of their loss and subsequent depression. We see a Westernised end-of-the-world version of this in Lars von Trier's film *Melancholia*. One way of interpreting the film is that Justine's depression originates with her knowing that the Earth will soon be destroyed and that there is no point to anything: entropy rules. As the catastrophe draws closer, she is completely incapacitated and bed-ridden. However as she accepts what is to be, and perhaps in empathic response to her sister's panic, she emerges to take care of her young nephew, comforting him with a "magic" tepee in which the sisters and the boy await the end: even *in extremis*, the film tentatively affirms the power of human connection as exemplified by Justine's loving holding. *Melancholia* suggests a very current reason for depression: it is hard to keep back the belief that we are living in end times.

The foundation myth for the Western world is Homer's *Odyssey*, which describes being separated from home and trying to find the way back against repeated obstacles. Some of the origins of Brampton's depression go back to a childhood accompanying her family to six countries round the world to wherever her father's work with Shell took him. This included times when she couldn't speak the language of her school or when she was bullied. At the age of eleven she was sent for five miserable years to a boarding school in England. In all of these moves she lost friends, home, country, pets and eventually her family. "A part of my depression lies, I think, in my unanswered question: Where is home? I feel a sense, always, of trying to find my way back to a place that doesn't exist" (Brampton, 2008, p. 141). Brampton's question crystallises an experience that is increasingly widespread in our globalised and liquid world. Home is more than a house or a country: it is an inner state that can be achieved only when we have internalised a secure base. It is both nearer and further away for the emotionally homeless like Sally Brampton than they can know.

Separation anxiety/insecure attachment

Separation anxiety can arise in the context of a cold and rejecting mother, but also in more benign and loving environments. Daphne Merkin fits into the former category, so I have placed her story in the section on "Rejection, neglect, and abuse in childhood", whereas here I will look at two examples of separation anxiety in the context of loving mothering (Haig and Mabey), one in an emotionally neglected and culturally shaming environment (Harding) and one individual who was rejected by her mother but had an initially good but subsequently anxious attachment to her father (Gask). Interestingly, both Mabey and Harding replaced inadequate human relationships with an intense attachment to the natural world, and in Harding's case to religion—especially the sacred mother—as well (2013, 2014).

Matt Haig was twenty-four years old in 1999 when he had his first and worst depressive breakdown—accompanied by intense anxiety—while living in Ibiza. It took more than a year for him to recover somewhat, but even in 2002 he was still highly phobic with severe separation anxiety (He has been diagnosed with generalised anxiety disorder and panic disorder). He had another bout in 2008 and had still not fully emerged from his depression in 2013. His mother had postnatal depression after he was born, making him insecurely attached and predisposed to depression, as we will see in Chapter Four. He was always a sensitive child whose imagination created untold anxieties (e.g., that he would wake up unable to see or hear), despite having loving supportive parents. He suffered intense separation anxiety when his parents went out: even as a ten-year old he imagined his parents getting mugged, killed, or eaten by dogs (Haig, 2015). But, as he points out, he was unintentionally teaching himself to be anxious in all these fantasies, for "fear breeds imagination, and vice versa" (ibid., p. 62). As an adult too he suffered separation anxiety with respect to his girlfriend, Andrea, even three years after the onset of his breakdown. One day when Andrea was accompanying her parents to the hospital for her mother's cancer treatment Matt begged to be taken along. But he decided to challenge himself and stayed alone in the house. "The first ten minutes my heart was pounding. I could hardly breathe. Andrea was dead. Her parents were dead. I was picturing the car crash too vividly for it not to have happened. Then twenty minutes passed. I was going to die. There was a pain in my chest ..." (ibid., p. 155). It is likely that his mother's post-natal depression after his birth gave him an anxious start in life and that anxiety fed his imagination, which created further anxiety.

Richard Mabey was also a sensitive child: "I suppose these days I would have been diagnosed as suffering from separation anxiety or rejection sensitivity, from some quirk of genetics or upbringing. But what I learned was the power of psychosomatic illness—... to get you out of unpleasant situations, get you *home* (Mabey, 2006, p. 53). He had an alcoholic father and "subdued" mother (p. 54). He nursed his mother through her last years, and after she died he worked on *Flora Britannica*. When it was published, he was in his mid-fifties but still living in the family home, which he shared with his sister. As he puts it: "I'd failed to go through a crucial stage of development, had never 'fledged'" (ibid., p. 55). He realised that he had run out of excuses for not taking that next step.

After leaving hospital still depressed and anxious, he went to stay with friends. Here he was given simple physical tasks and taken out into the wild. He was passed from friend to friend along the Norfolk coast and slowly began to improve. He met Polly, the woman who would become his partner. She asked him to keep a diary during her absence on holiday. This writing seems to have been a turning-point: "not just a relief in itself, the regaining of an identity, but a key that began to unlock pieces of me that had been dormant for years ... it was regaining that imaginative relationship with the world beyond" that was his "nature cure" (ibid., pp. 63–64). Eventually Mabey was well enough to live independently and left his beloved Chilterns and the family home for an attic in the East Anglian Fens. Less than six months later he was making a living from bits of radio and journalism and "supporting [himself] emotionally to a degree [he] never had in his life before" (p. 102). He went out into the Fens and eventually back to "the high Chilterns and their free-wheeling kites" (p. 113). He found he was not assailed by uncomfortable associations or regrets for leaving; he appears to have challenged his fear of separation without a defensive cutting off from what he loved. He has finally made the transition from childhood to adult attachment figures and places.

Unlike Haig and Mabey who appear to have the ambivalent form of insecure attachment (they cling to the attachment figure/place), Michael Harding displayed the avoidant, distancing form with his partner, where he lived in defensive denial of attachment needs (See Chapter Four for a systematic exploration of attachment styles and their consequences). His mother rejected him for not being a girl. He cried throughout his childhood, but was grateful for what the world gave him. "[My mother] may not have hugged me very much, but she gave me buns and apple tarts. And beyond that, I found a deeper mother in the world and in all its loveliness" (Harding, 2013, p. 290). He grew up soothed and nourished by nature: the lakes and woodlands of his native Cavan in rural Ireland.

In his mid-fifties, despite having a good marriage, Harding longed to escape its confinements and live out the freedom of which he had not taken advantage in his youth. It was "a sort of mid-life crisis. A desperate attempt to be a hunter at last" (ibid., p. 189). He contrived an in-between life where he lived apart from his wife during the week in the town of Mullingar and returned to the family home in rural Leitrim at weekends. Ultimately he realised that his freedom didn't make him any happier, that "there is no escaping the interior weather" (ibid., p. 212): "I felt sad that men run away from their loved ones in late middle age because they are afraid of death, but can't admit it, and then they end up alone in self-centred apartments and die anyway" (p. 114). He questions why men flee from emotional intimacy and then "need God to sustain them in their isolation" (p. 133). One clue comes from a brief comment about his mother who was "always threatening to leave" (p. 28) and his knowledge as a child "that love was the most important thing in the world, and that eventually I must fall in love with someone who would never disappear" (p. 29). He grew up in a non-touching family where his "personal space was more secure than a military bunker" (p. 148). After he left the priesthood and spent a summer in Italy with his partner, he found the pleasure "unbearable" (p. 74). "When the ecstasy was over, I felt alone and guilty each time. Not on account of having made love, but on account of having heard such a deeply solitary music on the inside and having not been capable of sharing it" (p. 76). Later on a trip to an Indian monastery with his wife, away from the world of mundane responsibilities, he felt that loneliness he experienced in their years together dissolve. At home again, he reverted to his old armouring and isolation. During his mid-life crisis years "I paced hotel foyers, and I was close to other people without being intimate. In hotels I wrapped myself in solitude, as I stood in the lift or sauna or lounge bar. It was as if at last I were a ghost in the world of others" (pp. 198–199). Here he lived out his avoidant attachment, surrounded by people, but safely distanced from intimacy with them.

In a follow-up memoir written—significantly—while his wife was away for six weeks, Harding (2014) reveals a lot more about his relationship with his mother. He now suggests ambivalent attachment with his mother—and also quite a needy dependence on his wife—and it is not unusual for one type of insecure attachment to be overlaid with another (Pollard, 2005). The change in the overt attachment style may be due to his depressive breakdown and the therapy he attended subsequently, which would have made continued denial of his attachment needs untenable. We hear about his mother's emotional rejection: "'If you want to cry, go upstairs', she'd said coldly … I was twenty-six … and yet I craved for her to hold me" (Harding, 2014, p. 75). In old age his mother was depressed, but though she could be enlivened, even vivacious with others, she could not or would not respond to her son. We hear of his need to please her then: "'Please tell me what's wrong, Mammy. Did I do something to annoy you?' Over and over again" (ibid., p. 120). Two years after her death he was still grieving and empty and couldn't let go of her because he hadn't received what he craved: "I needed her to approve of me and hold me as a child likes to be held" (p. 256). He believed that "she burned with love for her children, but she failed us" (p. 237). Yet, elsewhere he mentions distinctly unloving behaviour: "she'd turn to the audience and say, 'Sure, he's useless'. A tiny smile on her mouth as she became empowered by disempowering me" (2014, p. 234). The rejection and abandonment began early: "When I was nine months old, my mother decided that she had had enough. So a nurse was engaged. A teenager of exquisite beauty and tenderness who would steal me a little bit of bread at night, to the back bedroom where my mother had abandoned me. I loved this nurse. … But then at four years of age, the nurse vanished. She was let go. … As a result, I grew up with the uneasy suspicion that the mundane world was never quite dependable, and that the people around me were not quite reliable" (2014, p. 184). With a mother so distant and dismissive, even cruel, and with an alternative early attachment figure vanishing, it's not surprising that Harding is trapped in chronic sadness with an intense yearning for holding.

Linda Gask is a psychiatrist who has herself suffered from depression. Her book (2015) looks back on a working-class childhood in the 1960s and 1970s, her student years in Edinburgh and her working life in various parts of England and Scotland. Her own story is interwoven with stories of patients with features similar to her own. Gask's account, unlike the other memoirs, does not convey the subjective texture of depression, perhaps partly because it was written decades after many of the depressive episodes.

Her vulnerability factors from childhood include a family life that was full of dramas and stress on account of her brother's extreme obsessive compulsive disorder. Both her parents suffered from anxiety, and Gask herself started experiencing the symptoms (fear that something terrible was about to happen, churning stomach, sweaty palms, severe headaches) in her early teens. Her mother was rejecting and Gask could never live up to her unreasonable demands: she could never be the person her mother wanted her to be and retain her sanity, so she felt "guilty just for being alive" (Gask, 2015, p. 74). She was close to her father in her early life, but her attachment to him became increasingly anxious during her teenage years. She got married during her student years as a way of controlling her anxiety.

Gask's early adult life had its share of stress and loss. In 1980, her father died suddenly during her first year of medical practice, and her anxiety about her new job and about the hours she would have to work caused her to push away her grief. A few years later, she failed her exam for membership of the Royal College of Psychiatrists, which severely shook her sense of identity, since she acknowledges that psychiatry was "the single most important dimension of [her] life" (ibid., p. 88). Six months later after some psychotherapy (with "E"), she retook the exam and passed it. She left her seven-year marriage for a lover of three months who ditched her the day after moving into what had been intended as their new flat: "Like many people who have difficulty trusting in the fact that they can be genuinely loved, I had chosen men who were not available" (ibid., p. 148). In her thirties, while still in therapy with E, she met the man who became—and remained—her second husband. This despite her attempts at self-sabotage. Then came further loss when E without warning took time off for depression and never returned (She later heard that he was fired from his job for misdemeanours, and subsequently took his own life). Years of psychodynamic psychotherapy, some cognitive behavioural therapy (CBT) and antidepressants for more than twenty years all contributed to maintaining a functional mood stability. Later periods of low mood that required a change in treatment were almost all triggered by work stresses.

These examples show how insecure attachment generates anxiety in childhood and fails to provide the kind of psychofeedback on which a strong sense of self is founded (see Chapter Four), thus leaving the individual with a sense of emptiness, and often worthlessness, and a difficulty with relationships that is transferred into adulthood.

Overprotected childhood

Anxiety can be created as much through overprotection as through neglect, as revealed in *Cotton Wool Kids*, a critique of anxious parenting (O'Malley, 2015). One of my clients had loving bohemian parents and a fun-filled childhood, but whenever she was away from home and missed her family, her parents immediately went to retrieve her. Like Richard Mabey, she never learned that she could survive and adapt to separation. When, as a driven young adult, she forced herself to take a major career promotion outside of Ireland, she promptly suffered such severe anxiety that she was forced to return, despite the blow to her ambitions.

As a child Rachel Kelly had a constant need for reassurance and thinks that her parents may have been *too* supportive. As she says: "Unwittingly, by scooping me up and trying to soothe my worries, they had deprived me of the chance to discover that I could handle my fears myself" (Kelly, 2014, p. 289). However, the circumstances may have been more complex. Her mother "reflected that she herself wasn't a very 'huggy' person, or one who verbalised her undoubted devotion and approval" (ibid., p. 305). Whether Kelly failed to pick up the approval or failed to become independent of its constant provision, she grew up to be a perfectionist and people-pleaser. She was "polite, non-confrontational, hard-working and dutiful" (p. 289), and hypersensitive. Her school was highly competitive but "short on praise" (p. 292), which only increased her need for reassurance.

Solomon's account of his childhood suggests a happy and secure background, though one wonders about the impact of being a "much scrutinized" child (Solomon, 2014, p. 41). The degree of his mother's vigilance is suggested by her taking him to a psychiatrist before he had even reached puberty to find out whether he was gay. Again, this excess attention to the child carries the message that life is hazardous and must be guarded against.

Of course, overprotective parents are not securely attached to their children, and their pattern of anxious attachment is inevitably passed on to the next generation.

Rejection, neglect, and abuse in childhood

The examples of Lauren Slater and Daphne Merkin were selected to illustrate this category because of the severity of their relational trauma and the early appearance of mental illness in their lives. Of course, others could be placed in this section too: Harding, with his rejecting mother; Mabey, with his alcoholic father; Lewis, controlled by her mother's moods; Thompson, with her very anxious mother and transgenerational trauma; and Brampton, with her depressed mother and Asperger's father and repeated loss of home. All of them had childhoods which left much to be desired, but all got through this period without major psychopathology, though with a vulnerability to depression that was then triggered by later events.

Merkin (2009) has a lifelong history of anxiety. In her family there were "too many children [six] and too little attention to go around". She had an abusive nanny, an oblivious father, and a mother she describes as mercurial and Germanically cold with whom she was pathologically enmeshed. By the age of eight, she was unwilling to attend school because of a mixture of fear and separation anxiety. By the age of ten she had been hospitalised because of crying all the time, and she set out on a forty-year journey through psychotherapy, while at the same time having been on psychotropic medication since her early twenties (she is now in her fifties). She was unable to sustain romantic relationships, had a tortured attitude towards work, and suffered a number of bouts of severe depression. She notes that "the quiet terror of severe depression never entirely passes once you've experienced it" (ibid.). Her 2007 bout was precipitated by the death of her mother two years earlier, the anticipated separation from her daughter who was going to college, as well as both therapy and romantic relationships going wrong for her. She was not helped by her usual medication or six months of attempted distractions. She was "inert but agitated", unable to get out of bed, to concentrate, to eat, or communicate; she was entering a "neurovegetative" condition (ibid.). She had reached the stage where the depression had taken on a life of its own outside the reach of her will. It was only her love for her daughter that stopped her from killing herself, and it was to protect herself against taking her own life that she checked into a psychiatric hospital.

Slater grew up in a wealthy Jewish family in Boston. Her mother was disturbed, anxious, and over-controlled, and was cold, cruel, and rejecting towards Lauren. The only times she treated her daughter well was when she was sick, so Lauren learned the lesson that illness was rewarded. Her parents' marriage broke down when Lauren was eleven, and her mother began to cut Holocaust atrocity stories out of the newspaper and forced her children to watch movies about the concentration camps. Mrs Slater installed an alarm system in the house along with panic buttons spaced thirteen feet apart on every wall. She was a woman who could not rest, who was full of anxiety and intensity, and her daughter learned that "life was to be lived at operatic pitch, that love came in notes so high they hurt the ears" (Slater, 1999, pp. 82–83). Unlike her sisters, Lauren was badly behaved, evoking hard slaps from her mother, being forced to drink detergent and subjected to other cruelties that her more favoured sisters were not. Her father was placid and sad, and distanced himself emotionally and physically from the family. Slater was fostered out at age fifteen, and in adulthood saw little of her parents.

Slater suffered from mental illness from an early age. She engaged in self-harm including cutting, anorexia, and attempted-suicide, spent time in psychiatric hospitals at ages fifteen, seventeen, twenty-one, twenty-two, and twenty-three (for depressive and anxiety-related problems with a poor response to medication), and received diagnoses of borderline personality disorder and major depression. "I had experienced my various psychiatric conditions as devastating. I was five and the roses were red claws. I was ten and terrified to go outside. I was twelve and grew so thin the bones turned to blades in my neck. In secret, on our wide porch, I cut myself. I knew nothing of pleasure" (ibid., p. 32). But, she wrote stories and poems from her eight inner voices: "three men who taunted me, three nine-year-olds, a girl trapped in a glass case and a blue baby, sometimes dead, sometimes dying" (p. 45).

Terrifying parents generate a disorganised attachment style that is indicative of relational trauma, as reflected in Lauren's imagery of claws and blades. The mothers of Merkin and Slater both sound quite disturbed themselves, and such trauma can be passed on intergenerationally, as we will see in Chapter Four.

Sexual abuse

Karla McLaren suffered from depression since childhood resulting from—as she realised only in adulthood—years of sexual abuse as a toddler. She managed to put up a functional front with emotional suppression, the dissociation defence characteristic of trauma and the massive internal clashes of a fragmented self. Crucially, she regards her depression no longer as an enemy, but as an ally that "sent parts of [her] soul away to safety while it held fast in a combat zone" (McLaren, 2015, p. 28). McLaren healed her depression by being willing to hear what it had to tell her.

Summary

The cases presented here all show difficulties in the early relationship with parents. They demonstrate that love is not enough—many of the memoirists came from loving and supportive homes. For if parents are anxious or depressed themselves, unavailable because of illness or other causes, or unable to create a secure, mirroring, or stable environment, the child learns that parents can't be relied upon and attachment is insecure. The parents' behaviour may be benign but over-vigilant or overprotective, or they may be neglectful, rejecting, or abusive. In any event the child will learn to be fearful and sad, while in the more negating and hostile relationships there will also be severe damage to self-esteem, indeed to the child's self. The resulting sadness and anxious attachment renders the individual more likely to suffer future relationship difficulties. It may also make them more sensitive to future losses: whether ones impacting on the self, such as the loss of loved ones, home, or belief systems; or losses such as blows to career prospects or to other aspects of an individual's identity.

Sometimes only one aspect of the child may be rejected—gender (Harding), sexuality (Solomon), or independence (McEvoy)—in an otherwise loving and accepting relationship, but this generates an intense conflict between need for the parents' love and approval and the need to express the authentic self, as we will see in the next chapter.

CHAPTER TWO

The many ways of not being true to yourself

"No bird soars too high, if he soars with his own wings"

—William Blake, *The Marriage of Heaven and Hell*

A theme that runs through most people's experience of depression is not knowing or not acting on who they are deep down and consequently living the life that suits their adaptive self, but not the true organismic self. Thus, individuals fit well into their society, family, and friends, but their core impulses die unborn because, as a result of disapproval or lack of recognition or mirroring in childhood, they are unaware who they really are, or are afraid to act on it. A client, Susan, has no ability to make subjective choices such as which path to follow on a walk or what food she is drawn to in a restaurant. When left to her own devices, she cannot make valid decisions because her tool for choosing is rational argument rather than embodied preference. Susan has spent her life trying to please others but has no idea how to tune into her own needs or motivations. In reality she doesn't even please others: what she does is predict and respond to what she presumes are their wishes or requests. The pattern began with her narcissistic, demanding mother, but Susan's compliance only makes her mother more tyrannical without making her happy. Inevitably Susan is highly anxious because she feels powerless and is terrified of making people angry or letting them down. But as she repeatedly discovers, she is constantly letting others down because they *all* want her attention and time in conflicting ways; she runs herself ragged but gets no thanks for her efforts. Susan's anxiety is telling her that her way of living is unsustainable. Depression and anxiety are calls to attend to the fragile nature of the self: in the words of Thomas Szasz, mental illness is "a *self*-promoting strategy" (quoted in MacLeod, 1996, p. 81; italics added).

Living out of the false or adaptive self (Winnicott, 1990) may be expressed as people-pleasing or, equally, as over-achievement to impress others or just to try to keep up or feel good enough. There are varying degrees of awareness of how we put this kind of pressure on ourselves, with Mary McEvoy and Andrew Solomon, as we will see, being conscious of the compromises they make with themselves, while Mark Rice-Oxley, Mary Manning, and others are apparently quite unaware.

Being wilful or reacting against other people's wishes and doing the opposite—a common adolescent trait—is not, of course, to act out of the true self. Being true to oneself requires embodied awareness of one's impulses as a starting point. But these primary expressions of the organismic self must then be built into a coherent individual philosophy if we are to move beyond being a mass of unrestrained impulse and acting-out. An important part of this philosophy is finding a balance between our own needs and those of others in our social environment. If we are to maintain connection with the true self as we progress through life, there is no alternative to embodied awareness of our reactions to life's situations: do I feel authentic, alive, safe, stimulated, stressed?; is this a meaningful and ethical course of action? In practice most of the authors of the memoirs are overstressed and have failed to tune into the effect of their lifestyle on their bodily experience. Gendlin's concept of the felt sense (1996) is crucial to developing and protecting the true/organismic self. Here we are at the border between the conscious and unconscious: through proprioception we can access the flow of sensations, particularly in the throat, chest, stomach, and abdomen. The felt sense we experience in any situation tells us how safe we feel, whether we are in a comfortable balance between stimulus and relaxation, whether our hearts are open or closed, whether our spirit feels free or oppressed. Many or most people are driven by the will or ego and attend only to feedback from the social world on how well they are performing in life—which in our current society amounts to how successful they are. They pay little attention to the feedback available from their bodies every moment of every day telling them how stressed they are or how meaningless much of their activity is.

The combination of being social animals and living in any kind of monoculture (whether that of communism or technocapitalism) generates intense pressure towards conformity and hence inauthenticity. The starved true self reacts with depression, while the part of us that needs the security of belonging to the tribe experiences anxiety because of the impossibility of living up to the expectations of others. We thus fail the demands of both the true self and of the adaptive (i.e., socialised) self.

Living from an external locus of evaluation—to use Carl Rogers' phrase (1967)—is stressful. But a particular manifestation of it—working too hard, whether to please or impress others or to run away from inner emptiness—takes stress to a higher level. Stress in itself also leads to high levels of anxiety as well as depression. This is true not only of psychological stress, but also of physical stress derived from lack of sleep, from infectious illness, or pain, as we will see in the next chapter.

High-achievers—and our society as a whole—struggle with what might be called the Icarus complex. In his flight to freedom, Icarus rose too close to the sun (the realm of the gods), the wax on his wings melted, and he plunged to his death. The depression of these high-flyers appears to arise, not out of failure, but out of success. As Mary Midgley observes, "Hubris calls for nemesis, and in one form or another it's going to get it, not as a punishment from outside but as the completion of a pattern already started" (2011, p. 148). Exhaustion from being driven by the unconstrained ego is one possible reason for this, but another is that individuals are unclear what it is they are really striving for. If they amass material wealth or public recognition, but what they really—though unconsciously—want is their parents' love and appreciation, no amount of money or fame will compensate for the real deficit.

Demanding parents and the adaptive self

For many of the memoirists there is a whole network of causes behind their episodes of depression and anxiety, but for two—Mary McEvoy and Gwyneth Lewis—the conflict between their own needs and the demands of their parents stands out. Compromising the demands of the true self to keep their parents happy (thereby protecting the attachment relationship) is the dominant reason for their depression.

McEvoy explicitly demonstrates the tension between two incompatible needs: the need to be true to herself and the need not to upset her parents. She is an actress who starred in the rural television series, *Glenroe* (Ireland's number one TV drama for much of the 1980s) for sixteen years as well as acting on stage during the annual three-month break from filming. A spirited girl who grew up on a farm in Co. Meath, McEvoy was the only child of older parents who, she felt, loved her and whom she loved. The problem was, what she wanted for herself and what they wanted for her were incompatible. In addition, what her father wanted of her and what her mother wanted were also incompatible (but that is my observation, not hers). Her father wanted her to remain at home and manage the farm and didn't hide his displeasure when, after she left school, she wanted to explore the world. Her mother wanted her to be as elegant and ladylike as she herself was. But Mary was "wild, unruly and questioning" as a child, while at the same time wanting to please her parents: "I began to try my very hardest not to be who I was. That created a terrible inner tension, which was the cornerstone for the depression that would develop later" (McEvoy, 2011, p. 19). Later, as an adult, the same belief that she wasn't good enough, alongside pressure from people in her Buddhist group, drove her to overdo her chanting practice so that it became like "a third job" (p. 78). The fear, shame, and guilt of her Catholic upbringing, especially in relation to women and sexuality, further damaged her self-esteem: "I picked up very early from the faith I was born into and wanted so badly to embrace, that to be a woman, was in some ways, a compromised position" (p. 91).

As a young adult, she was a natural Bohemian and fell into a life in acting that fitted her like a glove. She would like to have been slim, beautiful, and soignée, but wasn't gifted by nature with great beauty. Driven by guilt, she tried farming alongside her father for five years in her early twenties. But she became hypochondriacal, and depressed by her loneliness and isolation from like-minded people (actors and musicians) and from stimulating city life. At the same time, her spiritual seeking sank into inertia: "for the five years I was at home, there was no prayer, there was no meditation, there was no enjoyment in nature, there was a void inside me that I couldn't even begin to contemplate filling" (p. 74).

Despite her early success and fame, McEvoy couldn't separate from the world of her parents, to whom she returned every weekend. She ended up living two incompatible lives without being entirely comfortable in either. The extent of the split is illustrated by the fact that her father "never mentioned a word about *Glenroe*" (p. 61) and her mother's reaction to a play was to protest at McEvoy always getting parts with bad language. Her mother was also unhappy about her living with "a married man" (though he was already separated when they met but couldn't get a divorce in the Ireland of the day). But McEvoy was also aware that she herself kept her mother at a distance because of "the unbearable fear of losing her" (p. 103).

McEvoy's depression took the form of "crippling self-loathing" (p. 46), anxiety and restlessness. She believes that some people are born predisposed to the condition, and she has learned to contain her depression, but not to cure it. She treats the symptoms with medication, and Buddhist chanting at the beginning and end of each day prevents her condition from "spinning off into black infinity" (p. 85). McEvoy's underlying sadness never goes away, but she also has "moments of wonderful happiness and joy" (p. 163). She distinguishes between depression and unhappiness, and says that she was often depressed and happy (able to enjoy the current moment) at the same time.

One thing McEvoy is very clear about is that love (from her partner) cannot heal the condition, and this contention is echoed again and again in the other memoirs. I would conjecture that there are two reasons for this. One is that major depression, once established, takes on a life of its own independent of the initial trigger. The second reason is that with depression founded in inadequate parental relationships that fail in mirroring and acceptance—and so generate a false self—the individual has learned that "love" is deeply flawed and compromising. The "love" they have known is the very thing that has generated the depression in the first place, so they may be too confused or frightened to receive or even recognise authentic love. Love is not enough: it does not repair developmental deficits. What such people most need is accurate psychofeedback and acceptance of who they really are, not a projection on to them or a demand that they be someone else.

What is striking to me is McEvoy's lack of anger and her maddeningly moderate and balanced view, as if she still doesn't want to offend anybody. She never names her parents' selfishness, and while she externally lives the life she wants, she hasn't done the inner work that would fully give her the permission to do so and ease the conflict between her needs and the wishes of her parents. In therapeutic terms, she retroflects her anger into self-hatred instead of propelling it outwards to where it belongs.

For the poet Gwyneth Lewis, a depressed mother and an entangled relationship with her, along with the help of school bullying created a vulnerability to depression; while burnout provided the immediate trigger. However Lewis, in what is by far the most psychologically astute of the memoirs, sees the core of depression as "a civil war between your ego and your soul" (2002, p. 211). The will may be viewed as the executive of the conscious ego, and if the will gets too much of its own way and is out of line with the soul, depression is inevitable: "Severe depression happens to those so wilful that they ignore whatever goes contrary to their conscious desires" (p. 117). For a long time Lewis convinced herself that she had to choose between humanity (being unselfish, putting mother or boyfriend before her own needs, having children) and being a poet. "Experience had presented me with a choice between being acceptable to others and being a poet and I'd chosen the former" (p. 51). But as she recovered, she realised that what she believed about the effect of her writing on others was "just a form of my own doubt, a projection of my own uncertainty and laziness" (p. 176). She had to learn to pay no attention to the inner guilt voice and realise that she—and not her mother, former boyfriend, or others—was the one torturing herself. If you "learn to treat yourself kindly, … [depression] could and should change your life" (p. 183). This treating yourself kindly includes taking the trouble to develop embodied awareness and then acting on the messages received.

Cultures of conformity and inauthenticity

The difficulty of accessing the true self is particularly pronounced in conservative cultures, such as 1950s middle-class New England (the milieu for Plath's protagonist). But in contemporary times too, certain classes and locations place restrictions, particularly on women or anyone outside the norm, such as gay men. Thus Thompson refers to fake Southern politeness, emotional dishonesty, and the pressure of fundamentalist Christianity; Slater points to the emotional lies and denial in her Boston Brahmin home; while Andrew Solomon discusses the pressures against him living authentically as a gay man.

Sylvia Plath in her autobiographical novel, *The Bell Jar* reveals through her protagonist Esther Greenwood both the phoniness and the implicit limitations on the lives of women in the USA of 1953. "It was a queer, sultry summer, the summer they electrocuted the Rosenbergs, and I didn't know what I was doing in New York" (Plath, 1999, p. 1). This sentence, heavy with dread, opens the novel about Esther's/Sylvia's breakdown and early unsuccessful attempt at suicide. Esther is one of a group of young women who have won a writing contest for a fashion magazine. The prize is work on the magazine for a month in the summer along with tickets to a whirlwind of social and cultural events. Esther is a winner according to the values of the time and place, a scholarship girl in a first-class college who gets straight As and doesn't know what it is to fail. The world is at her feet, but she feels "very still and very empty" (ibid., p. 3) and is "letting up, slowing down, dropping clean out of the race" (p. 30). She simply can't go on doing what she "should". When her boss confronts her and asks what she wants to do with her life, Esther, who has hitherto always been clear about her career trajectory, finds herself saying she doesn't know. "I felt a deep shock, hearing myself say that, because the minute I said it, I knew it was true" (p. 34). But then for a moment, she recovers herself enough to try her "old, bright salesmanship" (p. 35).

In the background is the charade of her relationship with her boyfriend, medical student Buddy Willard, the son of a friend of her mother's. Mrs Willard's view of men and women is that a man is an arrow shooting into the future while his wife is the place the arrow shoots from, but Esther wants to shoot off in all directions herself. However, she feels no good at anything except "winning scholarships and prizes, and that era was coming to an end". It's like being "a racehorse in a world without race-tracks" (p. 81). Her mother is constantly urging her to learn shorthand and mould herself into her own and society's ideal of womanhood, and Esther knows that, after college, there will be no further opportunity for ambition, adventure, or self-esteem.

Likewise, there is the double standard that a girl will be good, won't have sex before marriage, but that a boy may explore. Early on we see some of Esther's inner conflict in her fascination with adventurous bad girl Doreen (who enthusiastically has sex the first night she meets a man), but her desire to be loyal to good girl Betsy.

Back home, she finds that she hasn't been accepted on to a writing course that she was relying on as a "bright, safe bridge over the dull gulf of the summer" (p. 121). Amid the loss of structure, the hollow core inside her knowing she is not capable of taking another course, the lethargy of the suburbs, and the anti-role model of Catholic Dodo Conroy with her six children (and pregnant again), Esther's depression deepens. She fails to move beyond page one of a novel and can't make progress with her impossible thesis on *Finnegan's Wake*. When she finally goes to a doctor, she hasn't slept for seven nights or washed her hair for three weeks because it seemed so pointless when it would just have to be done again. Eventually, she attempts suicide but is rescued while in a coma.

It seems clear that the cause of Esther's depression is the suffocation of her authenticity—and with it her life and vitality, sitting under the "glass bell jar, stewing in [her] own sour air" (p. 195). While skiing downhill for the first time, she plummets down "through year after year of doubleness and smiles and compromise, into [her] own past" (p. 103). Partly the problem was the brainwashing and expectation that her only possible role in life was to serve men. Partly the problem was that Esther was such a bobby-soxer, wanting everything and wanting to be the best at everything. "I saw myself sitting in the crotch of this fig-tree, starving to death, just because I couldn't make up my mind which of the figs I would choose. I wanted each and every one of them, but choosing one meant losing all the rest" (p. 81). She has ambition, but untethered to passion or a deeply held belief. She doesn't know who she is and therefore just wants everything that society holds to be desirable. In this sense Esther is a very modern figure and strongly resembles the contemporary narcissist who burns out from the stress of trying to have it all. She differs from them in assuming she has to make a choice, whereas our current belief is that it is actually possible to have it all. The twenty-first century person would grab all the figs and try to eat them simultaneously.

Tracy Thompson was born in 1955 and grew up in Atlanta, Georgia in a fundamentalist religious home with parents who had traumatic childhoods (see Chapter Four). At the age of thirteen, she was hit by a passing car and sustained major internal injuries and broken bones, but the worst damage as far as she was concerned was that to her face. In such a fundamentalist church and family there was no place for Thompson's anger, and it became so repressed that for years she was unaware of it. From then on—because of the accident and her failure to be the kind of Christian her mother and church prescribed—she felt herself to be defective.

Even before the accident, signs of chronic depression were emerging in frequent psychosomatic symptoms. She was filled with doubt about her religion and hated the emotional coercion to rededicate her life to Christ. She was riddled with anxiety and with a fury she could not express, and was reliant on sleeping pills for whatever few hours of sleep she could achieve. She went on to have her first major attack of depression as a college student at the age of twenty-one.

Thompson was brought up, as a Southern female, to stifle and dissemble her emotions, for example, "hiding hostility behind a smile, a razor hidden in a bouquet of flowers" (ibid., p. 182). Likewise, her neediness for male attention had some cultural roots and ensured that when she finally found a man, she clung to him and appeased him in response to his deeply controlling, emotionally abusive manipulations.

Born in 1962, Lauren Slater grew up as the middle daughter of a wealthy family in New England. (There was at least one brother as well). But all was not well in the family, particularly between Lauren and her mother. She grew up in "a home of lies and denial" (Slater, 1999, "Reader's guide", p. 8). She was unable to reach her mother. "Maybe she moved at a pace too fast. Maybe she was too sad. She held herself stiff, a lacquered lady" (Slater, 1999, p. 16). Her mother was a woman of "manic intensity" (ibid., p. 82). "Nothing was ever enough, for there was no plug to stopper the hole in her soul, no pill" (p. 9). In this culture, "women had hair as hard as crash helmets. In my world, girls did not play. They practiced: the piano, the flute, French, manners so refined they made all speech stiff". Slater loved getting sick as this brought out her mother's tenderness and "a release from the demands of an alienating world" (p. 22).

Though the causes of Elizabeth Wurtzel's depression are complex, the relationships with her parents being notably problematic, one of the aggravating factors was the American culture of enforced conformity (she was born in 1968). The trigger that began the depression may have been the eight-week-long camps to which Elizabeth was sent for five summers between the ages of nine and thirteen. "I can't get away from the suspicion that it all went wrong at summer camp, that my exile began back then, that my spirit broke—and broke and broke and broke—a little bit more with each passing summer. Everything ended for me at camp. I stopped writing my books, stopped collecting grasshoppers, stopped feeling pretty, … stopped wanting to know if there was a God … expelled from that place where possibility still existed" (Wurtzel, 1996, p. 70). The campaign to make her normal filled her with depression which turned into "a militant rage" (p. 77) by the age of thirteen.

Andrew Solomon's account of his childhood suggests a happy and secure home background. However, he was unathletic and unpopular in elementary school, where his interests in books, opera, and glamour were reviled. In later years, he attempted to overcompensate for what he perceived as a deficiency in masculinity, despite having built a large circle of enduring and rewarding friendships in high school and young adulthood. His mother was sufficiently concerned about his development that before puberty she took him to a psychiatrist and asked if Andrew was gay. His closeness to and dependence on his mother was complicated by her homophobia, and his greatest emotional challenge concerned his confused sexuality, which later resolved into a primarily homosexual identity.

His first novel had "explicit gay content, and surely that too was implicated in the breakdown" that followed. "Perhaps, indeed, that was the dominant anguish: the forcing myself to make public what I had so long immured in silence" (Solomon, 2014, p. 207). Furthermore, he was conflicted over his mother's valuing of reticence, causing him to feel guilty that he was posthumously defying her when he published his overtly gay novel. His mother had died from cancer three years earlier, and that bereavement as well as the loss of two romantic relationships through break-up contributed to his first depressive breakdown.

Like Mary McEvoy, Michael Harding is the product of the essentially tribal mindset of rural Ireland in the 1950s and 60s, where emotional separation and differentiation were perceived as a threat to one's own and the family's and community's very existence. It was a highly conservative culture of conformity to the demands of the Catholic Church, where guilt and shame were the main tools ensuring obedience. In his mid-fifties Harding became ill, and a bed-ridden depression followed. The inner conflict and melancholy he had felt throughout his life came to a head. Grief, shame, the belief that: "Year after year, I ruined my life. I made the wrong decisions. I took the wrong road" (Harding, 2013, p. 25).

We hear of the shame-making of his teacher, Father Fingers; his nameless grief, grieving the loss of his innocent childlike faith; shame at being a man; regrets for a life not lived; his shame amongst artists and writers at being a priest at the time when clerical sex abuse was being exposed in Ireland; his shame at being so inadequate as a priest: "But I felt only shame in their presence. I felt like a charlatan to be with them in their grief" (ibid., p. 51); shame at needing religion; later shame at his breaking-down body. As with McEvoy, the rage that could release him from shame and guilt is never contacted. They both take full personal responsibility for the inevitable results of a toxic culture.

External locus of evaluation, exhaustion, and burnout

Having an external locus of evaluation ("I am only as good as others perceive me to be") is a manifestation of the adaptive self, where your self-esteem derives from your perceived impact on the people around you. For Mark Rice-Oxley it is evident that severe stress was the immediate trigger for his depression, and at least some of this stress was generated by his people-pleasing habits. This tendency doesn't become clear in his memoir until he does schema therapy, the term schema referring to a cluster of "preconceived ideas, prejudices and reflexes" (Rice-Oxley, 2012, p. 265). He recognises himself as falling primarily into the schema of other-directedness, which includes the traits of recognition-seeking, subjugation, and self-sacrifice. These are both the cause and effect of a fragile sense of self: if you look to others for direction, it is because you are not in touch with the true self to guide your own life; equally, as long as you look to others you won't find your true self.

People-pleasing and competitiveness are often combined: both derive from an external locus of evaluation where your self-esteem rests in the hands of other people. In a culture where there is a widespread belief that everyone can become exceptional (Ehrenberg, 2009; James, 2008) and where there are no limits on what the workplace permits or expects its ambitious workforce to do, this other-directedness/competitiveness generates massive stress, which leads to depression. In Japan, overwork, depression, and suicide are seen as a chain-reaction (Kitanaka, 2011). Overwork stress appears to have been the immediate trigger for the depression of Mark Rice-Oxley, Rachel Kelly, Richard Mabey, Gwyneth Lewis, Martha Manning, Linda Gask, at least some of Tracy Thompson's breakdowns, as well as for the bipolar memoirists (below). In several cases (Lewis, Mabey, Rice-Oxley), it was when a long period of intense stress came to an end that breakdown occurred. Breakdown may then be seen as the organism grabbing the first opportunity for decompression, recovery, and homeostasis. Depression may be seen as shutdown, the opposite pole to prolonged and demanding overwork.

Undercurrents is a memoir by an American clinical psychologist in her mid-thirties who developed severe depression in 1990. Martha Manning's maternal grandmother suffered from depression: "the weariness, the passivity, the cutting-to-the-quick anger" (Manning, 1994, p. 26); and Manning's brother also "inherited the curse" (p. 179); so they shared familial contributions from genes or the shaping environment of childhood.

But it seems to me there was an adult lifestyle cause too. It is clear throughout the book that Manning is a doer, somebody who consistently takes on too much and then can't cope. She is even an overachiever at church: offering to write the litany of prayers, to teach Sunday school, and to sing in the choir, despite having a lousy voice. When she is trying to relax, even after she has recovered, she is still full of "shoulds", which suggests she hasn't learned what she needed to. On a retreat a year after her hospitalisation, she says: "I find myself growing quieter over time. But I'm so unused to it that I still equate it with being overwhelmed or depressed". She appears to be still running in spite of all she needed to learn. But on this retreat, she admits to all the "sand castles" (ibid., p. 193) she has worked so hard to build and how the waves sent them crashing into the beach. "I thought achievement was the express route to happiness and that competence guaranteed contentment. … When the career in academics was not as bright as I had hoped, a castle crumbled. When my work as a therapist became unsatisfying and draining, a castle crumbled. When I lost the babies I'd always assumed that I would have, a castle crumbled." She concludes: "You have to plant your feet solidly in the sand and get yourself anchored. … You loosen your body and you move with each wave" (ibid., p. 194). But she didn't convince me that she really understood or heeded the message. She refers several times to the emptiness that she feels within that no amount of work can fill and appears to understand that emptiness as a *symptom* of the depression, without considering that it might be the *cause*—that she isn't living her life from her true self. She tells her young daughter she doesn't know why the depression happened.

In 1986, Manning went to a therapist and stayed for three years. As someone who should know better, she has an astonishing view of therapy for therapists. "Being a therapist myself, I found consulting a therapist a bit strange at first. But I comforted myself that most therapists have their own psychotherapy at some point in their professional lives and rationalized that this was not some personal failing on my part, but rather a quest for personal growth. It was bullshit, but I find a self-deception quite comforting" (p. 57). It appears that personal therapy did not constitute part of her training, and it shows in her lack of self-awareness: the "constricted rigid vertical" perspective (p. 58) that was shaken up by psychotherapy. Or so she claims. But she says in August 1990: "Until last year I lived with the innocent arrogance that my life was the simple product of effort, will and design" (p. 97). She's a therapist and appears not to believe in the unconscious! It seems to me that her pattern of avoiding her inner emptiness through constant activity was still undented a year after she ceased therapy, which brings us to 1990 when a really major depression hit. She does acknowledge the need to "let go" (p. 104), but fears "drowning" if she does. She ends up going to a psychopharmacologist and another therapist (Kay Redfield Jamison) because her previous one was on sabbatical. Her book is frustrating in that she tells us nothing of her therapy with Jamison and little of her family history.

Overwork and stress were breakdown triggers for Kay Redfield Jamison and Stephanie Merritt who both have bipolar diagnoses (though Jamison is more delusional in her manic states), as well as for Elizabeth Wurtzel whose condition was diagnosed as depression initially, though she raises the possibility that she is bipolar. The distinction between unipolar and bipolar depression is not clear-cut: many diagnosed with depression have some bipolar tendencies (Nesse, 2009) and there is a continuing risk that unipolars will switch into bipolar illness (Young, 2009).

Jamison has done a great deal of research into bipolar disorder, has published extensively on the subject, and practices as a clinical psychologist and therapist—and yet reveals no insight into the environmental conditions that may have contributed to or triggered her own episodes of depression. Her family tree reveals repeated occurrences of "manic-depressive illness" (her preferred term) in the three generations of which she had knowledge in her father's family: this included her father as well as herself. She believes that genetics is the cause of bipolar disorder and that it should be treated with both drugs and psychotherapy—but she says little about the role of the latter.

Jamison reports a wonderful childhood in a military family. Her father was a meteorologist working for the US Air Force, so they moved round a lot, but he was twice posted to Washington DC and there was another family who moved with them—to Washington, then Tokyo, then Washington again—and from whom they were inseparable. She loved school and was successful academically, athletically, and socially. Her father was "ebullient, funny, curious" (Jamison, 1997, p. 15), her mother "kind, fair and generous" (p. 17), and she had a much-loved older brother as well as a sister with whom she had a difficult relationship. Her life fell apart in 1961 at the age of fifteen, when her father retired from the Air Force and took a job in Los Angeles. She missed Washington, her friends, boyfriend, and the close-knit military way of life, and found it hard to adapt to an academically competitive school where most of the other students had parents who worked in the film business. Her brother had gone to college before the move and her parents were now estranged, though still living together. Her father's moods began to dominate the household: especially his rage and screaming, which terrified her, and his immobilising depression, made worse by his beginning to drink heavily.

By the time Jamison was sixteen or seventeen, her moods too began to veer between elation and darkness. She had her first major attack of manic depression when she was a senior in high school. The mania in this first attack was relatively mild, but swung into a depression where she was unable to make sense of or remember what she was reading; she was exhausted, yet restless; lost all interest and confidence; and thought obsessively about killing herself. She had been brought up to keep her problems to herself, so she said nothing, put an enormous effort into not being noticed, and after a few months, gradually got better.

Her college years were a recurrent nightmare of dreadful, black moods interspersed with intoxicating, productive states. After two years, she took a grant-funded year out at the University of St Andrews in Scotland that "provided a gentle forgetfulness over the preceding painful years of [her] life" (ibid., p. 52). When she returned to UCLA, she once again had to work twenty or thirty hours a week in order to support herself financially, and she returned to the turmoil of her mood swings. How can we not conclude that overwork played a major part in her illness—at least as much as genetic makeup?

In graduate school (also in UCLA) she had a remission of her symptoms, which she says is common in the early years of this "disease". This coincided with being free of the "highly structured existence of undergraduate studies" (ibid., p. 57) and being married to a steady, kind, and gentle man, when she lived for a time in a safe and quiet world. After completing her PhD she was hired as an assistant professor in UCLA's department of psychiatry: "I had a glorious—as it turns out, too glorious—summer, and within three months of becoming a professor, I was ravingly psychotic" (p. 63). That summer, "a lack of sleep, a deluge of work and exquisitely vulnerable genes eventually took me to the back of beyond, past my familiar levels of exuberance and into florid madness" (p. 70). Her work pace was feverish; she craved excitement and rebelled against her husband's stability so that the marriage began to fall apart; she went on a spending spree; became delusional; began to hallucinate; and was agitated, paranoid, and physically violent. Her thoughts were so fast that she couldn't remember the beginning of a sentence halfway through. Finally, she sought help from a colleague and was prescribed lithium and told to take a short time off work. Again, Jamison doesn't make any connections between her feelings—about becoming a professor or the breakdown of her marriage and dating other men—and the onset of her mania. If anything, she sees such possible triggers as excuses to avoid the "truth" that she had a medical illness. She appears to see these as alternative, rather than mutually reinforcing explanations. Despite her apparent resistance to environmental triggers, she believes in the importance of psychotherapy in making sense of what was happening and in easing her back into reality.

Transition from high to low pressure—the aftermath of stress

Most of us are familiar with the phenomenon of staying well for as long as we have work and other pressures that demand our attention, but as soon as the Christmas holiday arrives, we succumb to flu. Our bodies keep going in the face of external emergency, but when the crisis is over, we withdraw and repair. This makes adaptive sense: we cope with external threats that occasion acute or chronic stress, and it is only when the danger is past that we can collapse. Many of the episodes of major depression were triggered, not during periods of high stress, but *after* the stress lifted.

Mark Rice-Oxley describes a pretty idyllic 1970s childhood in rural Hampshire in a loving and fun family, spending a lot of time outdoors in games of the imagination and long walks. Early on he is aware of two sub-personalities: the adventurous, playful Roxy and the cautious, dutiful Marko. He had a period of freedom, adventure, and hard-drinking sociability working abroad in his twenties as a reporter and foreign correspondent. By his mid-thirties he had achieved all he wanted in his life: a highly prized staff job on the *Guardian* newspaper, a wife he loved, and three healthy children. But in the months leading up to and after his fortieth birthday, he found himself sliding into depression, with its symptoms of "loss of weight, energy, patience, appetite, concentration and joy; ... panic attacks, rumination, headaches, stomach troubles and cognitive dissonance". The reader is initially confounded by the question he asks himself: "What do I have to be depressed about?" (Rice-Oxley, 2012, p. 24). There seems to have been very little warning that he might be prone to depression, though he mentions a lonely time in Switzerland on his gap year and a period during his student years when "suddenly everything seemed flat and stale" (p. 36). His only family history was of his father suffering an episode of depression when his four children all left home at the same time.

The crisis came in Rice-Oxley's thirties. He had three young children and a working wife, while serving as night foreign news editor on the *Guardian* and continuing his freelance journalism during the day. Reading the hair-raising description of his schedule, it becomes clear that a breakdown was almost inevitable. He endured not just long hours with insufficient sleep, but also the lack of control over his life that comes with needing to respond to news events. He was trying to be the perfect father, perfect husband, perfect employee. He had no time for himself and less and less time for sleep. After speaking to fellow depressed dads he began to wonder if his own descent into depression coincided with becoming a father, but unlike his friends (who admit to exhaustion, a life out of control, or loss of a wife's appreciation) he doesn't reveal exactly which elements of fatherhood were his nemesis. After being released from five years on the night-shift and at a time when the children began to sleep better, just when he had the opportunity to "repair [his] biorhythms" (p. 81), Rice-Oxley found that he was waking in the early hours of the morning and rarely getting back to sleep. After panicking during his fortieth birthday party and acquiring a long list of physical and emotional symptoms, he became too ill to work. He went on to do mindfulness-based cognitive therapy and schema therapy, but while he dutifully completed his homework assignments, he appeared to gain little or no insight into why he had become depressed. Rice-Oxley comments that he waited until he could afford to be ill, but I see it rather as his organism grabbing the first opportunity for recovery and homeostasis after prolonged stress.

Richard Maybey's depression struck *after* finishing his magnum opus *Flora Britannica* on the folklore of British plants: 250,000 words with 10,000 contributors! The book was well received and the work on it had been a joy, so he was not expecting to be hit by depression at such a time of achievement and status. However, he had not allowed for the exhaustion caused by the project and the vacuum opened up afterwards. For the first time, he came to the end of a book without a new idea ready to take him over. He had a growing sense of being an "ecological voyeur" with a wish that he had been "the conker-player, not the census-taker" (Mabey, 2006, pp. 51–52).

His depressive symptoms included heart arrhythmia, body aches, crippling anxiety and panic, and drinking too much. Medical treatment had little impact: the drugs didn't work and the talk therapy, "though diverting and convivial at times" (p. 53) didn't alter the basic problem. He spent a few weeks in the same hospital as the poet John Clare a couple of centuries earlier. Here he dried out and improved somewhat, but went downhill again after being discharged. His hearing became distorted, his panic increased, he stopped taking care of himself, and his unpaid bills led to debt collectors appearing. His sister was insisting that they sell the house and part company. He returned to hospital, but this time was discharged on the proviso that he go into the care of friends.

In the lead-up to her breakdown, Gwyneth Lewis had been trying to have/do it all: hold down a demanding job (chief assistant to the Controller of the BBC in Wales) and in her spare time give poetry readings worldwide. Her depression taught her the effect of greed: of wanting "too much" (e.g., alcohol) and doing "more" (e.g., two demanding careers). She went through a transition from high to low pressure in her life and likens the shock to "emotional bends" (Lewis, 2002, p. 10). Lewis quotes Saul Bellow on sloth: "Sloth is really a busy condition, hyperactive. ... These slothful sinners ... labor because rest terrifies them." She says, we must find the strength to give time and space so that the listening soul "can hear the essence of things" (ibid., p. 126). At the same time, Lewis and her husband had made the decision not to have children, which left her feeling "an immoral, hurtful and unacceptable human being" (p. 199). She had to learn to accept that the decision was the right one for their situation, but also that she needed to grieve for the children she would not have.

Stress from overwork played a triggering role in some of Tracy Thompson's depressive episodes (Thompson, 1995). When she got a prestigious job as legal affairs correspondent on the *Washington Post*, she found Washington to be a city of workaholics, obsessed with power and contemptuous of weakness. She began to sink into a second episode of depression (her first arose at college) heralded by losses of concentration and all feeling except anxiety, and by a drop in her weight. At the same time, she began a relationship with a deeply controlling man who was alternately supportive and abusive. The depression deepened as the cracks in the relationship began to show, and she checked herself into a psychiatric hospital where she was put on suicide watch. She was discharged after only two weeks, still only slightly less depressed, and returned to work. With various CBT tricks (learned from a book), Thompson was able to struggle through the next few months. Because stillness laid bare her mental pain, she always put work ahead of her health—she could only endure one week of the instructed three weeks for recuperation from a gallstone operation. After a gruelling summer covering the mayor's (Marion Barry) cocaine possession trial, when all was over she suffered a three-day crash, again while attempting to take a holiday. She returned to Washington and replaced the imipramine and lithium she had been taking with Prozac. After only three days she got, in a moment of silence, the first hint that she was going to get well: "The buzz in my brain was there, and then it was not." She makes the distinction that Prozac "didn't make me well. It made it possible for me to get well" (ibid., p. 249).

Depression generating the manic defence and low self-esteem

The overactivity that generates stress and exhaustion is what Keedwell (2008) calls the manic defence, where the individual compensates for inner emptiness or the terror that his core feelings of worthlessness will be exposed. It differs from the mania of bipolar disorder in the absence of extreme elation. While stress causes depression, the reverse is also true. Some depressed people use overwork and over-partying/acting-out to run away from their depression. This in turn generates stress, which leads to further anxiety and depression. Thus stress and depression/anxiety are parts of a self-reinforcing vicious circle. This was true most extremely for Elizabeth Wurtzel, but also for Stephanie Merritt, Tracey Thompson, Martha Manning, Mary McEvoy, and Tracy Thompson. McEvoy writes of herself as an "anxiety-ridden lunatic, running from invisible demons all the time, desperately trying to distract myself from the darkness" (p. 161).

A second vicious cycle—interwoven with the first—connects depression with low self-esteem; it is difficult to work well when depressed, so self-esteem is further diminished, which deepens the depression and so on. The attempt to run away from depression through overwork and over-socialising is in part an attempt to bolster self-esteem and in part an attempt to be so busy there are no gaps where self-awareness might seep into consciousness.

Wurtzel's memoir of her depression (1996) was written from the age of nineteen and was published in 1994 when she was just twenty-six. Her depression starts at the age of eleven and by the end of the book it has become controlled by a combination of lithium and Prozac. It's a fascinating read and contains a lot of insight, but the character she describes in her worst episodes is not sympathetic. She was flagrantly self-destructive and narcissistic. In her attempts to run away from her depression she had many alternative strategies: she worked manically and went without sleep and food for days on end, she cut herself, took cocktails of drugs, had meaningless sex, obsessed over boyfriends (and drove them away with her endless phone calls and need for reassurance), and alienated her friends with her acting out and frequent visits to the emergency room. Her therapist/psychiatrist was saintly and forbearing, tolerating phone calls in the middle of the night, or every few minutes. Wurtzel's fleeing took a literal form in the crackpot conviction that if she could only get somewhere else she would be okay: this took its most delusional twist in her trip to London to stay with her roommate's ex-boyfriend (whom Wurtzel had never met) on the grounds that he had been good to her friend when she was going through a tough patch. Needless to say, the trip was a disaster. Throughout this frenzy of activity alternating with being unable to get out of bed in the morning, Wurtzel screams and moans about her pain and her need for help. But we must conclude that we are being shown the worst of her because somehow she got prodigious amounts of work done in high school, gained a scholarship to Harvard, won prizes for her journalism, and attracted a large circle of friends.

The acting out may have been a desperate attempt not only to run from depression but to fill its void: "Depression is ... a complete absence: absence of affect, absence of feeling, absence of response, absence of interest. The pain you feel in the course of a major clinical depression is an attempt on nature's part ... to fill up the empty space" (Wurtzel, 1996, p. 19). The build-up to Elizabeth's extreme attention-seeking may be understood from her therapist's feedback: "Typically, in your household, the only way anything got attended to was if it had reached a point of complete desperation" (ibid., p. 289). She was conditioned early into hysterical acting-out.

What struck me about my own response was how little sympathy I felt. Certainly, I was gripped by her story; but I didn't feel for her, I wanted to shake her. And indeed I may be picking up the specific nature of her need for containment. Thus one boyfriend, who was—for a time—very sympathetic, caused her to wallow in her depression. But another, who demanded that she shape up and make an effort, stimulated her to rise to his expectations. Admittedly, at this stage, she was finally being treated with antidepressants and therefore more capable of pulling up her socks.

In Stephanie Merritt's case, we can see that her adult partying may have been an attempt to overcome and compensate for being bullied at school/depressed about it, while her later depressive breakdown may have resulted from the stress of overwork and over-partying (Merritt, 2009). Thus we see her cycling back and forth between the two sides of the coin: depression leading to hyperactivity/stress; stress/hyperactivity leading to depression.

Merritt grew up as the older of two children of loving parents, both teachers and in a stable marriage, in a small village in the Home Counties. In trying to make sense of the depression that started in her teens, she mentions quite severe bullying and rejection by her schoolmates at her comprehensive between the ages of eleven and fourteen. While she eventually learned to fight back, she concedes that "I left with the highest exam results in the school and my self-esteem shredded; ... I had no coherent sense of self; I only existed as a series of awards strung together" (Merritt, 2009, p. 39). At age seventeen she dieted, initially to lose some weight, but this morphed into starvation to punish herself, alongside a fear of company and of making small talk, then anxiety attacks and phobias about mirrors and eating. By this stage she had moved to a different school, a sixth form college. She loved her school work and had a boyfriend, but she was having doubts about her faith and managed to conceal this from everyone, including herself, until she went to university. Merritt emerged from her first crisis following a church exorcism and sessions with a church counsellor, and she questions whether she recovered as a result of belief, or just as part of the natural cycle of depression. During a gap year in Spain working for a Christian charity, she experienced what she would later recognise as an attack of hypomania: "a growing agitation had bloomed into a kind of frenzy that manifested itself in a need for urgent flight, as if there was a force in me that could not be contained but had to be given its head … driven by a sudden extraordinary surge of voltage" (ibid., pp. 65–66).

Later, at university, she reinvented herself in a hard-drinking, frenzied, partying, road of excess: she was now "revealed to be funny, outspoken, flirty, daring" (p. 70). But, after graduation, she spent ten unemployed months mired in torpor, followed only weeks into her new job by the frenetic agitation she had experienced in Spain. This time it was accompanied by grandiosity about the novel she was writing, which—when she got some constructive criticism from a literary agent—inevitably swung into furious self-hatred expressed by slashing her arms with scissors. As a journalist in London, she returned to wild drinking and partying with too little food or sleep, and occasional disturbing and even aggressive behaviour, followed by the inevitable guilt the morning after.

During her student and young adult days she fell painfully in love with various unavailable men, including a Jesuit sworn to celibacy and a man on the other side of the Atlantic, who eventually vanished from her life, leaving her plummeting again. In the meantime, there were the events already mentioned and taking on extra work responsibility while raising a child as a single mother.

Lorna Martin's book (2008) describes a year she spent in psychoanalytic psychotherapy (three times weekly) in her mid-thirties after finally accepting that her life was chaotic, that she was chronically in denial, and unable to form long-term relationships with men, instead replacing them with obsessive romantic day-dreaming. She was brooding over a married man with whom she had an affair and who she suspected of moving on to a second affair. She was repeatedly getting speeding fines and missing flights; "crying became a sort of second career" (p. 22); her life seemed meaningless. She admits that psychoanalysis was a last resort. "I've tried everything else—fresh air, pills, exercise, changing jobs, drinking, not drinking, going out, staying in, new hobbies. I have no energy and no passion anymore and I'm afraid of the way I'm feeling" (p. 30). She had been on Prozac intermittently since the age of thirty after completing an online depression questionnaire and finding that she scored highly for feeling sad, hopeless, worthless, anxious, and with dysfunctional attitudes. Her GP diagnosed her as clinically depressed and prescribed the drug. Martin's account shows that you can be depressed while having a great career, loving family, and close friends and appear to be functioning well—when she started on Prozac she had never missed a day at work and wasn't suicidal or unable to get out of bed. Hers is a tale of functional, relatively low-level but chronic depression, unlike the severe major depression of the other memoirs.

Martin's account is laugh-out-loud funny, which was part of her problem since she has a highly developed capacity to turn the worst situation into a self-deprecating joke. She was competitive in her career (couldn't bear to be average) and relationships (e.g., she had to give the best present); unhealthily identified with work; constantly apologising for people or situations where she was not at fault; in denial of any shadow feelings, particularly anger and jealousy; and a people-pleaser, at times destructively impulsive.

She was transformed by her year in therapy—facing up to the reality of her feelings and able to feel and regulate them. Her identity was no longer tied up exclusively with her job; she was no longer driving recklessly or obsessing over her ex-lover; she was more emotionally contained and apologised less. Most impressively of all, as she tells us in the epilogue, she was secure enough in herself to tell a man to whom she was highly attracted that she "liked" him. When he rejected her, she was able to feel the full force of her feelings and get over them in a few days, instead of calling forth her old arsenal of defences.

Postnatal depression as a result of stress

Stress and exhaustion are particularly likely to be followed by depression when the pressure and responsibility of bringing a child into the world is added to the mix.

Rachel Kelly was a (London) *Times* journalist, on maternity leave following the birth of her second child, when she suddenly broke down with a major depressive attack (Kelly, 2014). Her depression was characterised by physical agony, terror, insomnia, and a complete inability to make the smallest decision. She was bed-ridden and unable to work or play any part in her children's lives, and completely cut off from others, except in her need to cling to her mother and husband. Her husband had a demanding career with Goldman Sachs and had stood for parliament during her pregnancy and the birth of their second child. Her exhaustion, and panic over how she would manage her return to work, appear to have been the immediate trigger for the depression. She gave up her job when expecting her third child and all went smoothly. However the birth of her final two children (twins) following a difficult pregnancy—with the final trimester spent in a wheelchair—appears to have been the trigger for another episode. It was only when she finally began to examine her patterns that she got to the bottom of how a—if not *the*—major contributor to her depression was her lifestyle. Kelly wanted to be a high-achieving career-woman *and* the perfect wife, mother, daughter, friend.

The opportunities for and pressures on her generation of women to combine successful careers with children generate a very stressful package. Kelly was constantly torn between children and work. A career in journalism is particularly difficult to combine with young children since they have opposite paces and demands, children requiring a slow-paced routine and journalism demanding you operate at high speed and drop everything when news happens. Work can boost self-esteem and help the recovery from depression, but it can be detrimental if it is not flexible, and "there are few workplaces less flexible than a newsroom" (p. 162). The pressure of all these conflicting demands alongside a lack of awareness or compassion for her own needs and the complete repression of her anger is the classic cocktail to produce crushing levels of stress.

Arguably, Stephanie Merritt's most self-destructive behaviour (fuelled by denial) was having a baby as a single mother while emotionally dependent on her excessive partying and working lifestyle, and without any of the emotional, social, or financial resources for parenthood. A long episode of depression started while she was pregnant, and escalated and lasted for about two years after the birth. In the midst of this period, she agreed—again in an act of massive self-destructiveness—to take over the job of literary editor of her newspaper for six months, while at the same time researching an appeal to the Child Support Agency. This led to breakdown, while she was still managing to act the part and convince others that she was functioning. It was only when she came very close to suicide shortly after her son's first birthday that she finally sought help.

Women who are pregnant or have just given birth are more likely than all others to suffer from depression. Severe postnatal depression affects about one in ten mothers, with a milder version (postnatal blues) in about one in two or three (references in Wolpert, 1999; Solomon, 2014). The milder version may be caused by hormonal changes and is usually restricted to the first week after birth, whereas the more severe condition can persist for as long as two years. The likelihood of postpartum depression is lower amongst women whose partners share childcare and is particularly high amongst women under severe stress (Solomon, 2014). This can include stressful life events or stressful living conditions: for example, lack of social support, poor relationship with the partner, and poverty. Women who suffer anxiety or depression before the birth are particularly vulnerable to postnatal depression (Wolpert, 1999).

Only about four per cent of mothers in Hong Kong suffer postnatal depression. This relatively low frequency may result from the practice of "doing the month": a form of social support provided by family and friends so that for a month after the birth the mother has no household chores (ibid.). In families where fathers share substantial responsibility for childcare and household chores, fathers are more vulnerable to depression resulting from stress, as appeared to be the case for Mark Rice-Oxley (2012).

The unsatisfied needs underlying depression

When an individual is motivated by the embodied true self, it is not possible to push herself beyond her organismic limit: this is the wisdom of the healthy animal. It is only when coming from the disembodied, ego/superego-based false or adaptive self that one can override one's true (organismic) needs. Increasingly we live in an age of the false or adapted self: ego-based, disembodied, and narcissistic. From this stance we judge ourselves according to what we are told to value by a commodifying culture. Most of the cases of depressive breakdown explored in this book were to a greater or lesser extent caused by the stress of living out of a false self based on extrinsic values.

Just as a false or otherwise fragile self is the distal origin of depression, stress is the common proximal trigger for low mood. People with a fragile self are driven by extrinsic motivation, have an external locus of evaluation, and thus are prone to overachieving. The stress of burnout is characterised by an excess of doing and having at the expense of being, so that the individual is unable to rest or to be present to the very inputs that would satisfy his true needs (see Chapter Eleven). However, we are inherently motivated towards non-goal-directed doing—in other words, play and exploration for its own sake. The fundamental need to move out of our own separated and alienated egos into a state of I-thou contact with the world was discovered by many of the memoirists during their depressive breakdowns. This might be the beauty of art or the natural world—as Rachel Kelly found with poetry, Richard Mabey with nature study, and Michael Harding with his landscape of lakes. Equally, to renounce our narcissism can be a move into altruism: Tracy Thompson found that in helping others she relieved her own depression. In such ways did the memoir writers begin to heal the divorce from the self, embrace their embodied needs, and live out of a more authentic identity.

Summary

Depression and anxiety are consequences of a fragile sense of self. The individual is out of touch with the true needs of her organismic self, but instead, with varying degrees of awareness, lives out of the need to please or impress others, or expel her own inner emptiness or sense of worthlessness. This may entail living the life demanded by parents or society at large or exhausting herself compensating for poor self-esteem or filling up the vacuum within. In any case, life is lived from an external locus of evaluation and an inner sense of lack, and is therefore highly stressful.

We will return in Chapter Eight to the links between fragile self and depression and anxiety.

CHAPTER THREE

Depression as consequence and cause of somatic conditions

The symptoms of depression and anxiety manifest somatically as well as psychologically. In some cases, they are experienced as bodily symptoms before their psychological origins become evident: this is particularly true for the men in this sample, possibly because men are often less aware than women of their emotional process. We can see the difference between the genders in Lewis Wolpert's and his wife's differing views on the trigger for his first depressive breakdown: he attributed it to a new heart drug, she to reminders of his father's murder (Wolpert, 1999). However, the relationship between the body and the psyche is not clear-cut, and infectious disease and physical pain can independently generate low mood, so that physical illness may be understood as both cause and effect of depression. Cleare (2009) views depression as a condition "exemplifying … the indivisibility of body and mind" (p. 249); thus bodily symptoms, of which the most common are pain and fatigue, can both originate in and generate depression. There is little doubt that in Solomon's case, physical pain triggered renewed attacks of depression (Solomon, 2014); while for Ann Marie Chiasson, chronic pain from an undiagnosed malformation of one of her kidneys led to her becoming depressed. In her case, her family doctor thought the pain might be a symptom of unacknowledged depression, until an organic reason for it was discovered (Chiasson, 2015). For other people such as Kelly (2014) and Wolpert (1999), pain seems indeed to have been an outcome of depression. It turns out that the neural mechanisms underlying the emotional pain of depression and the sensitivity to physical pain are very similar (Wiech & Tracey, 2009). In addition, the part of the brain—the insula—that mediates awareness of body sensations is activated in depression (Wiebking et al., 2010), thus making the individual hyper-aware of body problems.

The stress and inflammatory responses that are overactive in depression can also be induced by infectious disease (see Chapter Six), suggesting a basis for some people's slide into depression during the course of an infection. Sickness behaviour is an adaptive response that helps us to get well when ill by making us eat less, become less active, withdraw socially, and other familiar effects, and is similar to the withdrawal observed in depression. However, they are not identical: sickness behaviour ends with the somatic symptoms, whereas depression lasts a great deal longer. One reasonable hypothesis is that sickness behaviour only turns into depression if there are primary causes for depression rooted in childhood experience. According to this model, physical illness is a secondary trigger for depression only if a primary susceptibility is already present.

Depression triggered by drugs and alcohol—and by withdrawal from them

Physical factors were the immediate triggers of Matt Haig's breakdown: heavy drinking, smoking, and partying with a poor diet and very little sleep signalled a process in which he was running away from himself, "scared of having nothing but my own mind to listen to" (Haig, 2015, p. 243).

William Styron abused alcohol as an enhancer of creativity—"the magical conduit to fantasy and euphoria, and to the enhancement of the imagination" (Styron, 1992, p. 40)—for most of his life. As he approached his sixtieth birthday, he found that even the smallest amount made him feel nauseous. He gave up alcohol abruptly, and this may have precipitated his subsequent breakdown. Another contributory factor was the benzodiazepine tranquillisers—first Ativan and then Halcion—he had begun to consume two years previously. At the time of the breakdown he was taking large doses of Halcion, which is known to depress mood and even precipitate breakdowns. However, he also realised that "depression had clung close to the outer edges of my life for many years. Suicide has been a persistent theme in my books …" (ibid., p. 78). So he concedes that the condition probably had earlier origins, citing his father's depression and his mother's death during his boyhood.

Styron had a wide range of symptoms: confusion; memory lapses; dread; alienation; anxiety; insomnia and a complete absence of dreams; a voice like a ninety-year-old; loss of self-esteem and of self-reliance along with an acute fear of abandonment; and finally, suicidal ideation. He became utterly dependent on his long-suffering wife who was endlessly patient and wise. He checked into hospital because he knew he was in danger of killing himself. He stayed for nearly seven weeks and puts his recovery down to time and seclusion and coming off the Halcion sleeping medication. He discovered that he had been on three times the hypnotic dose, so it is likely that the drug played a major role in triggering his depression, alongside giving up alcohol.

One of Stephanie Merritt's breakdowns also coincided with her giving up drinking, as well as smoking, caffeine, sugar, red meat, wheat, and dairy products (Merritt, 2009). It seems that an abrupt change in physiology—even in a healthy direction—is challenging to the system and can precipitate depression.

Wolpert's depression began when the drug he was taking to control his heart arrhythmia stopped working (Wolpert, 1999). Thus the regular rhythm of his heart was lost, which in itself can make you feel low. Then his already well-established anxiety and hypochondria caused him to worry about the real possibility of a stroke. An alternative drug gave him unpleasant side effects, and that along with his distress at letting down several groups (by cancelling an important trip to South Africa) increased his anxiety. Another change in heart drug to flecamide made him feel "very weird" (ibid., p. 40) and suddenly unable to sleep. His skin seemed to be on fire, he developed uncontrollable twitches, was unable to work or take physical exercise, and panicked if left alone. He was diagnosed with depression, which he describes as "the worst experience of [his] life" (ibid., p. vii).

Wolpert was convinced that it was the flecamide that was the cause of his depression, but his wife's view was that it was his plan to visit his old home of South Africa where his father had been murdered some years before. He already suffered from anxiety before he took the drug, so I am more inclined to his wife's interpretation. Wolpert's dismissal of the idea of the unconscious as nonsense and his contempt for psychoanalysis (Cohen, 2013) suggest an entrenched resistance to psychological causes.

Four years after his recovery from his first depressive breakdown, some of his symptoms came back "for no obvious reason", Wolpert tells us in an update (2009, p. 2). He continued to get worse despite being put on Seroxat. His new partner (his wife had died) encouraged him to try psychoanalysis, but he found the interaction "unfriendly", which perhaps explains his later attack on the profession. After several weeks the analyst took a break, and Wolpert didn't go back since he got much better. Since then he has had further minor episodes. He takes Effexor and also finds that exercise works well.

Wolpert's father also suffered acute depression as a result—according to his son—of taking the blood pressure medication, reserpine, which reduces the concentration of serotonin. However, it seems more probable that familial psychological patterns (see Chapter Four) are the common denominator underpinning the depression of father and son.

Antidepressant drugs can have terrible side-effects, sometimes nearly as bad as or worse than the illness itself, as was the case for Sally Brampton. Several (but not all) of my own clients who have been prescribed antidepressants for anxiety have reported negative reactions worse than the original symptoms, including an exacerbation of their anxiety. After just two days of taking a half tablet (7.5 mg) of Mirtazapine, Paul developed depressive symptoms: increased anxiety, exhaustion, slowing down in psychomotor activity, insomnia, florid dreams, agitation and rage combined with a sense of a heavy duvet covering him, and physical aches that caused him to pull a muscle. Previously, Escitalopram (10 mg) had also increased his anxiety and after four weeks this didn't diminish, though he got used to the experience of anxiety. Paul's anxiety resulted from early relational trauma and was not linked to depression. It is perhaps not surprising that drugs designed to counter the under-arousal of depression pushed him further into the over-arousal of anxiety.

Somatic conditions as contributing factors

While Solomon's first episode of depression and anxiety was primarily caused by loss, an aggravating factor that pushed him deeper into anxiety was the pain from kidney stones that severely limited his sleep.

When he left the hospital he was hysterical and constantly afraid, and his libido and appetite dried up. Solomon rapidly slid into complete breakdown, which he describes graphically: he took to his bed and couldn't remember how to talk, how to turn over, nor could he explain what was wrong. He went on medication and moved back into his father's apartment. With the help of Xanax, friends, and his father he somehow got through a reading tour to promote his first novel, "the most difficult endeavour of my life" (Solomon, 2014, p. 66). A third but brief breakdown followed abandonment in love and the severe pain of a dislocated shoulder. In Solomon's case, intense physical pain with its shock and insomnia contributed to depression.

Michael Harding had a range of somatic symptoms that he acknowledges were psychological in origin. However, he suggests that the reverse could also be true—that his depression coincided with being diagnosed with colitis and was induced by the shock (Harding, 2013). Thus, it is not clear whether Harding and Solomon are in different categories, or whether in both cases depression was induced by pain and illness.

Depression somatised

At the age of fifty-seven, Harding's body began to break down. He had an enlarged prostate, an attack of impotence, digestive and breathing problems, flu-like symptoms, a swollen back, an extensive skin rash, and finally colitis. He spent most of a four-month period in early 2011 in bed, apart from the days in which he forced himself to perform in a one-man show on a long tour throughout Ireland. He realised that the somatic symptoms were coming from the inside and that the immediate cause was overwork, following a lifetime of inner conflict, shame, and low mood.

In virtually all cases of depression, many of the symptoms are somatic, and include: disruptions to sleep and appetite; stomach or bowel problems; muscle tremors and shaking; body aches; heart arrhythmia (Mabey, and one wonders also whether Wolpert's arrhythmia was effect as much as cause); physical pain (e.g., Wolpert's burning sensation, and in Kelly's case a physical agony "worse than tearing in childbirth with a faulty epidural" (Kelly, 2014, p. 25); tinnitus (Mabey, Rice-Oxley); slowing down in psychomotor function (e.g., Lewis). In Rice-Oxley's case, his depression announced itself with "headache, lethargy, bowel problems, panic attacks, anxiety, muscle tremors and shaking, tinnitus, black moods, [and] insomnia" (Rice-Oxley, 2012, p. 99). Depression must indeed be regarded as a condition of both the psyche and the soma.

With respect to somatisation, Wolpert (1999) examines the contention that this is more pronounced in non-Western societies. This does appear to be the case in countries, such as Japan, where there is a stigma attached to depression which makes it more acceptable to admit to physical symptoms like stomach ache, headache, dizziness, lack of energy, backache, and loss of appetite (Wolpert, 1999; Kitanaka, 2011). In China, it is considered impolite to talk about feelings, so it is difficult to acknowledge emotional problems. There, depression is often considered morally unacceptable so that instead of reporting sadness, many depressed Chinese people complain of "boredom, discomfort, feelings of inner pressure, and symptoms of pain, dizziness, and fatigue" (Kleinman, 2004, p. 951).

Amongst the memoirs reviewed here, it is notable that somatisation was more frequent amongst the men than the women. Indeed, apart from Rachel Kelly, whose physical pain was agony, none of the other women pay much attention to somatic symptoms, whereas for the men, there is a marked emphasis on the somatic as both attributed cause and outcome of the depression. Western culture is more open to women talking about emotional difficulties than men, so it is not surprising that men are generally less aware and less open about psychological problems. Thus they can more easily present with physical pain or disease and are more likely to ascribe their condition to drugs, alcohol, somatic illness, or physical pain. This is not to deny that pain or illness can bring about depression, but they are likely to be one of a number of factors including emotional health that contribute to this multifactorial condition. So attribution of primary cause is a matter of emphasis on what the individual is aware of, or what disturbs him most. Nevertheless, depression has evolved for a reason (Chapter Five), and like any emotion or mood, it carries a message from the unconscious. I would expect the intensity of the somatic symptoms to be proportional to the denial of the psyche. The less we heed the message, the more the signal has to be amplified.

Attempts to escape the pain of depression

In Chapter Two we saw how people use work as a way of escaping minor low mood. But when they work themselves into exhaustion, the stress leads to a more severe depression. In a similar fashion, a large number of depressed and anxious people try to run away from their condition with alcohol, drugs, self-mutilation and other destructive behaviours. These inevitably deepen the depression, both through the depressing effects of alcohol and some drugs and through the continuing avoidance of the underlying problem.

Brampton, Mabey, Merritt, and Martin all self-medicated with alcohol. Styron and Lewis drank heavily but gave up alcohol before their breakdowns, though they had perhaps been previously attempting to soothe themselves against chronic milder depression. Martin tried drinking and not drinking before facing up to her difficulties in psychoanalysis. Merritt's drinking was part and parcel of her self-reinvention as one of the in-crowd, but it was also part of her running away from her depression. When she decided in one too-extreme step to detoxify her system, she became more severely depressed, as we saw above.

Brampton and Mabey are both clear that for them the depression came first: they then attempted to self-medicate with alcohol, thereby generating a second problem. Indeed, this is likely to be the case with many people who are labelled as alcoholics: they may in fact be suffering from depression, and drink to combat the pain. Brampton drank to dull the (emotional) pain of treatment-resistant depression, but as part of her recovery she went into rehab and found AA meetings useful as a kind of regular group therapy in which she could engage with her feelings—rather than ignoring them as was her default position. Likewise, Mabey's depression wasn't dented by either drugs or therapy, and he drank to cope with the symptoms (2006). In hospital he dried out and improved somewhat but went downhill again after being discharged.

Wurtzel acted out using legal and illegal drugs as well as relieving her emotional pain by self-mutilation. In her attempts to run away from her depression she had many alternative strategies, both behavioural (work, sex, relationships); and body-focused: she went without sleep and food for days on end, cut herself, and took cocktails of drugs. Slater engaged in regular self-mutilation and anorexia, while Merritt too reports lashing out at herself with scissors in a fit of self-hatred.

Physical treatments for depression

Depression can be linked to a range of deficiencies including micronutrients, light, and exercise. Our recent ancestors spent most of the time outdoors, where even on a cloudy day in winter the light intensity is greater than indoors. Similarly, hunter-gatherers and farmers had far more exercise than humans in the technological era, and the decline in vigorous exercise in modern society may contribute to the increasing incidence of depression. Young (2007), in an editorial reviewing non-medicating solutions, finds that positive mood induction, exercise, light, and diet are all useful in raising serotonin levels and combatting depression.

Exposure to bright light is effective in treating both seasonal affective disorder (SAD) and non-seasonal depression; if spending more time out of doors is not possible, a full-spectrum light box is an alternative. Patients recovering from spinal surgery had a higher tolerance for pain when moved to sunny rooms (Walch et al., 2005).

Aerobic exercise improves mood in the subclinical population, and cycling on a stationary bike for just fifteen minutes is enough to raise serotonin levels and increase activity in neural circuits involved in emotional regulation (Fumoto et al., 2010). Tango dancing—a practice of embodied relatedness if ever there was one—was compared to mindfulness meditation (six-week programmes) and a waiting-list control. Depression levels were significantly reduced in the two treatment groups relative to the controls, while stress levels were reduced in the tango group only (Pinniger et al., 2012).

Exercising, being exposed to daylight, and working with the soil are all elements of the way of life for which we have evolved but of which we are deprived by modern, urban, indoor lifestyles. Rachel Kelly and Sally Brampton both found that gardening helped in their recovery. The experience of feeling relaxed and content while gardening now has a scientific explanation: soil bacteria *Mycobacterium vaccae* have been found to have antidepressant (Lowry et al., 2007) and anti-anxiety (Matthews & Jenks, 2013) effects in rodents. Whether applied in the trachea or by injection, they activated a subset of serotonergic neurons and altered stress-related emotional behaviour. Gardeners inhale the bacteria, have topical contact with them, and can get them into their bloodstream through cuts, thus being exposed to their mood-lifting effects (Grant, 2015).

Depression can be associated with a deficiency in nutrients such as B vitamins, omega-3 fatty acids, and polyunsaturated fatty acids (see references in Gerhardt, 2015, p. 136, 141), and supplements of micronutrients can help some people (Holford, 2010). The amino acid tryptophan is a precursor of serotonin, but to increase levels of the neurotransmitter in the brain it is essential to consume purified tryptophan rather than tryptophan-rich foods (Young, 2007). We will see in Chapter Six the kind of diet that promotes a healthy diversity of gut bacteria that is helpful in combatting stress, anxiety, and depression. Stephanie Merritt (2009) consulted Patrick Holford's Institute of Optimal Nutrition and was told that her low carbohydrate diet was contributing to her mood swings. She was given dietary advice and a combination of supplements, including 5-HTP, which increases levels of tryptophan. Despite having little faith in the treatment she took the supplements. About a week later, her dark, crushed mood lifted, not into elation, just an "unspectacular" sense of clarity and resilience. Sally Brampton found that omega-3 oil and B vitamins helped, and that acupuncture healed some of her most distressing somatic symptoms.

There is limited research available on the effectiveness of acupuncture for treating depression, but MacPherson et al. (2013) found that it significantly reduced symptoms within three months compared to usual care alone.

Suicide

Suicidal ideation

Merkin, Thompson, Solomon, Styron, Haig, Manning, Wolpert, and Merritt all thought about or became obsessed with killing themselves, and some, such as Merritt and Haig, got within a hair's breadth of jumping off a train and a cliff respectively. Several of them make it clear that they didn't actually want to die: they simply couldn't endure to go on living with such agony. As Styron says: "the pain of severe depression is quite unimaginable to those who have not suffered it, and it kills in many instances because its anguish can no longer be borne" (1992, p. 33). Jeff Foster too saw suicide as release from his pain until he realised more deeply that his urge to die was in reality an urge to live: "*I wanted to live, but I didn't know how*. I wanted rest, so deeply and profoundly, but I didn't know how to get there" (2015, p. 207).

In Matt Haig's case it was fear of death that held him back, but the others mention neither fear nor the hope of recovery as the ultimate preventative. It was the feeling of responsibility towards loved ones that stopped Merkin, Solomon, Manning, and Merritt from taking the ultimate step. Merkin, Thompson, Styron, and Wolpert were all sufficiently alarmed by their desire to kill themselves that they checked into hospital so that the means of suicide would be removed from them. In Wolpert's case, the thing that helped reduce his suicidal thoughts was his wife agreeing to help him die if he wasn't better within a year (Wolpert, 2009).

Andrew Solomon's suicide plan was particularly bizarre. When he reached a state of half-recovery from his first breakdown he became suicidal: "I didn't particularly want to die, but I also didn't at all want to live" (Solomon, 2014, p. 69). He pulled back for big reasons, like not doing that to his father, and reasons of vanity, like not revealing his misery to the world. One of the most extraordinary episodes in his account concerns the period when he came off his antidepressants very fast, plunged into a second episode of agitated depression, and felt that he could not go on living. But he needed an excuse for killing himself and he felt that depression wasn't a sufficiently visible illness. So he sought out unsafe sex in public places in a bid to become infected with HIV in order to generate an adequate excuse for killing himself. He stopped after four months with the sudden realisation that he might be infecting other people, but fortunately his efforts to become HIV-positive were unsuccessful anyway.

Suicide attempts

Out of the twenty-one writers, it was Plath, Brampton, Slater, Jamison, and Wurtzel who carried their fantasies into actual attempts at suicide. Of course, all were unsuccessful at the time or their memoirs would not have been written.

Wurtzel's action appears to have been a cry for help more than a serious determination to end her life. It was after the Prozac started kicking in that she made an impulsive bid to kill herself. She herself was startled by it, but as she says "a little bit of energy, in the hands of someone hell-bent on suicide, is a very dangerous thing" (Wurtzel, 1996, p. 279). Despite her mood lifting and being able to get out of bed in the morning, she believed that her life "sucked". But two parts of her struggled: "I tell myself I really want to die, and it never occurs to me until the last possible moment that what I really want is to be saved" (ibid., p. 280). Her psychotherapist was finally taking her suicide threats seriously and suggested taking her to a psychiatric hospital. Wurtzel, scared of the threatened confinement, ran to the bathroom at her therapist's office, swallowed a full bottle of Mellaril (an antipsychotic medication) that she carried round "just in case" (p. 283), was discovered by her therapist and brought to the emergency room. Wurtzel describes her suicide attempt as "the purest and most deliberate act of hatred I have ever committed. It doesn't matter if I never really figured on dying: I still feel that I've crossed a line, and that in doing so I now can actually return from the other side of that border. A sudden and nearly manic lust for life overcomes me" (ibid., pp. 285–286).

A person who self-injures has a hundredfold greater risk of suicide according to the psychiatrist Linda Gask (2015). Lauren Slater attempted suicide during childhood, and it needs to be seen as an extreme of her ongoing self-mutilating behaviour in response to her mother's rejection and *de facto* reward of illness (the only time her mother treated her with tenderness). It was only when Slater was treated with Prozac at age twenty-six that she learned to move from an illness-centred to a health-based identity. In the case of Sylvia Plath's protagonist Esther Greenwood, after some failed medical intervention, she swallowed a bottle of pills and hid in a blocked-up hole in the cellar, where she was discovered after being missing for a few days. When she emerged from her coma and recovered from her injuries, she felt no better and was placed in an asylum where she was uncooperative and angry.

When Kay Redfield Jamison gave up the lithium treatment for her bipolar condition, "a floridly psychotic mania was followed, inevitably, by a long and lacerating, black, suicidal depression" that lasted more than a year and a half (Jamison, 1997, p. 110). She refused to go to psychiatric hospital and—in her unrelenting pain and with the intention of being fair to others—she decided to kill herself. Jamison's suicide was carefully planned: she took an anti-emetic medication along with a massive overdose of lithium and removed the telephone to another room (but left it plugged in!). When the phone rang, in her semi-comatose state she instinctively answered it and her brother initiated a rescue mission. She went back on the lithium. Jamison tells us little about the long-term impact of her suicide attempt, other than saying that she had to reconcile her image of herself with how she actually was in her depressed and manic states: a step towards integration of fragments of the self.

Sally Brampton had major depression of the agitated variety, which was resistant to drug treatment. Likewise the psychoanalysis and CBT she tried were of no help. Her despair became so great that she couldn't go on. She made a half-hearted and then a precisely planned attempt at suicide, but failed. She saw the second attempt as a turning-point in which she gave up on any expectation that anyone else could help her and began to look for ways in which she might help herself. Brampton said that her road to recovery took three years, but eight years after her account of her depression was published (2008), it appears that the depression again became too severe to tolerate. Like Plath, who succeeded in killing herself at the age of thirty-one, Brampton's tragic and untimely death in 2016 is believed to have been suicide (www.heavy.com).

Summary

Depression is a condition of the psyche and soma. For some, the origins are psychological, while a number of the effects are somatic. For others, the immediate trigger (but probably not the primary cause) for the depression may be physical: due to somatic illness, pain, or abrupt changes to the physiology through starting or stopping drinking, changing prescription drugs, or radical changes to the diet. In some cultures, it can be more acceptable to admit to physical symptoms than to psychological "weakness", so that depressed patients are more likely to present with somatic symptoms. Lack of self-awareness is a contributing factor, no doubt bound up with cultural stigma, which may make men ignore emotional distress until a variety of physical symptoms intrude.

Once a depressive episode is under way, many people try to self-medicate with alcohol, drugs, or self-mutilating behaviours, including starvation. In the end many contemplate or attempt suicide—or successfully carry it out—as a way of escaping intolerable pain and anguish.

The treatment of depression can benefit from a variety of physical interventions, including nutritional supplements, acupuncture, exercise, light, and even working with the soil.

CHAPTER FOUR

Childhood development: what does it take to build a self?

Such is the dominance of the biomedical model in public awareness that many of the memoir writers unthinkingly attribute to genetic susceptibility what are more likely to be learned and internalised familial patterns of depression. For example, Styron, writing of his father being hospitalised for depression during William's boyhood, concludes: "The genetic roots of depression seem now to be beyond controversy" (1992, p. 79). However he concedes that his mother's death when he was thirteen was probably more significant. We cannot rule genetics out as a contributing factor, but as we will see in Chapter Six, genetics plays a relatively small role in depression in the population as a whole. Parents supply not only genes—nature—but early nurture as well, so the existence of familial depression does not in any way prove or imply genetic origins. Having depressed relatives with whom you don't live is still no indication of genetic causation, as extended families share patterns of child rearing and emotional processing, including those that generate low mood, for example, the tendency to please the other instead of being true to yourself, or withdrawing in the face of interpersonal conflict.

The ideology that propagates the view of people as self-determining monads is blind to the impact of the familial and socio-cultural environment on the individual. In this chapter, we will explore the relational context in which the child builds a self, the consequences for the child if the mother is depressed, and the intergenerational transmission of depression.

The memoirs show that two major themes run through the aetiology of depression: loss and a fragile or false sense of self. However, it should become clear in this chapter that these are not truly separate causes, but are linked through insecurity in early childhood relationships. Anxious (insecure) attachment can be caused by loss or separation, or more often by unattuned parenting. In either case, a fragile sense of self is the outcome. Thus I argue that the core reasons for depression and anxiety are a weak or empty sense of self generated by impoverished relationships with caregivers in early childhood. What Winnicott (1990) called the facilitating environment provided by the mother depends on the current family and social conditions as well as the environment in which the maternal self was organised a generation previously.

Attachment

Babies are born with immature brains that grow in the early years after birth: the way they develop and the emotional and relational capacities of the individual depend on the relationship with the carer; it is at this time that the seeds of anxiety and depression are sown. In the optimum case of a securely attached infant, the parent is "perceptive, sensitive, responsive, and predictable" (Siegel, 2012, p. 203), and the child experiences safety and self-esteem and learns to regulate his feelings and to mentalize. He thereby develops emotional intelligence and empathy, grows up according to the healthy blueprint of his relationship with his parents, and becomes adept at managing the social realm. He is more resilient to stress, which has positive downstream consequences for his mental and physical health (Gerhardt, 2015).

Insecure (anxious) attachment can arise from extended separation between parent and child (e.g., due to hospitalisation of one of them) or, more commonly, because of unattuned parenting of either the abusive or neglectful kind (see Dowds, 2014; Gerhardt, 2015; Holmes, 2010; Siegel, 2012) for summaries of the consequences of insecure attachment). Here "the internalized mother, instead of being a source of security and autonomic regulation, becomes organized as a destabilizing state of mind and body" (Cozolino, 2010, p. 205), as Richard Mabey experienced with his separation anxiety and sensitivity to rejection (Mabey, 2006).

In the avoidant kind of insecure attachment the individual distances herself from relationship and avoids intimacy. This pattern is generated by parents who are uncomfortable with feelings and fail to respond sensitively to the child's needs, with the result that the individual has little expectation of or capacity for closeness, trust, or comfort in relationships. The avoidant individual has grasped that feelings will distress the parent and will be ignored or punished, so she learns early on to repress and negate them. This leads to chronic, underlying depression—albeit often out of awareness. But avoidant behaviour merely covers over the alarm felt when a child is emotionally or physically abandoned, so in fact the avoidant person merely *denies* the anxiety that is more explicitly manifest in the ambivalent (anxious) and disorganised (traumatised) patterns. An avoidant child separated from the parent may look unconcerned, but her heart rate and the arousal of the sympathetic nervous system show that her physiology is reacting to threat with the same alarm as any other child who has been abandoned (Gerhardt, 2015). Michael Harding, with his distant and rejecting mother and consequent fear of intimacy, is a clear example of some of the problems of avoidant attachment (Harding, 2013).

The other major class of insecure attachment is the ambivalent or resistant type, who is clingy and anxious but also resentful in relationship, and therefore highly entangled with others: for example, Gwyneth Lewis and her mother (Lewis, 2002) or Tracy Thompson and her partner (Thompson, 1995). This is believed to be generated by inconsistently available parents, so that the child learns to focus very closely on the responses of others (codependence) and/or to exaggerate his own feelings to get attention. My client Susan (Chapter Two) fears rejection and abandonment, having had an avoidant father, a narcissistic mother who was blind to or dismissive of her daughter having any needs, and a childhood history of repeated moves to new neighbourhoods and hence a succession of schools. Susan compensates for her fears by a debilitating over-adaptation to what she imagines are the needs and desires of others, particularly her mother. She believes that privacy is equivalent to telling lies, which further strips her of boundaries between self and other. Not surprisingly, in the absence of any assertiveness or control over her own life, she is a highly anxious individual.

The avoidant is in denial of his need for the other, whereas the ambivalent's anxiety is balanced by his anger about his dependence. They are mirror images, one in whom the dependence is more obvious, the other with the autonomy on the surface, but each with the counter-side in the unconscious (Gerhardt, 2015; Pollard, 2005). Under pressure the repressed function emerges, so that the avoidant personality is a veneer over anxious dependence, while the anxiety of the ambivalent overlies a desire to reject the other. The avoidant whose partner leaves him will feel the full blast of terrified abandonment. When Harding's wife went away for six weeks, he began to feel his dependence on her (Harding, 2014), though when she was available to him, he felt the urge to leave and live alone (Harding, 2013). Equally, when stressed by too many demands, the helpful, agreeable ambivalent may move into avoidant or rejecting mode. We see a particularly cruel balance between avoidance and ambivalence in Mary McEvoy's description of her relationship with her parents (McEvoy, 2011). In living true to her own guiding light, her weekday life in the city, acting, mixing with the creative bohemian set, is quite cut off from the lives of her parents. On the other hand, to maintain contact, she spent weekends—and also five years full-time—with them on the farm during which she lived out their demands. Their rejection of her true needs set her up for avoidant attachment; but their selective love for the imago they projected on to her trained her for ambivalence. Acting out a false self for her parents was inherently depressing, but being her true self generated guilt-depression. Anger is strikingly absent from the memoir, making me, the reader, feel irritated with her. It is likely that McEvoy will remain caught in this no-man's land between true and false self until she can feel her anger at her parents.

A third, more rare kind of insecure attachment is the disorganised class, where the innate need for the parent is countered by the fear of unpredictable, terrifying and/or dissociated behaviour caused by psychosis, addiction, or trauma (West, 2016; Yellin & White, 2012). This group is characterised by a disorganised self, where "the fear and chaos of the mothers' internal worlds can be observed in their children's behaviour" (Cozolino, 2010, p. 200). Here the disorder has more severe and fragmenting consequences for the self than is the case for the insecure but organised defences of avoidant and ambivalent attachment. Lauren Slater, with her terrifying mother and her own extreme depression and signs of trauma, is a probable example of disorganised attachment (Slater, 1999).

In all three kinds of insecure attachment, children—and the adults they become—are more anxious and stressed than securely attached people because they have not been able to rely on their carers to see and respond appropriately to their fundamental survival needs. Since the parenting that generates insecure attachment fails in accurate mirroring, the children suffer a deficit in psychofeedback (Gerhardt, 2011, 2015). This is crucial, because it is adequate psychofeedback that guides the individual in learning that he is real, acceptable, and intelligible. But the insecurely attached (particularly those in the disorganised class) receive less of this mirroring, which therefore generates a weak sense of self. Such people are less resilient to stress in the face of life's vicissitudes. They don't learn to identify or give meaning to emotional states or even become aware of being a self: the necessary preconditions to understanding that one has mental as well as physical agency.

Beatrice Beebe and colleagues have studied communication patterns within mother-child dyads, examining how well the response of one partner corresponds to that of the other (Beebe et al., 2005). Avoidantly attached pairs were markedly independent of each other in vocal rhythm matching, while ambivalently attached dyads were excessively well matched. Securely attached pairs, on the other hand, fell into the midrange of corresponding with each other while also having the freedom to vary responses. Siegel points out that this balance between "interpersonal linkage" ("Intimacy" in Table 4.1) and "individual differentiation" ("Autonomy" in Table 4.1) allows integration and maximal complexity to be achieved (2012, p. 204).

Whatever relationship model we internalise in childhood is likely to be replicated in our primary adult relationships: we will react in the same way as we did as children to closeness, loss, stress, or unattuned communication and behaviour. In adulthood the attachment styles are renamed as autonomous (equivalent to secure), dismissing (equivalent to avoidant), preoccupied (ambivalent), and fearful or unresolved (disorganised). The three insecure types differ from each other and secure attachment in their capacities for autonomy and intimacy (Table 4.1). Each of these has a default mood setting, internalised from the responses of parents and other caregivers. The secure/autonomous adult can respond flexibly to environmental conditions without getting stuck in any one particular mood, whereas the basal state for insecure attachment is either anxious or sad, which renders the individual prone to depression in the face of stressful demands, blows to self-worth, or threats to security.

Table 4.1. Default mood settings in different attachment styles.

Attachment style	*Autonomy*	*Intimacy*	*Default mood*
Autonomous/Secure	High	High	Balanced, flexible
Dismissing/Avoidant	High	Low	Sad
Preoccupied/Ambivalent	Low	High	Anxious
Fearful/Disorganised	Low	Low	Anxious and sad

Depressed people are particularly vulnerable to feeing unwanted or ineffective, and depressive episodes often begin with rejection or other loss of self-esteem, or with failure to get emotional support. The study of Brown and Harris (1978) found that those who lost their mother before the age of eleven and those with insecure attachment had little ability to repair wounds to self-esteem. Indeed, infants lucky enough to establish secure attachment with their parents do better on a range of measures later in life (Sroufe et al., 2009).

Affect attunement and self formation

Stern (2003) observed that babies are born with capacities for coherence (organising experience), agency (making choices), continuity, and affectivity. During the first eighteen months of life, these potentials become more complex and refined through relating to their carers: this is the pre-verbal period in which the individual develops a sense of self that does not depend on either words or other forms of representation. Crucially, the sense of self develops within a sensitised relationship with the carer where parents empathically attune less to the baby's particular emotional quality (category affects of sadness, anger, fear, etc.) and more to the kinds of arousal, the way the ebb and flow of emotion, sensation, thought, image, or movement *feels* (vitality affects) (Stern, 2003; 2014). These may include "less differentiated primary emotional states, such as surges of energy, a sense of deflation, images of one sort or another, diffuse fogginess, or nervous agitation" (Siegel, 2012, p. 154). This process is replicated—and repaired—when the psychotherapist tracks their client's energy patterns rather than merely responding to the emotional content.

Expression of the inner state through such vitality affects is the primary mode of communication between infant and caregiver during the early pre-verbal years. Vitality affects are elicited and shared by both caregiver and child: they constitute an interactive intersubjective field. Mother conveys vitality by her facial expression, the tone and intensity of her speech, the firmness of touch, timbre of voice, and how she moves. Infants sense themselves through these fluctuations in stillness, sound, comfort, joy, or pain. Adequate emotional resonance between mother and child leads to secure attachment, where the sharing of primary emotion doesn't simply allow the child to feel good, but also facilitates him in feeling experienced by others, and thus learning that he exists and who he is. This is crucial to becoming somebody and knowing who that somebody is—in other words to the development of self.

Affect regulation

One of the main consequences of secure attachment is the internalisation of the capacity to regulate affect, in other words the ability to maintain a homeostatic balance between arousal mediated by the sympathetic nervous system and calming via the parasympathetic. It is regulation that allows us to feel comfortable in our skin, to keep our feelings within a tolerable range of intensity, to soothe when over-aroused and to stimulate when under-aroused. This is achieved by sensitive attunement of the parent to the child's emotions, with external soothing by the parent gradually being replaced by the infant acquiring the capacity to self-soothe (Pearmain, 2001). The absence of this kind of affect regulation is highlighted in the story of Kay Jamison whose father's manic ebullience shaded into screaming rage before plunging into its opposite of immobilising depression (Jamison, 1997). While Jamison's bipolar disorder may be strongly familial, that does not imply that it is entirely genetic. Inheritance probably plays some part, but the other feature must be the highly charged and emotionally dysregulated environment in which the child grows up. Other memoir-writers who suffered affect dysregulation include Wurtzel, Merritt, and Martin. Unfortunately, when affect regulation is inadequate, this carries over into adult relationships, where even those connections that begin well can rapidly become a source of dysregulation.

Emotion is the organising process that shapes the self towards coherence; at the same time interpersonal relationships are the primary way in which emotion is regulated and integrated by the developing mind (Gerhardt, 2015; Schore, 2003a, 2003b; Siegel, 2012). As this implies, emotion is both the subject and the object of psychic processes. Thus, in the absence of attuned relationships, particularly in childhood, we remain fragmented, because the emotions that could integrate us are dysregulated.

In the attention even a good enough mother gives to her child, she doesn't always understand the child or even notice his signals, and indeed sometimes the child is giving conflicting messages, for example of both being tired and wanting more play (Pearmain, 2001). Attunement is never perfect but an ongoing process of good or bad fits, and Schore (1996) believes that it is the *attempt* to adjust that is important for the baby's learning to regulate affect and manage transitions. This is because such an attempt confirms the child in a number of ways: I exist, I am real, because seen by the other; my needs matter to the other; I can trust the other and her responsiveness to me. Repair following misattunement involves the parent soothing the distressed infant so that he is not left stuck in stressful feelings. If disruption is followed by repair, the baby internalises security and resilience; but if the child fails to evoke a positive response to a communication, he feels shamed (Schore, 2003a). With an adequate disruption and repair cycle, the child learns that it is possible to restore a positive relationship even after misunderstanding or conflict and thus he acquires a core of social confidence: that is, the confidence to seek contact and communicate his feelings openly.

Mentalization

The caregiver's ability to attune to the mind beneath the behaviour of the child leads in turn to the child developing her own capacity for what Fonagy (2006) calls "mentalizing": the ability to understand other people's minds. The mother who realises her infant had a tantrum because he was tired after being dragged round town all day is mentalizing; the parent who attributes the tantrum to him "deliberately trying to embarrass me" is not. The insecurely attached don't learn awareness of their own feelings or those of others and can't accurately attribute motivation to behaviour, so that when they or others are distressed it is very difficult for them to understand why. Essentially they live in a state of chronic bewilderment, blame, and projection. Stress and depression are frequently the outcome because the unmentalized are poorly aware of their own needs.

Table 4.2. Consequence of caretaking patterns on relationship expectations.

Caretaking pattern	*RIG*
Overstimulating	Relationships too demanding
Understimulating	Relationships unrewarding or rejecting
Selectively Attuned	Rigid and narrow sense of self
Misattuned	Relationships confusing or frustrating
Inauthentic	Relationships disorientating, leading to withdrawal

Sally Brampton felt loved by her parents, but she didn't feel seen or understood. Her mother lived in a state of low-level chronic depression, while her father, she believes, had undiagnosed Asperger's syndrome, making both parents incapable of seeing or understanding her (Brampton, 2008). This deficit affected her ability to know who she was or believe that her needs would be noticed and met, so that she learned to ignore and override her needs in adulthood. Her parents' blindness to her must also have contributed to her loneliness and sense of homelessness, which she attributes to their repeated moves from one country to another.

Internal working models

We unconsciously acquire non-verbal patterns and expectations of relationships, called internal working models by Bowlby, or representations of interactions that have been generalised (RIGs) by Stern (2003). These experiences of relationship affect not only what we come to expect of others, but also how the self is organised. Table 4.2 shows the kind of RIGs generated by various patterns of poorly attuned caretaking (assembled from Mearns & Cooper, 2005).

It is apparent that most kinds of misattunement by the parent will bring about withdrawal from relationship on the part of the child. This in turn leads to sadness, loneliness, and anxiety for the now isolated individual.

Maternal depression and its consequences

"When I was a child of nine or ten years old, I was so depressed that I used to wish I could die in my sleep", the novelist Margaret Drabble remembers (1996, p. 91). There was nothing in her external circumstances that made sense of her being tailed by the black dog at such an early age, until she realised—later—it was her *mother's* depression that was "mother to [her] gloom" (p. 94).

We are in constant interaction with our social environment, and being around depressing people is, it has to be admitted, depressing and exhausting: Gwyneth Lewis's husband, who nursed her through depression, fell apart after she recovered; Rachel Kelly's nanny "collapsed for several days" (2014, p. 249) after returning home to Australia. These effects cannot be attributed to genetics, but are the consequences of absorbing low mood from the depressed person. After merely reading twenty-one memoirs of depressive breakdown one after another, I felt like Persephone descending to a dark underworld from which I was not sure I would ever return. Being marinated in somebody else's depression is risky for adults. How much more so for the unboundaried child, who is being formed through his interactions with parents and other adults? The younger and less-formed the child and the closer the relationship, the greater the danger.

Having a depressed mother is predictive of depression in children, especially if they are insecurely attached: forty per cent of children of depressed mothers experience depression themselves before the age of sixteen (Gerhardt, 2015). The prognosis for children with a depressed mother is much worse than for a physically sick mother, with over three times more developing an emotional disorder (ibid.). An overreactive stress response underlies chronic depression (see Chapters Five and Six), and this system is programmed in the womb and the early months of life. After birth, breastfeeding inactivates the mother's stress response and facilitates her ability to calm baby's distress when it arises. But if the child doesn't have this experience, or if mother is absent, unresponsive, or herself stressed or depressed, the baby's levels of the stress hormone (cortisol) escalate, and eventually the cortisol receptors close down (ibid.). A research study showed that four-year-old children had high levels of cortisol if their mothers were stressed, "but only if their mothers had also been stressed or depressed when they were infants" (ibid., p. 95). Most of this stress has interpersonal causes—and consequences—and results from poorly adapted primary caregivers lacking in attuned attention to the infant. So while stress in adult life may trigger a depressive episode, it is early childhood stress that is a fundamental cause of depression in generating an overactive stress response in the first place. Most adults—those with a good start in life—do not become depressed in the face of bereavement, loss, humiliation, illness, or any of the other events that trigger depression in the vulnerable person. Conversely, a person who has experienced early childhood stress is less resilient even in the face of life's more mundane challenges.

To repeat: early stress leads to vulnerability to depression later in life. It can lead to greater susceptibility to anxiety, and permanent alterations in cerebral lateralisation and dopamine activity (Cozolino, 2010), both linked to depression as we shall see in Chapter Six. Infants of depressed mothers have a range of physiological effects characteristic of stress and depression, including greater right frontal lobe activation and higher cortisol levels (ibid.). If mother's depression lasts more than a year, the child is more likely to have prolonged impairment in left-hemisphere activation in the future (Siegel, 2012). Children aged ten who have grown up with a continuously depressed mother have a larger amygdala than controls; but even when maternal depression only lasts during infancy, the children were more prone to stress when tested at age thirteen (Gerhardt, 2015). Depression is linked to a smaller prefrontal cortex (the social brain), particularly the dorsolateral part that is involved in putting feelings into words, and to a less active orbitofrontal cortex, which makes it harder to infer the states of others or to regulate emotional reactions (ibid.).

Attunement in depressed dyads

Depressed mothers are more likely to be angry with their babies and spend less time in matching emotional states, including shared positive affect (Siegel, 2012); and such "loss of maternal presence, engagement, and vitality may all be experienced as life threatening" (Cozolino, 2010, p. 268). Normal mothers spend about equal amounts of time in positive or neutral interactions with their children; however, depressed mothers are switched off about forty per cent of the time, and angry, intrusive, and rough the rest of the time (Gerhardt, 2015).

To facilitate the development of the self the child has an absolute need for active emotional engagement, so that babies protest even more when mother is disengaged than when she is hostile (Gerhardt, 2015). Anger is an attack on the self, but cutting off contact negates the self: in this void, the baby (and even adults) can lose the sense of existing.

The importance of communication to the child is illustrated by Tronick's "Still-face experiment" (Tronick et al., 1978), in which a (non-depressed) mother switches from normal responsive contact to an expressionless face. The infant reacts by trying to evoke a response in ways that have worked before, until she rapidly gives up and begins to cry. In the extreme case of Romanian orphans who had virtually no emotional contact at all, the parts of the brain involved in stress management developed very poorly (Gerhardt, 2015).

Infants may be regarded as "open dynamic systems [who] must constantly garner information to increase their complexity and coherence" (Tronick & Beeghly, 2011, p. 107). While doing so, they are engaged in non-symbolic meaning-making, which depends on what they can *do* with objects (Piaget's sensorimotor stage) and how they *feel* about interpersonal experiences. Mental health problems arise when meanings that are adaptive in the short term "limit [the infant's] subsequent engagement with the world, and in turn, the growth of their state of consciousness in the long run" (ibid.). By being sad *together*, the infant and depressed mother stay engaged and thus produce "states of consciousness [that] can be coherent and complexity-enhancing" (ibid., p. 115) in the short term, thereby to some degree fulfilling the infant's developmental needs. However, over time, this depressed way of being together becomes stabilised, so that the child's self-organisation and relationships become rigid and constricted. What is missing from such an individual is the "flow" of a healthily developing sense of self, which is characterised by being "*flexible, adaptive, coherent, energized, and stable*" (Siegel, 2012, p. 336, italics in original). Not surprisingly, given the disengaged way in which they are parented, children of depressed mothers are less interactive, even with non-depressed adults. This has downstream consequences for further development of the self as well as for future relationships (Cozolino, 2010). When the parent is depressed, low energy and negative tone in the vitality affects are absorbed by the child and internalised as his way of being in life. In this respect, at an energetic level, we all become our mothers.

There is inevitably less psychofeedback from the depressed mother to her child: indeed the child can end up attuning to the mother rather than the mother showing the child who he is. One consequence is that the child will feel protective towards mother, and his life may become devoted to healing her: "to enliven her was my living" wrote Winnicott of his relationship with his depressed mother ("The Tree" quoted in

Phillips, 1988, p. 29). This establishes a pattern of attending to the needs of the other at the expense of the individual's own authentic organismic aliveness. Here lie the beginnings of a false or adaptive self and an external locus of evaluation, the shaky foundations that precede depression. Lewis and Solomon amongst the memoirists shared this desire to please and heal their mothers, as we will see later in this chapter.

Depression can be characterised, not just as *low* mood, but also *stuck* mood. Vitality affects are then less fluid and become anxious or down *states* where, in the adult, "the various thoughts and perceptions and memories may be skewed towards down, deprecating, low-energy forms … [and the] overall state's lack of flexibility, its lack of transitions [are] the primary problems in a person's life" (Siegel, 2010, p. 210). Children of depressed mothers don't expect mother to support, comfort, or soothe them out of negative moods, so they become caught in ruminating on how stupid or bad they are or how nobody likes them. In general they are less able to respond to negative events with problem-solving or self-distraction. Depression is cumulative and self-reinforcing because the more times a person fails, the more they feel hopeless and lacking in the confidence to react creatively to the next challenge in life (Gerhardt, 2015).

The young child of a depressed mother finds it more difficult to recover from negative affect and return to the positive (Schore, 2003b). Such a child's capacity to experience joy or excitement is markedly reduced, especially if maternal depression lasts beyond the first year of life. In depressed dyads, the normal amplification of positive affect is missing, so that not merely the experience of, but also the capacity to regulate and tolerate, such intense states may be underdeveloped (Siegel, 2012). In addition, as Drabble notes about her own experience: "depression is often linked to an unexpressed and inexpressible rage. The child has no strong person to kick against" (1996, p. 94), which in itself could be part of the reason for the depression if, as Freud believed, depression can be generated by repressed anger. I am myself familiar with the frustration and cycles of rage and despair that come from a mother perceived as vulnerable and fragile, and hence needing to be protected at the expense of my own life force.

In the face of ongoing misattunement, according to Allan Schore (1996), the infant's sense of self becomes equated with shame, the opposite of self-esteem, and the child learns to expect "humiliating narcissistic assault from a primary object" (Pearmain, 2001, p. 26).

For depressed people who have not experienced the potential for repair of misattunement, emotional regulation following interpersonal conflict is based on strategies of fight or flight, either attack or withdrawal (Gerhardt, 2015). In reparative therapy, it is crucial that the therapist comes clean when they make a mistake; this is a vital opportunity for the client to learn that misunderstandings and inappropriate responses can be worked through and that the repair process actually *deepens* trust and depth in the relationship.

A client, Shelley (Chapter Seven), who was severely depressed, brought therapy to a halt without explanation and by text message. I can only assume that she was hurt or anxious about how I had responded to her on some occasion, but I don't know when or why—though of course I have some hypotheses. She didn't pick up my telephone calls or reply to my texts. I had thought we had developed a warm and collaborative alliance, so I was shocked by her abrupt departure, but I was aware from her description of other relationships that she "knew" that once there was a rupture of the smallest kind, there was no possibility of return from that place. She described a large, schismatic family where alliances were constantly shifting, conflicts escalated rapidly, and where two brothers had already cut off from parents: this was the path that Shelley herself had just taken with her family and with me.

In conclusion, maternal—and also paternal—depression is a "communicable condition" (Tronick & Beeghly, 2011, p. 114) that profoundly affects children's emotional development. However, when mothers are treated and recover within three months, the prognosis for the children is good (Gerhardt, 2015).

Anxiety in infancy

Depression usually carries the co-symptom of anxiety, as was indeed the case for most of the memoir writers. Anxiety is a universal emotion given the helpless state in which we are all born (Cohen, 2013): the transition from a womb state where all needs are effortlessly gratified into a state of separation where we are utterly dependent on others for our survival generates inevitable shock and anxiety. The real danger isn't so much the helplessness itself as our *awareness* of it, Cohen observes. Part of a mother's job, according to Winnicott (1990), is to shield the infant from perceiving his total dependence; she does this by giving him the "illusion of omnipotence" and hence an experience of safety.

Anxiety will be greatly exacerbated if there are difficulties at birth, if the newborn's mother is unresponsive because of stress, postnatal depression, her own insecure attachment or narcissistic needs, or because of excessive demands on her attention such as caring for other young children or needing to return to work immediately. Sometimes the infant will give up trying to have his needs met and lapse into uncomplaining withdrawal. One client, who was known by her busy mother as a "good baby" because she never cried, became a depressed adult out of touch with her needs. Anxiety is the first reaction to an awareness of being helpless, but it may be followed by depressed withdrawal as a secondary self-soothing long-term defence. However unpleasant or alarming it can become in the long term, depression may be easier to sustain than anxiety, which is bearable only in brief doses.

It should be clear by now that insecure attachment leaves us anxious about fear of abandonment, rejection, and not having our fundamental needs met. Separation anxiety, which is always lurking for the insecurely attached, can be provoked in adulthood when a spouse, partner, or parent is lost through divorce or death, as we can see in Andrew Solomon's reaction to his mother's death. Indeed, losses of job, home, neighbourhood, country, school, friends, and other elements of our secure environment can provoke attachment-related depression in both childhood and adulthood. Sally Brampton's plunge into suicidal depression in her early fifties coincided with a series of losses that replicated insecure attachment to her parents and her repeated loss of home when she was a child (Brampton, 2008).

Developmental needs

There has been a need for an integrative model that would bring together early developmental stages, the determining qualities of the relationship with the caregiver, and their impact on the soma as well as the psyche. This is fulfilled by the NeuroAffective Relational Model of development (NARM), which knits together relational needs and self-organising principles at different stages of childhood with the impact of deficits in the provision of these needs on our emotions and neurophysiology (Heller & LaPierre, 2012). At the core of the thinking is the belief that the capacity for connection defines emotional health. This connection embraces self and others, and is fundamental both to identity and to the regulation of the nervous system. The authors postulate five core needs or organising principles: connection, attunement, trust, autonomy, and love–sexuality, which emerge in a developmental sequence. Coupled with each of them is a "survival style" through which people cope if they have suffered relational trauma at any of these stages. The crucial point, especially in the context of depression, is that this survival adaptation protects the attachment relationship at the expense of the child's other needs (see also Tronick & Beeghly, 2011). Initially, if a need is not met the child protests; but if the neglect is chronic, the rage can threaten the attachment relationship and therefore the child defends against the ensuing anxiety by splitting or projection. In response to an escalation of unmet needs the child goes into freeze mode, with its attendant dissociation, helplessness, chronic fear, and toxic shame. Thus a potentially healthy life force of expansion, aliveness, and self-expression becomes compromised, first by symptoms of the sympathetic nervous system and then of the parasympathetic. Each survival style has shame-based identifications and pride-based counter-identifications. Frequently the shame is held in the shadow while the persona plays out the pride characteristics, but some people fail to develop the pride defences to any great degree and display their vulnerability throughout their lives. In presenting examples of each of the survival styles below, I don't want to imply that anyone lives solely out of one style. However, in many cases one organising principle has been markedly more compromised than others. We have already explored the role of attunement in self organising, but will now briefly examine the four other core needs according to Heller and LaPierre's model.

Connection

The type of connection we experience governs our capacity to be in touch with our body and emotions and to connect with others. The time in which connection is established is the period encompassing gestation and the first six months after birth: the period when the stress response is laid down (Gerhardt, 2015). Shock (e.g., in the womb, at birth, or subsequently) can generate a "connection survival style", in which there is a lifelong disconnection from the body and emotions and difficulty relating to others. Such people have severe boundary ruptures, can't filter the environment, and therefore dissociate as a primary coping mechanism. Their nervous system is highly activated: "Unresolved high arousal becomes the source of a relentless, nameless dread, a continuous sense of impending doom that never resolves" (Heller & LaPierre, 2012, pp. 37–38). Because of their early and profound dysregulation, connection types are prone to many different syndromes including anxiety, depression, and stress-related somatic conditions. The way in which one life difficulty builds on another is most clearly represented by people traumatised at this early stage. For example, a traumatised foetus will have a more difficult birth so that the newborn goes into a freeze response, which in turn makes attachment difficult. Later, these children are more vulnerable to their peers because they don't have access to the fight/flight response.

One difficulty for the connection survival type is that the trauma occurs before any capacity for explicit memory has developed, and indeed the trauma may have been inflicted on the mother or father rather than the child, as we will see later. Women who are pregnant when trauma occurs can transfer the threat physiology to the foetus—it is known, for example, that the stress hormone cortisol crosses the placenta (Gerhardt, 2015). People who conceive children after a trauma can pass on an overactive stress response either behaviourally, or through epigenetic imprinting (see Chapter Six). In the absence of explicit memory it is difficult for the child or adult to make sense of his terror and other intense anxiety-related phenomena, such as hypochondria about normal body sensations, or extreme sensitivity and paranoia in relationships. Matt Haig (2015) suffered throughout his life from phobias and a whole range of anxieties (fear of going mad, hypochondria, agoraphobia, and intense separation anxiety) and then had a severe depressive breakdown at the age of twenty-four. His mother had post-partum depression after his birth, which may explain why he had symptoms of the connection survival type.

Trust

The third need (after connection and attunement) is for trust, which generates the core capacity for healthy dependence and interdependence. In its absence, we feel that we cannot depend on anybody but ourselves and that we always have to be in control. The "trust survival style" develops when a child's dependency is attacked, manipulated, or used against them. Thus they learn to associate dependency with being used, and later seek to dominate others and wrest power and control into their own hands. These people really feel small, powerless, exploited, and betrayed, but may have a persona that is strong, successful and/or ruthless—doing to others what was done to them; the politician Frank Underwood in the American television series *House of Cards* is a classic example. The parents of the trust types reward their children for becoming who *they* want them to be and punish them if they fail; they encourage competitiveness and one-upmanship and force the children to act out particular roles of their choosing. The child may be rewarded for taking on responsibility or power (mother's confidante or instrument of father's frustrated dreams) before he is ready, and may be punished if he doesn't, so is forced to grow up too quickly. The inability to trust develops in an extreme form when a child grows up in a household or community marked by abuse or violence.

Several of the depression memoirs indicate a trust survival style. Andrew Solomon's "greatest happiness" as a little boy was the impossible task of, like Winnicott, making his depressed mother happy (Solomon, 2014, p. 282), and as we saw, he was, as an adult, conscripted into helping his mother with her suicide. His feelings towards her were projected on to his psychoanalyst, by whom he felt betrayed when she told him of her plan to retire. Daphne Merkin exhibits the shame-based identifications (small and helpless, used, betrayed), remaining dependent on her numerous psychoanalysts (Merkin, 2010) without—after forty years—realising that healing herself and making herself "happy" is her own job. As a child she had an abusive nanny and a mother who was cold and unpredictable—in general, a childhood that generated intense separation anxiety. Others exhibit the pride-based identifications. For example, Sylvia Plath/Esther Greenwood was driven by the intense competitiveness that came from having a mother who was very ambitious on her behalf (Plath, 1999); while most of Martha Manning's identity was based on achievement as "the express route to happiness" (Manning, 1994, p. 194), until overwork and the emptiness of her dreams crashed into depression.

Much of Gwyneth Lewis's battle with depression was a struggle with her mother, who was ambitious for her talents as a poet (Lewis began writing at the age of seven), insisted she enter the eisteddfod, and even corrected her work. Unfortunately, Lewis's early success as a poet made her the victim of envy amongst her schoolmates, so she decided to give up writing. A later tentative return to poetry was nearly scuppered by a jealous and demanding boyfriend. Having two external loci of evaluation (mother *vs.* peer group/boyfriend) giving opposite messages made it even more difficult for her to discover her own needs and drives. Lewis, like Solomon, had the fantasy of rescuing her mother from her rage and despair: "It has made me do some very uncharacteristic things which didn't suit me, including writing a doctorate. I felt that if I dragged enough prizes back to our cave that she would be satisfied and not need to go through that hateful cycle again" (Lewis, 2002, p. 139). But as her mother said: "'What if I'm not a happy type of person?'" (ibid., p. 213). Between living a life not her own and blaming herself for her failure to make her mother happy, Lewis unwittingly carved a pathway into her own depression.

The struggle to discover and act from the true self—with its associated authenticity and meaning—is the growth direction for those drawn into depression by the sell-out of the self represented by the trust survival style. Those who don't move beyond this style live out of either their shame or pride-based identifications, such as the Machiavellian Frank Underwood luxuriating in florid, self-aggrandising defences against his inner emptiness.

Autonomy

The fourth organising principle concerns the development of autonomy, which if all goes well generates the capacity to set appropriate boundaries and limits and to speak our minds without guilt or fear. If, however, parents are highly anxious on the one hand, or rigid and authoritarian on the other, the child can become fearful of independence, or angry, rebellious, and resentful of authority. Despite this, they may appear on the surface to be sweet and compliant and might fear disappointing others. As adults they can become paralysed by the internal conflict between these parts and may associate intimacy with being controlled or overwhelmed. They will, of course, be ambivalent towards authority and have a tendency to ruminate after personal encounters about whether they did or said the right thing. This blocking of autonomy can also be played out within couples, where, for example, a husband blocks his wife from working or having friendships independent of him. This is a common cause of adult depression (Rowe, 2003). Despite—on the surface—following her own path, Mary McEvoy never achieved full autonomy, but instead returned home (from her work as an actress) every weekend to help on the family farm. Here is a vivid example of how the child, even as an adult, will continue to sacrifice the self if that is the price for maintaining connection with the parents, which was of course a life-or-death issue in early childhood.

Parents are asked to go through many transitions and developments as their children grow. Some may be well-equipped to provide for the needs of the infant, but can find it difficult to step back and allow the older child or teenager to take responsibility and find her own solutions. Indeed, it has been shown that not only hostile parental attitudes (perfectionistic expectations, criticalness, and poor care), but also overprotectiveness, correlate with depression tendencies in the children (Randolph & Dykman, 1998). If parents protect their offspring against all anxiety, the children don't learn that they can cope when something goes wrong—as was Rachel Kelly's experience (Kelly, 2014). Likewise, Richard Mabey's parents protected him against the challenges of growing up by allowing him to live with them until his mother's death when he was in his fifties (Mabey, 2006). The over-coddled individual doesn't learn confidence in his own power and autonomy, or how to react appropriately to challenge, frustration, disappointment, or imperfection. Thus the parents' inability to tolerate their own feelings is passed on to their children.

Love–sexuality

The fifth core need is to develop the capacity to live with an open heart and integrate a loving relationship with sexuality. The "love–sexuality survival style" develops at two stages: between four and six years of age and at the onset of puberty. Parents who reject, shame, or punish a child's developing sexuality cause a split between loving and sexual feelings. If things go wrong at these times, the individual may base her self-esteem on looks or performance and be unable to combine sexual attraction with love for the same person. Such an adult may feel hurt, flawed, and unlovable, but her defensive strategy is to appear perfect or to reject before she is rejected. People with this survival style may appear highly attractive and successful, "the doers and the winners of the world" (Heller & LaPierre, 2012, p. 79); but their self-esteem is conditional on looks and performance (There are two subtypes: the romantic, who is openhearted but disconnected from his sexuality, or may find that as a relationship deepens his sexual feelings diminish; while the sexual subtype fears real intimacy—and uses seductiveness to avoid it).

If these childhood needs are adequately fulfilled we develop an authentic sense of self and the capacity for intimate relationship and autonomy that will enable us to engage with the adult world with flexibility and resilience.

Intergenerational transmission of depression

Most of the authors of the memoirs pointed to previous members of their family who had suffered from depression. All attributed this familial pattern to genetics. However, while I am not denying some genetic contribution to susceptibility to depression, it is clear that it is handed down within the patterns whereby family members recognise, regulate, express, and defend against a range of emotions including sadness, fear, anger, shame, and joy. Thus a mother with a particular insecure attachment pattern will pass this on to her children; if avoidant she will pass on a distrust of emotions in general. The children of parents who suffer from chronic anxiety will themselves suffer anxiety through being marinated in a fearful atmosphere and receiving constant messages about the world being an unsafe place. Parents who have an active (frantic and frenzied) response to anxiety (Breggin, 2014) will be stressed and vulnerable to burnout and will pass this defensive pattern on to some of their offspring.

Research on the descendants of concentration camp survivors reveals how anxiety is passed on to subsequent generations, despite the later members of the family having suffered no direct trauma themselves. Alison Pick grew up believing herself to be Christian. She learned the truth gradually about her Jewish father, his parents who emigrated to Canada and hid their religious identity, and his mother's parents who died in Auschwitz. Not surprisingly after such terrible losses, Alison's grandmother suffered from depression. What may be less obvious is that her father too suffers, as does Alison herself. She attributes it to her family repressing the horror of the gas chambers: "The unfelt grief had been passed from my grandmother to my father to me, like an heirloom … The depression I suffer from has always felt pre-formed, ancient, like it was given to me in its entirety at birth" (Pick, 2015). Such intergenerational trauma and depression is passed on in the emotional timbre and culture of a family: in all that is not said and in how the spoken and unspoken feelings are processed, or not. Recent evidence suggests—alarmingly—that it is also passed on epigenetically, as we will see in Chapter Six.

A narrow escape can likewise generate chronic anxiety, as was the case for the Jewish parents of Ruby Wax whose American relatives got them out of Nazi-occupied Austria in a laundry basket just before the borders shut down. Connecting her mother's early experiences to her neurotic attention to cleanliness, Wax says: "This probably is what made her so unconsciously fearful, which she projected onto dust balls. … Whatever the case, I picked up the panic in her voice and that sound has never left my head" (2014, pp. 13–14). This was one of the background factors contributing to her depressive breakdown, whose proximal trigger was the decline in her career.

Anxiety passes from generation to generation, as with a woman client whose grandfather was knocked down by a car. This man had emigrated with his wife and children from an African country where it was dangerous to draw any attention from the authorities. He could never trust that England was more benign, and out of fear that the car belonged to the police, he did not seek medical attention and subsequently died. His fear was passed on to his daughter in the shape of such exaggerated "respect" for the authorities that she actually reported her own daughter (my client) when she drove over the speed limit. This recurrent pattern of anticipating the supposed expectations of external authority, which my client had experienced in her family of origin, manifested in her as an inability to take charge of her own life, despite moving to Ireland to get away from her mother.

Amongst the memoirs reviewed here, Tracy Thompson provides the best illustration of intergenerational depression. She absorbed some of the emotional patterns and behaviours of depression from her mother, who had a traumatic childhood. Thompson's mother's story was one of abandonment: she never knew her father and she lost her mother at the age of four. She was passed on from relative to relative and then abandoned on the side of a deserted road at the age of six along with her ten-year-old sister. The children were placed in a poorly funded children's home, from which Thompson's mother was adopted at the age of eight. "Not surprisingly, she lavished her unqualified adoration on the man who came to her rescue" (Thompson, 1995, p. 25). However, after four formative years of loss, rejection, terror, and poverty, it is hardly unexpected that, as an adult, Thompson's mother frequently sank into despair, suffered from chronic headaches and nightmares and, underpinning all of this, had an overreactive nervous system. When her husband died, she was "inconsolable, her grief frightening in its abject need" (ibid., p. 71), her adult bereavement no doubt carrying reminders of all her childhood losses.

Thompson believes she acquired a genetic vulnerability from her father. While this possibility can't be ruled out, it is certain that his family history influenced how he developed, and then how he related to his daughter in a manner that diminished her security and self-esteem. When her father was a boy, his sister died in a household accident. He was sent to live with his aunt while his older brother stayed at home to help care for his mother. His father later abandoned the family, and at some stage his mother took to her bed with depression for a decade, leaving her sons effectively parentless. Tracy "sensed a deep, unfathomable anger" (ibid., p. 28) in her father. Although she and her father adored each other, she also found him "remote", over-critical, and "impossible to confide in" (ibid., p. 59), indicative of a defensive distancing of himself in relationship. The result was that she sought out male mentors and was needy for male attention and approval.

Thompson's parents seem to have had a loving marriage, and she and her sister were brought up with love and laughter in a fundamentalist religious home, though in the presence of their dependent and depressing paternal grandmother, who lived with them and whose need for contact was insatiable. However there was a pervasive atmosphere of anxiety in the household, and quite a lot of pressure to conform to the demands of the Church on the part of her mother, so that Thompson grew up feeling defective. Thus, her upbringing infected her with fragile self-esteem and a dependence on men to boost it, as well as second-generation stress, and insecurity about the reliability of relationships.

Summary

Vulnerability to depression is laid down during the course of childhood development. We need sensitive affect attunement to build the self-structure and the capacities for emotional regulation, mentalizing, and resilience to stress. These are all outcomes of a securely attached relationship. Depending on our early relationships with caregivers, we can internalise to varying degrees: a connection to our embodied life force; understanding and acceptance of our own needs; trust in others; and a capacity for both intimacy and autonomy in relationships. Failure to have these fundamental needs met generates stress, poor self-esteem, anxiety in relationships, and a disconnection from our own needs. The parents who facilitate the expression of a child's natural impulses, meet his phase-specific needs and limit self-serving demands will support the development of the true self of their child. Conversely, those who ask the child to adapt to their needs, whether implicitly (e.g., the depressed mother) or explicitly (e.g., the controlling or manipulative parent), thwart the emergence of the child's authenticity, with the result that an adaptive or false self will predominate. Ways of emotional processing and of interacting are passed on from generation to generation, thus creating familial patterns of depression.

PART II

THE SCIENCE OF DEPRESSION

CHAPTER FIVE

Low mood as an appropriate adaptive response: an evolutionary perspective on depression

Has depression survived as an evolutionary inheritance because it protects us against something worse? Disease mutations persist in the population instead of being removed by natural selection when they are useful in particular genetic combinations (at the same or different loci) and/or under particular environmental conditions. All adaptations come with a cost, and it is only when the cost outweighs the benefit that the trait will be selected out of the population. Every environment carries a different cost-benefit ratio. Thus humans with dark skin were protected against the cancerous equatorial sunshine in our original African home, but as we migrated north, pale skin carried a selective advantage because it absorbs sunshine more efficiently and permits us to synthesise adequate amounts of vitamin D under the weaker light conditions. Likewise, a genetic make-up leading to susceptibility to type 2 diabetes in one dietary environment (rich and plentiful) enhances survival in another (the periodic semi-starvation conditions that characterised our evolutionary past and are still the case for millions of people today) (Diamond, 2012).

But why has natural selection not eliminated genes that predispose us to depression and anxiety? For them to be maintained at such a high level in the population they must carry a selective advantage. If we conceive of depression as a mood disorder, we need to focus on the adaptive functions of mood and emotions. It is clear that emotions such as sadness and anxiety are essential to our survival; it is more problematic to see incapacitating major depression as having a selective advantage. Thus, one key question concerns whether it is emotions or mood rather than depression itself that have a selective advantage (Nesse, 2009; Wolpert, 1999). A second is whether depression is a by-product inherited alongside another adaptation so valuable that it outweighs the allied cost of depression. The latter question of whether depression is "genetic fluff"- has been addressed by Keedwell (2008). He rules out the hypotheses of depression as a by-product of language acquisition, increased intelligence, or particular personality types. While there is no doubt that human depression is deepened by our capacity to think about our misery (rumination), there is no reason to believe that the capacity to think per se forms the foundation stone of depression.

The evolutionary biologist Randolph Nesse argues: "An evolutionary view suggests that we should expect evolved brains to be jumbles of incompletely differentiated, jury-rigged parts with multiple overlapping functions" (2009, p. 18). Thus a trait may initially evolve for one purpose and then be used in the same or a further adapted form (e.g., following gene duplication) for another function.

Extreme depression as the pathological form of useful functions

Evolutionary psychologists argue that it is low mood that carries a selective advantage and that the most extreme forms of major depression are a maladaptive spin-off (Keedwell, 2008; Nesse, 2009; Rottenberg, 2014). "Serious depression is not an adaptation shaped by natural selection. ... However, we do need an evolutionary explanation for why natural selection has left us so vulnerable to a disease as common and devastating as depression", Nesse contends (2009, p. 21). He lists six evolutionary explanations for why a "design feature" such as low mood may leave us vulnerable to a disease such as serious depression: (1) infection by agents that evolve faster than we do; (2) mismatch between our bodies and novel environments; (3) constraints on what selection can do; (4) trade-offs that limit the perfection of any trait; (5) traits that increase reproduction at the expense of health; (6) protective responses such as anxiety (analogous to pain, fever, and cough for physical disease).

That infectious agents—hypothesis (1)—can play a role is suggested by the facts that: depression can be induced by viral infections; inactive behaviour is beneficial in sickness; and there is a link between depression and inflammatory cytokines (see Chapter Six). One variant of Nesse's second explanation refers to the connection between depression and autoimmune reactions resulting from lack of childhood exposure to the diversity of pathogens found in our stone-age ecosystems. Other variants focus on the social environment: life under modern urban conditions is not only very different from the stone-age ones in which we evolved, but it is also changing at an ever-increasing rate as a consequence of social and technological development (see Chapter Seven), so it is virtually a certainty that we are imperfectly adapted to our current world. In our contemporary culture where people want and expect "it all", many—perhaps most—people pursue unreachable goals. (Nearly one third of American teenagers claim that they will be famous someday! (Rottenberg, 2014).) The theory emphasised in this book is that we are poorly adapted to our modern social environment. This is consistent with the increase in depression worldwide as well as with differences in incidence between cultures.

To understand Nesse's third hypothesis, we need to take into account that mood is regulated by a large number of genes (Flint et al., 2010; Gratten et al., 2014; Nesse, 2009; Plomin et al., 2013; see Chapter Six). Any polygenic trait follows a normal distribution (bell-shaped curve), so that the largest number of people have an average expression of the trait with small numbers at the two poles of extreme low mood and extreme high mood (Jang, 2005). Thus for a polygenic trait with inherently high variance it is not unusual to have a pathological version of the characteristic that carries no selective advantage, while the more moderate degrees of expression are adaptive.

In relation to the fourth possibility above, it has been observed that all protective responses can fail or operate in too extreme a manner. There is always a trade-off between costs and benefits in the optimal threshold for expressing a defence. Over-vigilance to threat may produce many false alarms as we shy away from blowing leaves or the sound of a breaking twig, but this is less costly than failure to respond to the sound of a predator. Support for hypothesis (5) comes from the finding that ambitious people may be both more successful and more prone to depression (Nesse, 2009; and the memoirs), and in certain societies would have more offspring. Evidence for theory (6) is that anxiety has an important protective role as shown by the problems of people who have hypophobia: some get into trouble and others die young. Likewise, people who don't experience low mood—such as those in the manic phase of bipolar disorder—can generate long-term chaos in their lives.

Nesse (2009) argues against the common assumption that depression is a brain disease because this ignores the role of life events in triggering it (Keller et al., 2007) and the advantages of low mood in certain situations.

> In contrast, an evolutionary perspective recognises that depression symptoms can be normal or abnormal depending on the situation …, that multiple factors may combine to cause a single case of depression, that etiological factors may differ markedly from case to case …, and that different depression symptoms may have been shaped to cope with different precipitating situations. (Nesse, 2009, p. 22)

That mild depression is advantageous is indicated by the finding that it is associated with increased longevity in women (Blazer, 2005) and by studies that claim that mild depression protects against suicide (Leader, 2009). In this view, depression is a message that something is wrong that must be attended to, not medicated away. An evolutionary perspective on psychological processes has often been reductive. However, in this case it both widens our understanding of depression and grounds it in concrete environmental and experiential realities. In the next section, we will examine the selective advantage of low mood.

The selective advantage of emotions and moods

What is the role of emotion and mood in fitness? Jaak Panksepp (2010) has identified seven "primary-process affective systems" in mammals, namely seeking, maternal care, pleasure/lust, play, anger, fear, and panic-grief. The four positive affects indicate that the individual is moving towards a comfort zone and the three negative ones are associated with discomfort zones that may impair survival.

Moods differ from emotions in that they last longer and are less tightly tied to specific cues (Nesse, 2009). They help us tune into and therefore relate to the world. The mood system "takes in information about the external and internal worlds and summarizes what is favorable or unfavorable in terms of accomplishing key goals related to survival and reproduction". Mood is "the great integrator" (Rottenberg, 2014, p. 13). It directs the individual's behaviour in relation to weather, time of day, safety of the environment, hunger, tiredness, need for exercise, practice or play, attracting a mate, caring for the young, and carrying out the multifarious goals of mankind. "Moods sculpt behaviors in ways that enhance fitness and do so without the animal's express permission or knowledge" (ibid.). The implications of this for life and therapy is that we go against moods at our peril because we thereby ignore our implicit regulatory processes. Moods are an integrated emotional response to our perceptions that then go on to shape our behaviour. They ensure that we avoid danger and maximise our resources instead of wasting time or energy on fruitless pursuits. An anxious mood narrows our attention to focus on threats; a relaxed but alert mood promotes exploration—of the social, natural, or intellectual environments. The necessity for low moods is illustrated by the problems of hypomanic individuals, who are unable to feel low mood. They make impulsive decisions, start too many projects, get into debt and complicated social difficulties—such as taking on commitments they cannot maintain or having a baby they have no way of supporting (Nesse, 2009; and the stories of Jamison and Merritt in Chapter Two).

Moods involve the body (micro and macro, visible and invisible), emotions, perceptions, cognition, and memory. Thus, an anxious mood while speaking in public might involve a rigid, alert posture, a staring, vigilant expression in the eyes, "butterflies" in the stomach, a highly active amygdala, the release of adrenal hormones, a scanning of the social environment for threat, a restless search for an explanation for the anxiety, an inner self-critical monologue, memories of similar occasions in the past, feelings of embarrassment, shame, and anxiety—amongst many more phenomena, all happening simultaneously.

Different adverse events lead to different depressive symptoms (Keller & Nesse, 2005; Keller & Nesse, 2006). Keller et al. (2007) correlated symptoms with nine adverse life events: death of a loved one, romantic loss, failure, chronic stress, health problems, conflict, distress over future events, other events, and no known cause. Their findings followed the patterns expected. Thus losses were followed by sadness, anhedonia, and appetite loss; while chronic stress and failure were associated with fatigue and hypersomnia. By examining the symptoms of individuals that had experienced more than one episode of depression as a result of different adverse events, Keller and colleagues showed that the symptom patterns did not result from stable interpersonal differences, but were caused by the specific nature of the adverse situation. This research demonstrates that depression is neither a single condition nor a disease; rather it is a context-dependent and *appropriate* reaction to environmental conditions. As Gilbert says: "different depressions can be associated with different physiological profiles, different types of thinking and behaviours, different life histories and current stresses" (2007, p. 22). Thus psychotherapy must be individualised for each unique case.

Adaptive value of low mood

There are multiple theories about the adaptive value of low mood (Keedwell, 2008; Rottenberg, 2014; Solomon, 2014; Wolpert, 1999) but we don't have to choose between them; rather, low mood "*is a state that is potentially useful in many different situations*" (Rottenberg, 2014, p. 24). The various hypotheses are summarised below, ending with the two that are most plausible, most widely applicable, and that match the findings from the memoir accounts in which loss and stress were the primary triggers for depressive breakdown. The different propositions are really just sub-branches of an overarching theory of depression as a reaction to chronic stress due to frustrated needs. Nesse suggests that selection may have "shaped different subtypes of depression to deal with problems in different domains" (2009, p. 25).

While it is clear that anxiety plays an important role in physical survival, in general it is social situations that are the strongest drivers of mood (Rottenberg, 2014). Peter Breggin links the emotions of guilt, shame, and anxiety to our social nature: "No other social creature is as violent as we are. No other violent creature is as social as we are" (2014, p. 19). It is not surprising that "our [human] lineage is marked not just by male dominance and xenophobia but also by a love of harmony and sensitivity to others", given that our genetic relationship is as close to bonobos as to chimpanzees (de Waal, 2013, p. 12). Breggin maintains that guilt, shame, and anxiety are *needed* to keep us from destroying each other within our families. However, when excessive, these emotions can damage self-esteem and are frequent accompaniments to depression.

Status depression and the social competition hypothesis

The social competition hypothesis posits that the function of depression is to inhibit aggressive behaviour towards rivals and superiors among lower-status social animals. This would help explain the triggering of depression by humiliation (Nesse, 2009), as well as the observation that many people prone to depression place a high value on social ranking (Gilbert, 2000). Depression is associated with submission, not just to other people but also to one's own inner attacker, thus creating low self-esteem (ibid.). High status animals have improved reproductive success and higher serotonin levels, which are associated with an absence of depression, and also with increased aggression (Keedwell, 2008). Status depression would have the function of restraining unrealistic ambition, thereby conserving energy and avoiding physical harm from a stronger opponent. However, as Wolpert (2009) points out, yielding to the opponent would be sufficient to meet this goal, and indeed depression would have been selected out of the gene pool (because of the effect on reproductive success) if low status were a main cause for depression. The existence of depression in children and its higher incidence amongst women than men also provide arguments against this theory (Wolpert, 2009). Turning the social status hypothesis on its head, a counter theory proposes that tendencies to negative emotions may have been selected because they motivate a compensatory high ambition (Nesse, 2009).

Research shows that "it is humiliating defeat that triggers depression, not being in a lower rank per se" (Keedwell, 2008, p. 89). Other studies show that it is the discrepancy between unrealistic expectation and actual achievement that is important in causing depression. Finally, depression is seen in solitary mammals such as cats that do not live in social hierarchies, implying that social competition cannot be the primary selective force for depression, though this behaviour (of withdrawal in the face of a higher-status rival) could have hijacked a depression capacity already in place.

Social navigation and allied hypotheses

The social withdrawal typical of depression may serve to preserve limited cognitive and emotional resources and to motivate others to provide help (Blazer, 2005); and indeed where social support is available, the bereaved (Rottenberg, 2014) and mothers of newborn babies (Wolpert, 1999) are less likely to become depressed. Postnatal depression is less frequent in societies where there is substantial help provided to the new mother—four per cent in Hong Kong *vs.* ten per cent in the West (ibid.).

Dysphoric people are better at solving social problems, and one outcome of depressive navigation of the social world may be the discarding and replacement of unhelpful old alliances. As Keedwell concludes: "mild to moderate depression makes us more attentive to the quality of our social relationships, the structure of our social network, who has power, who has what opinions, how these opinions differ from our own and whether they facilitate or hinder essential change in our lives" (2008, p. 121).

The depressed individual in stone age times would be less capable of fending off predators and hunting or foraging for food. On the other hand, immobility reduces the risk of attack; slowing down reduces the need for food; and the depressed state might elicit increased support from other members of the tribe. Hunter-gatherer groups probably consisted of forty to fifty people of whom up to a half might have been children, so the loss of any one individual to illness would have had serious consequences. Keedwell suggests that small tribal communities might have traded a short-term withdrawal of an individual for recuperation against the long-term gain of retrieving them as active members of the group. He presents anthropological evidence from a present-day Ugandan village that "depression may indeed trigger a caring response in more traditional communities, and extort concessions with regard to normal responsibilities" (2008, p. 102).

Support for the view that depression is "a device for the elicitation of altruism" (Watson & Andrews, quoted in Solomon, 2014, p. 410) comes from the memoirs, which reveal astonishing amounts of self-sacrificing behaviour on the part of the families and friends of those suffering from clinical depression (e.g., Rachel Kelly, Michael Harding, Richard Mabey, Matt Haig, Gwyneth Lewis, and Andrew Solomon). However, if depression is indeed a strategy for evoking help and sympathy, it is a costly one since many more people respond with revulsion, fear, incomprehension, impatience, and judgement, as Solomon and Kelly also noted. Indeed combatting the stigma around depression was cited as one of the reasons for writing the memoir on the part of several of the authors. In contemporary Western neo-liberal society, where individual goals tend to trump community needs, there may well be much less acceptance and support for the depressed individual than amongst our hunter-gatherer ancestors.

Depressive realism

Mildly depressed individuals are more realistic than non-depressed people in judging their degree of control over events—the phenomenon of depressive realism (DR) (Feltham, 2016). There is a selective advantage in being better at analysing the environment, but the DR effect is probably limited to a predictable environment and is likely to discourage exploration where there is a possibility—albeit a low probability—of success. The original research (Alloy & Abramson, 1979), and most subsequent experimentation, was done under zero contingency conditions (i.e., having no control over events), which may simply match the pessimism of the mildly depressed group. Non-depressed people are more likely to attribute their successes to ability and their failures to chance (Blazer, 2005), whereas depressed subjects are realistic about themselves but have a positive bias about others. This supports a depressive pessimism, rather than a depressive realism hypothesis (Dowds, 2016). An alternative explanation for DR is that these people have a heightened sensitivity to deception—whether issuing from themselves or from others (Allen & Gilbert, 2000).

Oliver James (2008) has alleged that self-rating surveys of mood are worthless because of the repressor personalities who claim to be happy whatever their state (as shown by physiological indicators). In one study, DR was accounted for solely by the repressor phenomenon. If, on the other hand, we accept participants' accounts of their emotional state, a meta-analysis of research to date revealed a small DR effect, though one below Cohen's convention for a small effect (Moore & Fresco, 2012). Depressives do better than others on tasks involving social problem-solving (see Blazer, 2005), and a brief change in mood induced in the laboratory changes how well people can argue, the sadder people being able to argue more persuasively with more concrete detail (cited in Rottenberg, 2014). The same researchers found that a sad mood increased a range of cognitive performances including memory, judgement, detecting deception, and better interpersonal strategies. This is not true for people in the state of major depression, where cognitive functions can be quite severely impaired. However, transient low mood may well be more adaptive in some situations than happy mood. People with normal mood tend towards illusions, overconfidence, and blindness to their faults.

It is tempting to see a parallel between the optimist/depressive realist divide and the distinction between extraverts and introverts. Extraverts have been shown to take more risks and to be overconfident, with less realism or concern about, for instance, incipient financial disaster. The comparison group in the research were people with a variant of a serotonin-regulating gene linked to introversion and sensitivity, who took twenty-eight per cent less financial risk than others (Cain, 2013). Introverts' quiet restraint helps them to outperform extraverts on cognitive tasks such as acquiring knowledge and critical thinking. Extraverts perform better under pressure of time or information overload, whereas introverts "think before they act, digest information thoroughly, stay on task longer, give up less easily, and work more accurately" (Cain, 2013, p. 168).

Depression as a stone-age relic

It has been suggested that depression served a useful function in stone-age times but that it is now a relic without function. We do indeed have many vestigial emotional responses: even those of us living in temperate zones often fear snakes and harmless spiders far more than cars (Solomon, 2014).

One hypothesis is that depression is a modern-day version of hibernation (Keedwell, 2008; Solomon, 2014). The advantage of withdrawal into a state of quiescence is that it conserves energy in times of seasonal hardship—cold weather and low food supplies. Depression, like hibernation, causes a slowing down in thought, speech, and movement, and withdrawal into a state of torpor. Antidepressants have been found to reduce or eliminate hibernation in hamsters, lending support to the idea of depression as a relic of hibernation (Keedwell, 2008). Hibernation bears a particular resemblance to seasonal affective disorder, both states occurring during cold, dark winter months and being characterised by increased sleeping, carbohydrate craving, and weight gain. Generic depression, on the other hand, is associated with weight loss and insomnia and probably has different evolutionary origins.

The dramatic and continuing rise in depression in the twentieth and twenty-first centuries strengthens the case against the vestigial function hypothesis. The statistics suggest the opposite—that depression is a malfunction generated by social conditions that were substantially less prevalent in our evolutionary past.

Cultural evolution outstrips biological evolution

The theory that our cultural evolution has vastly outstripped our biological evolution is indeed supported by the current rapid increase in depression. Humans evolved about 300,000 years ago, lived a hunter-gatherer lifestyle until the development of agriculture 10,000 years ago, and then led fairly simple agricultural lives until the advent of the Industrial Revolution in the eighteenth century. One estimate is that we lived as hunter-gatherers one thousand times longer than in any other way of life (Rottenberg, 2014; see Keedwell, 2008 for a slightly different figure). Biological evolution occurs at a slow rate, particularly for organisms that, like humans, have a long generation time. Thus our brains have evolved for stone-age living, vastly simpler, slower and more socially supported than the technologically accelerated, unstable, crowded yet disconnected lives of the typical twenty-first century urban dweller. Conditions in the wild involve occasional acute stress that ends with survival or death. In modern societies, by contrast, stress is chronic. Excessive freedom of choice, atomisation of society, materialism, decline of religion, and increased pace of change have been posited as some of these stressors. In a longitudinal study, adolescent girls who became less engaged with goals reported lower levels of depression, which suggests that one of the cultural causes of the rise of depression is our increased expectations (Rottenberg, 2014).

However the fact that depression has existed throughout history (see Solomon, 2014; Keedwell, 2008), in all cultural groupings including traditional settled agricultural communities (Keedwell, 2008), and also in our mammalian relatives (Keedwell, 2008; Rottenberg, 2014) does not support the hypothesis that depression is caused solely by the gap between our stone-age brains and our modern lives. It implies that low mood has always had an adaptive role to play. But there is, equally, no doubt that the frequency of depression is increasing rapidly worldwide, which suggests that at least part of the epidemic is caused by changes in social conditions. Support for this hypothesis comes from the finding that rates of depression are usually low in hunter-gatherer or purely agricultural societies. Conversely, they are higher in industrial societies, and higher still in societies in transition (Solomon, 2014).

Separation and loss

In the accounts of depressive breakdown discussed in Chapters One and Two, it was clear that loss and stress were the proximal triggers for depression (in people who are already vulnerable to it because of fragile self-organisation and attachment difficulties). This finding provides support for the two dominant theories for the adaptive value of low mood described in the next two sections.

Mammals have evolved to form long-term attachments to caregivers, sexual partners, children, and social groups. We experience separation distress or panic when parted from our attachment figures, and it is the fact that separation feels bad that encourages us to form and maintain attachments that are essential for survival (Panksepp, 2010; Solms, 2012; Watt & Panksepp, 2009). The loss of a mother, child, or sexual partner through separation or death leaves the abandoned individual with reduced fitness: the child has a greatly reduced chance of surviving and the adult without their lover or who has lost a child has compromised their reproductive fitness. So there is a strong selective advantage in the emotions of grief and anxiety, which keep us close to our attachment partners. For adults, the most severe grief is brought on by the death of a child, and even more so by that of a child nearing reproductive age (Rottenberg, 2014). Loss leads to depressive symptoms in other mammals and other relationships too. For example a chimpanzee who lost his playmate displayed a drooped posture, reduced play and interest in other pleasures, less sleep, low energy, slower movement, poor attention, and loss of weight (ibid.).

Three of Panksepp's emotions are particularly associated with depression: panic-grief, seeking, and play. Panic-grief is the emotion induced by separation of the infant from the mother and may be the pivotal pain that precipitates a depressive cascade. The seeking system is the reward system and major source of life energy or libido. It is associated with exploration and anticipatory excitement and learning. It may be diminished seeking that pushes the emotional system into the prolonged dysphoria of clinical depression. Finally, stimulation of the play system has antidepressant effects and could thus have a potent role in psychotherapy.

The reason why depression is a negative feeling we want to avoid is that it was selected to encourage the formation of attachments (Solms & Panksepp, 2010). It has the second advantage of acting as a shutdown mechanism to terminate protracted separation distress; this minimises movement that would make the infant visible to predators, and conserves energy until the parent or other carer returns (Watt & Panksepp, 2009). The response of an infant to separation from her mother or of an adult to separation from his lover is similar to that following bereavement. The loss that follows separation is accompanied by a protest phase where we seek out the attachment figure. If we fail to find her, we go into the despair stage where the seeking impulses shut down to save energy and minimise the risks of straying too far or attracting the attention of predators. In other situations the frustration of seeking elicits rage, but in the context of the despair phase of separation distress this rage must be inhibited. Solms hypothesises that the key to depression is the "brain state that mediates the transition from 'protest' to 'despair' in the wake of social loss" (2012, p. 212). When we realise that protest is doing no good, we enter a state of prolonged helplessness/hopelessness, like the hospitalised child who moves beyond crying into a huddled-up silence and withdrawal.

In the similar process following death of a loved one, the grieving duration is variable and can last from days to years, with nearly one in three of the bereaved suffering clinical depression, and nearly one quarter of all depressions being bereavement related (Rottenberg, 2014). One of the precipitating factors is lack of support: bereaved people who receive less support from others are more likely to go on to become depressed (ibid.). Loss of a loved one often brings a cluster of other losses with it, such as compromise of financial security, social status, assistance with raising children, and other long-term goals.

Bereavement-related depression was found to be similar to other types of depression in psychological and somatic symptoms (electrical activity in the brain, endocrine, and immune systems) and in the clinical course of the depression (Rottenberg, 2014), though, as we have seen, the affect profile differs depending on the triggering event (Keller et al., 2007). Since loss most consistently predicts depression and since, in Rottenberg's view, there is no substantial difference between bereavement and other depressions, he proposes that reaction to loss can be used as the key to understanding the meaning of depression. This seems helpful provided we define "loss" in very broad terms.

Entrapment in a threatening situation/chronic stress

An all-encompassing view of depression is presented in this section: that it is a reaction to chronic stress, or frustration of our fundamental needs. Loss of an attachment figure, discussed in the previous section, can be understood as one particular example of a severe attack on an archetypal need.

Paul Gilbert (2007) views depression as an effect of processing threats. Some protective strategies mobilise activity (fight or flight) while others involve deactivation (freeze/immobilisation). When the threat comes from a social source, the mobilisation may manifest as avoidance and the deactivation mechanism is submissiveness. It turns out that the amygdalae of depressed people are more reactive to threat, and this is what narrows the focus of attention and creates the preoccupation with the negative. Immediate defence strategies are followed by plans to avoid future threats and then the pursuit of safety. This last phase depends on our safety beliefs, many of which are learned in childhood: people will like me if … I am entertaining/work hard/don't get angry, etc. Gilbert understands depression as an interaction between the negative emotions associated with threat processing and two branches of positive emotions: those that drive us to seek rewards and those associated with contentment that switch off the seeking impulse. His approach to therapy is to down-regulate the negative emotions and tune up the positive ones.

Mankind has needs for specific kinds of relationship (e.g., for care or support), but we often have to compete in the social space and therefore need a range of protection strategies to cope with social threats. These outer and inner threats include loss of control over aspects of our lives; entrapment (e.g., in a marriage that can't be left for economic or other reasons); not being able to unleash anger (e.g., because of a belief that anger is shameful) and therefore hobbling ourselves in situations of conflict; inability to access or ask for support; or not feeling valued. If our fundamental social needs continue to be frustrated, depression can ensue.

Many of the stories examined in this book support the view that depression warns us off risky activities and behaviours by making them too unpleasant to tolerate. For a majority of the authors, it was extreme stress that triggered the depression, and there is now substantial evidence that it is a chain of stresses that marks the genesis of initial episodes of major depression. Mild depression causes introspection and self-examination. More severe depression can be a paralysing block against damaging behaviour and a strong motivator to change one's life.

Most first episodes of major depressive disorder (MDD) are preceded by acute stress or an adverse life event; but as the number of depressive episodes increases, they are triggered more easily in the absence of significant stress. Chronic stress, especially if accompanied by entrapment or humiliation, is particularly predictive of depression (references in Claes et al., 2009). Furthermore, early life stress from abuse or severe neglect generates vulnerability to later life MDD and anxiety disorders (Kendler et al., 2004; and references in Geschwind et al., 2009 and Claes et al., 2009). One study found that twenty per cent of women sexually abused as children had psychiatric disorders, mainly depression, compared to six per cent of the non-abused population (in Claes et al., 2009). In another study, more than one third of depressed patients had a history of childhood emotional, physical, or sexual abuse (Young, 2009). The greater the number of adversities encountered—of which the most potent are those that occur in childhood—the greater the stress sensitivity.

Familial factors (genetics and/or upbringing) play a role in sensitivity to adverse events, and higher maternal neuroticism—a personality trait that is partly genetic and partly environmental in origin—predicted greater vulnerability to depression in the face of stressful life events (in Geschwind et al., 2009). It is not simply the nature of the stress, but rather how we perceive the event as well as our beliefs about our ability to cope that determine the outcome (Maier et al., 2009). To summarise: the proximate causes of anxiety and depression can be the dysregulation of the stress response by current adverse events interacting with a vulnerability to stress that may have origins in genetics, or in the events or relationships of childhood.

Depressive behaviour can be seen in animals subjected experimentally to threats they cannot avoid: when they discover they cannot escape they soon cease struggling and conserve energy, which enables them to survive longer. When Seligman administered electric shocks to dogs from which they could not escape, the dogs lost weight, moved less, and slept badly—all symptoms of depression. When the conditions changed so that they *could* escape, the dogs nevertheless passively endured the shocks in a state of learned helplessness that lasted a few days beyond the experiment (Rottenberg, 2014). Rats subjected to a variety of unpredictable mild stresses over a period of weeks secrete more stress hormones, are less reactive to an acute stressor, and have a reduced drive to seek pleasure that lasts for many months. However, if they are fed antidepressants their responsiveness to rewards returns. Importantly, there is variation between individual animals in their response to chronic stress, just as there is amongst humans (ibid.).

For humans, in many cases "entrapment is virtual not literal" (Keedwell, 2008, p. 90): the door of the cage is open but the bird is too frightened to fly to freedom. A common human form of inescapable stress occurs in codependent marriages where the partners can't live with and can't live without each other. One may be blocking the needs, authenticity, and independent life of the other (e.g., wife blocking man from playing golf/going to the pub, or husband forbidding wife from working/seeing her friends) and the oppressed spouse is too unassertive to take a stand, so fearful are they of being alone. Equally—for instance when giving up an intolerably stressful job, relationship, or country—people may fear the unknown or the loss of what must be forfeited. Ceasing to struggle may have an adaptive value here, because a solution can spontaneously appear from the unconscious under low-anxiety conditions, as in therapy when exceptional insights or energetic shifts emerge from the client's process in what seem like moments of grace. For example, a more creative third way that transcends the dualistic options (stay or leave) may reveal itself so it may feel possible to stay in the same situation under new conditions after one has revised one's expectations of the job or spouse. Alternatively, change itself may seem less daunting after sufficient time spent calmly imagining life under different conditions.

In humans, as in other mammals, chronic stress from a variety of sources predicts depression more than a single event (Keedwell, 2008; Rottenberg, 2014). Adverse life events are more likely to trigger depression in women if they have young children to take care of (Keedwell, 2008). A single stress often multiplies into a bundle of stresses. For example, loss of a job in an economic downturn could lead to repossession of one's house, emigration, loss of country, family, cultural identity, language, and familiar surroundings. On the other hand, an adverse event can arise in a background matrix or causative chain of chronic stresses, such as an adolescent who gets into trouble with the law when there is conflict between his parents that has been partly generated by the strain of caring for an older relative with dementia. The arrest of her son may be the final straw that pushes the mother in the middle of this multigenerational chain of stresses into depression.

Relationship stress is the major driver of mood, which may explain the high incidence of depression and anxiety amongst women, twice the rate seen in men (see also Chapter Seven). Because of having evolved to rear children and sustain close-knit community living, women have higher levels of empathic attunement to others—as well as its pathological downside—called confluence in Gestalt therapy or lack of differentiation in family therapy. Excess sensitivity to others can leave the individual anxious, exhausted, stressed, overwhelmed, and overburdened by responsibilities—in fact, burnt out, and the reaction to this can be withdrawal and ultimately depression. By comparison, men can seem to live in blithely unburdened freedom. Many of my women clients need to learn to distinguish between self and other and to switch some of their attention away from the needs of others and towards their own.

Frustrated needs

Nesse argues that mood is "an adaptation that regulates goal pursuit" (2009, p. 23); in Keedwell's terms (2008), mood ensures we meet our "archetypal needs". Low mood stops us from pursuing an unreachable goal, but if we persist in this unattainable ambition, ordinary unhappiness can escalate into pathological depression. Such objectives may often involve attempting to change somebody else, such as getting your rejecting mother to love you or persuading your alcoholic spouse to stop drinking. When the individual *accepts* that their goal will not be achieved (e.g., the woman who cannot have children), "negative affect decreases abruptly" (Nesse, 2009, p. 23). Despite this, humans persist in pursuing unreachable destinations, often because these goals are what we have decided, in our particular cultural context, give us meaning and identity: as we will see in Chapter Eleven, we are constantly engaged in balancing one need against another. People who are least prone to low mood include those more flexible in giving up on blocked aims and ambitions, and those who can re-engage more quickly after a loss (ibid.).

A challenge to the stress/loss model of depression comes from the finding that negative mood is aroused more easily by obstacles to positive goals than by an inability to escape danger (Nesse, 2009). However, frustration of positive goals is not easily distinguishable from threat when our goals actually represent archetypal needs such as having children or finding work. Frustration of such needs traps us in chronic stress. This may be involuntary, as in bereavement or in our inability to get others to meet our needs, or it may represent a voluntary but misguided way of life, where the individual is so obsessed with one set of needs that he ignores other equally important ones. It is the self-inflicted forms that are probably on the increase in our atomised and ruthlessly competitive social environment. Many a marriage breaks down because the husband is so intent on career success or because the wife is so preoccupied with her children. But human life is complicated and we pursue multiple goals simultaneously. "Success depends on judiciously allocating effort among diverse enterprises, including getting material resources, getting and keeping a partner, taking care of children, making and keeping friends, and gaining social status" (Nesse, 2009, p. 24). No wonder that as we lose energy with age and have achieved our limited potential, we gratefully relinquish struggling with many earlier goals that we now deem no longer necessary.

The comorbidity of depression and anxiety (see also Chapter Nine) may be explained by anxiety and low mood both being elicited by failure and loss. Goal frustration is accompanied by sadness, anxiety, anger, guilt, envy, or jealousy, and the unpleasant nature of these emotions drives us harder towards achieving our objectives. The goal frustration state becomes drawn out when we live in denial of our other needs and continue to pursue the same course with the same strategy. For example, the successful businessman may recognise that his marriage is in trouble but continue to put his relationship needs second to his ambition at work and attempt to pacify his wife with expensive gifts. He may then lose his wife as well as his wealth in a divorce settlement. Depression forces us to surrender in these situations and reassess our lives and agendas.

The selective advantage of low mood depends on the environment. In a favourable environment, high mood and risk-taking carry a selective advantage—as during an economic boom. "In an unpropitious environment, costs and risks are greater than benefits, so low mood and anxiety *increase* fitness" (Nesse, 2009, p. 24, italics added).

The above generic theory of the evolutionary value of low mood/low-moderate depression suggests that it provides a useful trigger for withdrawal and reassessment of our lives when our archetypal needs are frustrated (Keedwell, 2008). The failure to give up on unreachable goals leads to more serious depression (Nesse, 2009). Depression can thus be seen as a self-protective response: it immobilises us, takes us out of chronically stressful situations, and forces us to reassess our lives so that we gain a new perspective.

Emotional processing

Beck's negative schema and Seligman's learned helplessness/hopelessness theories are major cognitive models of depression. There are conflicting studies on whether negative thinking follows or precedes depression: in other words, whether it is a cause or consequence of the condition. In one study, negative cognitions did not precede episodes of depression, while in others negative thinking in combination with a negative event did (references in Davison et al., 2004, p. 276). Negative cognition has dynamic qualities that are dependent on the mood state as well as stable trait-like properties (Beevers & Miller, 2004); but this does not imply that individuals with the trait of negative thinking are any more vulnerable to depression. Indeed, it has been found that while cognitive bias is mood dependent, formerly depressed subjects in remission are no different from never-depressed controls with respect to cognitive bias (references in Leahy et al., 2011). The majority of the twenty-one memoirists do not appear to have had prior negative thinking that made them vulnerable to depression: rather they developed negative thinking once they became depressed.

Depressed people, and women in general, are more likely to have an attribution style that keeps their self-esteem down: they attribute success to luck, but in the face of failure they take all the blame (Billings & Moos, 1985; Radloff, 1985). Furthermore, even in the late twentieth and early twenty-first centuries there is much less expectation that women should be or can be competent: thus they are trained in helplessness (Radloff, 1985), which may partly explain why women have a higher incidence of depression. Women are also more likely to make use of an avoidance coping style, which is associated with depression (Billings & Moos, 1985). So, depressed people are set up so that they cannot win: they may feel incapable of taking charge; they prevent good things happening; or if they are successful they don't take any credit for it.

The belief of Beck and others that depressed people are more reactive to negative stimuli has been shown to have no basis in fact. Indeed Rottenberg (2014) discovered that depressed people were actually less reactive than others to sad stimuli: they displayed emotion-context insensitivity. Nevertheless, depressed people have been reported to display a negative bias in processing emotional information, (e.g., showing increased attention to sad or fearful facial expressions); and in remembering self-descriptors, they recall a higher proportion of negative and a lower proportion of positive words (Leppanen, 2006). Cowen and Harmer (2009) subjected healthy volunteers to a sufficiently short-term treatment with antidepressants so that their mood was unaffected. Any changes in emotional processing were therefore directly due to the antidepressant rather than a secondary effect of mood changes. Both the serotonin (citalopram) and noradrenaline (reboxetine) promoting antidepressants generated positive bias in emotional processing. The researchers concluded that mood improvement generated by clinical use of these antidepressants is a secondary and longer-term effect of the immediate positive bias in emotional processing.

Emotional processing may be divided into: positive affect (PA): behavioural approach and feelings such as enthusiasm, interest, and happiness; and negative affect (NA): behavioural withdrawal and feelings such as distress, sadness, and hostility. Increased NA and a decreased capacity for PA have short-term effects in terms of immediate mood, but also long-term consequences such as an increased risk of depression. Research participants with the greatest genetic risk of depression reacted to daily life stressors with more NA than did subjects with low genetic risk (Geschwind et al., 2009).

Conversely, PA has multiple protective effects, speeding up cardiovascular recovery from stress, improving immune system functioning, increasing longevity, giving greater resilience to chronic pain, and facilitating accomplishment (Fredrickson, 2001; and references in Geschwind et al., 2009). The experience of positive emotions during daily life stress was found to protect against stress sensitivity and attenuated the effect of genetic vulnerability to low mood; and it was found that the distinction between antidepressant treatment responders and non-responders depended on restoration of the ability to experience positive affect (Geschwind et al., 2009). In discussing ways of increasing PA, the authors noted that people report more PA in mindful than in non-mindful states and that advanced meditators experience more positive emotions.

Psychological health is not the absence of low mood; it is, rather, flexibility of mood, where there is an appropriate emotional response to the inner and outer environment and a capacity to listen to the message inherent in the depressed feelings. Part of the flexibility depends on the capacity for PA, which allows the individual to bounce back instead of getting stuck in a prolonged state of low mood.

Summary

This chapter has summarised the major theories about the selective advantage of depression. It is likely that it is the low mood of mild or moderate depression that increases fitness in at least some contexts, but that severe depression may have no selective advantage. Depressive symptoms of reduced activity, decreased appetite, and withdrawn behaviour are advantageous in many situations that threaten our basic survival and reproductive needs. These situations may include failure to meet our life goals, rejection, neglect or abuse in childhood, separation distress, loss of or threat to parent, child, mate, health, job, home, social resources (love), or even status resources—in other words an attack on any of our fundamental needs. These threats are often involuntary, but are sometimes self-inflicted through over-attention to some needs at the expense of others. Chronic stress from a source such as overwork can frustrate our basic drives towards fun, exploration, pleasure, and caring for others (Panksepp's basic positive emotions) as well as the fundamental physical need for rest and rejuvenation of the nervous system. A solution for such people is to regulate their aspirations and desire for status or for pleasing others—their extrinsic motivations—in favour of intrinsic needs and goals: in other words, the satisfaction of Panksepp's positive emotions. This may require one to challenge unsustainable and often culturally transmitted beliefs about oneself and one's place in the world.

It is probable that under conditions of chronic stress, withdrawal and reassessment of our situation and eliciting help is our best evolutionary strategy. More incapacitating, long-lasting major depression is unlikely to be beneficial, but represents the cost that is the flipside of the adaptive benefits of any trait influenced by multiple genes.

CHAPTER SIX

What science can tell us about depression: neuroscience; genetics and epigenetics; gut microbiota

"There is no single theory to account for the many facets of the biological psychiatry of major depressive disorders," conclude the authors of an article that links stress and immune activation to depression (Dantzer et al., 2009, p. 133). Accordingly, in this chapter, I will bring together the main elements that have been identified in the biological matrix, while recognising that the origins of depression lie in how the psychosocial interacts with the biological. The recurrent theme will be that causality is multiple, complex, and only partially understood.

Neuroscience of stress and depression

To grasp the neuroscience of depression requires an account of: the architecture of the brain (including different affect-regulating structures such as the hypothalamus, amygdala, and hippocampus); the nervous system (especially the autonomic nervous system with its sympathetic and parasympathetic branches); the hormones (e.g., adrenaline, noradrenaline, cortisol) and neurotransmitters (e.g., serotonin, dopamine, and again, in a different role, noradrenaline) that serve as chemical messengers between the different levels and systems.

The neuroscientist Alex Korb (2015), writing for the layman, provides an integrative view of the parts of the brain and neurochemicals that play a role in depression. Parts of the brain implicated are shown in Table 6.1.

In relation to affective neuroscience, the most important part of the nervous system in the body is the autonomic nervous system (ANS), which connects the central nervous system (brain and spinal cord) to the rest of the body, including the organs and glands. The ANS has two branches: the sympathetic nervous system (SNS), which controls activation of the nervous system in response to motivation (including a threat); and the parasympathetic nervous system (PNS), which balances the SNS by inhibiting arousal and thereby conserves energy and facilitates bodily repair and immunological function.

The brain with the rest of the nervous system is composed of nerve cells (neurons) that transmit information neuron to neuron via a chemical signal, the neurotransmitter. Neurons that release or react to a given neurotransmitter are part of that neurotransmitter system. Hormones are made in the endocrine glands, and, by being released into the blood stream, they have a widespread effect throughout the body, wherever there are receptors to bind to them. Neuropeptides may function both as neurotransmitters and as hormones, and their function is to modulate the effects of neurotransmitters (Hart, 2008). The neurochemicals

Table 6.1. Functions of parts of the brain relevant to depression.

Brain part	*Function*
Prefrontal cortex (PFC)—"thinking brain"	
Ventromedial PFC	Thinking about emotions
Dorsolateral PFC	Planning and problem solving
Limbic system—"feeling brain"	
Hypothalamus	Controls stress
Amygdala	Mediates anxiety and fear
Hippocampus	Creates long-term memories
Cingulate Cortex	Controls focus and attention
Upper (dorsal) striatum	Habits
Lower striatum (nucleus accumbens)	Impulsive behaviour: fun and excitement
Insula	Awareness of body sensations

Table 6.2. Neurochemicals relevant to depression.

Neurochemical	*Type*	*Effect*
Serotonin	Neurotransmitter	Arousal, motivation, mood
Noradrenaline (norepinephrine)	Neurotransmitter and adrenal hormone	Alertness, stress, fight-or-flight behaviour
Dopamine	Neurotransmitter	Enjoyment, inquisitiveness, reward reinforcement
Oxytocin	Bonding Hormone	Trust, love, connection, reduces anxiety
GABA	Neurotransmitter	Relaxation, modulates stress response
Cortisol	Stress Hormone	Stress response
Melatonin	Sleep Hormone	Sleep, circadian rhythm
Endorphins	Neuropeptides	Pain relief, elation, modulate activity of monoamines

most involved in depression are shown in Table 6.2 (see Cozolino, 2010; Hart, 2008; Korb, 2015 for details).

The brain, ANS, and neurochemicals form neural circuits that interact with each other. There are circuits for pain, worrying, forming habits, making decisions, for sleep, planning, enjoyment, and mood, among many others. Depression arises from the complex interactions between these circuits. Korb likens depression to a traffic jam or a tornado, both complex and dynamic systems where a large number of conditions must combine to create the effect. But "once the pattern starts to form, it causes dozens of tiny changes throughout the brain that create a downward spiral". However, the upside is that "in complex systems, small changes can sometimes have big effects" (ibid. p. 13), and the bulk of Korb's book is devoted to the kind of small changes (exercise, light, making decisions, contacting a friend, etc.) that can lift depression.

We can now move on to a more detailed description of different elements of these complex systems.

The impact of acute vs. chronic stress on the nervous system

As we saw in Chapter Five, depression is a response to chronic stress, whereas the fight/flight/freeze options provide an optimal response to acute stress. When in danger, the social engagement system of mammals is shut down and the SNS is activated. This releases the hormones adrenaline and noradrenaline for fighting, fleeing, or activated freezing. If it appears there is no possibility of escape, a portion of the PNS—the unmyelinated dorsal vagal nerve—is activated (Siegel, 2012). Blood pressure and heart rate dive and the individual goes into the flaccid freeze or paralysis of the helpless/hopeless, dissociated state. This is the option available to many animals in the face of predators who won't eat what they believe to be dead meat. It is also frequently the only option available to the abused child: one traumatised client described himself as a child as "a lump of meat" thrown into his predator-mother's cage. There are great individual differences in what and how long it takes to activate the vagus nerve. Diminished vagal activation predicts vulnerability to stress in infants and greater sensitivity to environmental stimuli. In abused children, diminished vagus activity leads to difficulties with affect regulation, depression, and hyperactivity; but in children reared in the opposite context of safety, this same low activity can lead to interest, empathy, joy, and attunement with the environment. Conversely, increased vagus activity has been found in withdrawn and fearful children and in those raised by depressive mothers (Hart, 2008). Thus there is a connection—albeit a complex one—between the flaccid freeze response to inescapable threat and sensitivity to stress and depression.

Link between depression and anxiety

As we saw in the memoirs, depression is frequently accompanied by anxiety: they are found together or sequentially, with the anxiety diagnosis typically preceding the onset of depression. However, it should be emphasised that anxiety is not necessarily linked with depression: while anxiety without depression is quite common, depression without anxiety is fairly rare (Davison et al., 2004). Depression exacerbated by anxiety has a much higher suicide rate and is harder to recover from than depression alone (Solomon, 2014).

What is it that connects the two responses of anxiety and depression, when they look at first sight to be such different, indeed opposite, states of over- and under-excitation of the nervous system? Depression can be understood as a defence against anxiety (Rowe, 2003), and it is not unusual for hyperarousal to be succeeded by a corresponding, protective hypoarousal in an involuntary attempt to return the ANS to homeostasis. Infants' response to trauma (e.g., in a disorganised attachment pair) is comprised of two stages. The first response is the hyperarousal of the SNS, expressed as crying, screaming, and even vomiting. A subsequent reaction to infant trauma is the opposite state, dissociation, which involves "numbing, avoidance, compliance, and restricted affect. … [This] state of conservation-withdrawal … is a parasympathetic regulatory strategy that occurs in helpless and hopeless stressful situations"—which induce depression—to avoid attention and conserve energy (Schore, 2003b, pp. 188–189). It is a regulatory process that is used throughout the lifespan.

Later in this chapter we will see that the same genes are involved in predisposition to both anxiety and depression; and though they have not yet been identified, we can speculate that they play a role in regulating the balance between the SNS and PNS to limit degrees of over- or under-arousal.

The HPA cascade

Most people develop major depression as a result of chronic relational and psychosocial stress. Early and prolonged stress is correlated with poor affect regulation, with memory deficits linked to a smaller hippocampus, and with other alterations in brain development. A key hormone involved in the stress response is cortisol, which if sustained at high levels weakens the immune system and actually halts neural growth. The organism responds to stressful stimuli by transforming stressful input into hormonal messages that adapt our physiology as needed.

Chronic stress is mediated through the hypothalamic-pituitary-adrenal (HPA) axis (Dinan & Fitzgerald, 2009). The latter can be triggered by either physical (e.g., hypotension, exercise, or circadian rhythm) or psychological (e.g., danger or stressful events) signals. Within the limbic system of the brain, it is the amygdala that evaluates an incoming alarm and sends a message to the hypothalamus, which then synthesises corticotrophin-releasing factor (CRF). CRF in turn stimulates the pituitary gland to secrete the adrenocorticotrophic hormone (ACTH). The next step in the cascade is that ACTH acts upon the adrenal glands to release three key hormones: epinephrine (adrenaline) and norepinephrine (noradrenaline), which mobilise the fight/flight response (by increasing the heart rate, blood pressure, glucose metabolism, respiratory rate, and muscle tone), and the glucocorticoid stress hormone cortisol, which inhibits the alarm reaction. The physiological outcome of glucocorticoid release is to mobilise energy and regulate carbohydrate, lipid, and mineral metabolism (Lucassen et al., 2009).

If the stress response is not limited by cortisol, the fight/flight response will remain mobilised, resulting in post-traumatic stress disorder (PTSD) (Rothschild, 2000). But in a healthy responsive individual, glucocorticoid secretion is tightly controlled by negative feedback affecting CRF and ACTH secretion and production (Young, 2009). An example of this would be somebody being alarmed by the news that their company is downsizing, but then immediately relieved to hear that they are not one of the staff being laid off. An unhealthy individual, on the other hand, would remain in the state of alarm, despite the (for them) reassuring news. Negative feedback of the HPA axis is highly complex and involves two kinds of receptors—with opposite effects on serotonin-mediated responses—differentially distributed throughout the brain (Young, 2009; Lucassen et al, 2009). Given that the hippocampus is an important site for regulation, the impact of chronic stress will lead to its shrinkage. Whereas cortisol is particularly toxic to the developing hippocampus, it is less so to the adult one (Gerhardt, 2015).

Severely depressed patients display hyperactivity in the HPA system. This is caused by decreased glucocorticoid signalling affecting the negative feedback loop to the hypothalamus (Chourbaji & Gass, 2009), as well as by disturbances at other levels of the HPA (Dinan & Fitzgerald, 2009). Cortisol levels are high in most severely depressed people, and the symptoms abate if the cortisol levels can be brought back to normal. Depressed subjects have been found to have elevated resting levels of cortisol—levels that in healthy individuals would be sufficient to inhibit the stress response (Young, 2009; Claes et al., 2009). Despite this, depressed patients respond to stress by further increasing their concentration of cortisol (Young, 2009), and numerous studies show that patients with major depression have an inadequate capacity to switch off the HPA axis (Claes et al., 2009). These high levels of cortisol leave the individual in a state of anxiety (Gerhardt, 2015). A study of discordant twins suggests that altered HPA axis functioning is more likely to be a contributing cause than a consequence of depression (cited in Geschwind et al., 2009, p. 183).

In the population overall, basal HPA axis function is determined by both environmental and genetic factors, the heritability for cortisol secretion being about sixty per cent. Genes involved in key stress regulatory steps are currently being studied as candidates that may contribute to genetic vulnerability to depression (Claes et al., 2009). Child abuse is an important environmental factor: for example, women abused in childhood were more stressed by public speaking, as indicated by greater increases in heart rate and an augmented ACTH and cortisol response (Geschwind et al., 2009). Babies securely attached to well-attuned mothers have low levels of the stress hormone and a brain densely populated with cortisol receptors, which will mop up cortisol released in the future. Thus an unstressed infancy protects the individual against future stress because the stress response is quickly turned off when no longer needed. Conversely, the absent or unresponsive mother is likely to have a child who has fewer cortisol receptors, particularly in the hippocampus and hypothalamus, along with a hyper-reactive stress response that remains turned on after the stress has passed (Gerhardt, 2015).

While stress induces a high level of cortisol, there is a twist in the story. Some people have a low baseline level of cortisol, which may be associated with an emotional defence of withdrawal and denial and is found in children with low-level emotional abuse and neglect. It is not yet clear whether it is early life exposure to stress or its duration that is significant in generating low levels of the stress hormone (Gerhardt, 2015). Pregnant women among the survivors of the 9/11 attacks on the World Trade Center in New York were assessed for their response to the event (Yehuda et al., 2005). Those who developed PTSD were found to have lower cortisol concentrations in their saliva, and these reduced levels were most apparent in mothers in the third trimester of the pregnancy. The work of this team suggests that low cortisol levels are a risk factor for developing PTSD. We will return to this study in the epigenetics section because of the downstream effect on the unborn children.

The HPA axis is activated not only by stress, but also during infectious disease and by pro-inflammatory cytokines (Lucassen et al., 2009). The converse is also true, with stress having multiple effects on the immune system (Gerhardt, 2015), one of which, the depression-inflammatory connection, is explored in the next section.

Inflammatory responses

The inflammatory response can be triggered by an infection or by stress. Normally, it is switched off by cortisol within a few weeks of the initial trigger; but when it fails to do so, the production of pro-inflammatory cytokines such as IL-6 can double (Gerhardt, 2015). Acute and chronic stress as well as early life stress are associated with increases in immune cytokines and their signalling pathways (Miller et al., 2009). Not surprisingly, given its activation by stress, major depression is also linked with changes in immunity and in inflammatory responses. Medically healthy depressed patients show differences in inflammatory biomarkers, and there is a correlation between the severity of depressive symptoms and measures of inflammation (ibid.). In addition, adults with high levels of inflammation or pro-inflammatory cytokines are at higher risk of becoming depressed. One eleven-year longitudinal study concluded that it was the cytokines that initiated the depression, not the depression that stimulated cytokine production (Gerhardt, 2015).

Whether immune activation has a causal link with depression or is an epiphenomenon is still being debated; but in any case it has negative health consequences, so that depression is associated with an increased prevalence of heart disease (Dinan & Fitzgerald, 2009). Indeed, a hypothesis is developing that inflammation may constitute a common mechanism of both physical disease and neuropsychiatric disorders (Miller et al., 2009).

When proinflammatory cytokines are released in response to infection, they act not only at the site of infection, but also systemically, provoking fever and sickness behaviour (Dantzer et al., 2009). Sickness behaviour includes adaptive responses such as decreased motor activity, social withdrawal, reduced eating and drinking, hunched posture, altered cognition and mood, fatigue, pain sensitivity, and fragmented sleep. You will have noticed that these symptoms are strikingly similar to those of depression. Such patterns are normally reversed once the pathogen has been cleared by the immune system. But in conditions of chronic inflammation or when the immune system remains activated, sickness behaviour persists and becomes pathological, with ongoing symptoms of depression, fatigue, pain, and altered cognition. One hypothesis is that proinflammatory cytokines induce depression by disrupting synaptic plasticity and neurogenesis (ibid.). Indeed stress, inflammation, and sleep deprivation all modulate adult neurogenesis, which can be normalised again by exercise, recovery periods, or antidepressant treatment (Lucassen et al., 2009). However "a lasting reduction in neurogenesis may be indicative of impaired hippocampal plasticity but is, by itself, unlikely to produce depression" (ibid., p. 149).

Dantzer et al. (2009) caution against the assumption that the biological causes of depression originate in the brain, since the molecular factors causing depression can be generated at the periphery and only secondarily enter the brain. The question is whether cytokine-induced sickness is the same as depression or a different phenomenon, and the researchers conclude that "it would be … very premature to make the cytokine signalling theory a universal theory of depression" (ibid., p. 133).

Monoamine neurotransmitters

The brainstem maintains breathing and heart rate and is the site of most of the functions required for affect regulation. Here is the link to the body's autonomic nervous system, and it is here too that most of the brain's neurotransmitters are synthesised and regulated. The monoamine neurotransmitters noradrenaline (NA), serotonin (5HT), and dopamine are all produced in the brain stem, especially in the reticular activation system, which regulates arousal and alertness. In the centre of this system are the serotonin-producing neurons of the raphe nuclei, which have connections to almost all areas of the central nervous system. Fearful stimuli trigger the release of noradrenaline from the locus ceruleus, while areas of the brainstem that contain high concentrations of dopamine and endogenous opioids are central to stress management and in regulating arousal, affect, attention, the startle response, and sleep (Hart, 2008).

The monoamine neurotransmitters are important for emotional and motivational processes, and the balance between them is determined partly by genetic makeup and partly by early life experiences. Cloninger's biosocial personality theory is built round three axes: the dopamine axis rewards seeking-behaviour; the noradrenaline axis regulates reward-dependency; while the serotonin axis is involved in the avoidance of emotional pain (ibid.).

Serotonin levels depend on environmental experiences and an adequate level in the diet of its precursor tryptophan. Serotonin promotes social behaviour and inhibits aggression, and its receptors are concentrated in the amygdala and orbitofrontal cortex. Repeated shocks will reduce the serotonin concentration, and when the levels are too low there is less capacity to modulate arousal. This correlates with a reduction in investigative behaviour, more aggression, impulsivity, suicide attempts, sleep deprivation, incoherence, and mania. On the other hand, raised levels are also problematic, being associated with less eating, play, and sex alongside rigid and compulsive behaviours (ibid.).

Noradrenaline (NA) triggers fight-or-flight behaviour, maintains high arousal, alertness, and efficient information processing, including the capacity to concentrate and filter out anything that is irrelevant. Raised levels of NA result in the anxiety, irritability, alertness, quick temper, and defensiveness characteristic of stress and trauma. Affect regulation depends on the balance between serotonin and NA. A stressful early environment leading to raised NA and reduced serotonin levels can generate impulsive behaviour later in life, while low levels of both cause hypoarousal (ibid.).

Dopamine generates inquisitiveness and positive emotions. Positive affect attunement in early infancy triggers the dopamine system and is important for healthy development of the nervous system. Likewise, in adulthood dopamine levels increase in response to natural rewards such as food, sex, or falling in love. Excessive activation of the dopaminergic system causes delusions, hyperactivity, aggression, psychotic symptoms, compulsive and/or high-risk behaviour; while a low level of dopamine is associated with feelings of meaninglessness, lack of motivation, and withdrawal (ibid.). A role for dopamine depletion in depression is suggested by the finding that dopamine reuptake inhibitors were highly effective antidepressants in some individuals (Watt & Panksepp, 2009).

Serotonin and NA are the neurotransmitters that have been most implicated in depression, not least because they are the targets for antidepressant drugs and therefore subjected to numerous well-funded research projects. The monoamine hypothesis arose from the clinical effects of monoamine oxidase inhibitors (MAOIs) and tricyclic antidepressants (TCAs), which affect the levels of monoamines by preventing their breakdown and blocking their reuptake respectively. While attempts to show that the levels of these neurotransmitters were lower in depressed subjects had mixed results, the best evidence for their role comes from experiments in which the levels were artificially lowered. In a healthy control group, depletion of serotonin and NA had no depressive effect, showing that low monoamine levels were not in themselves sufficient to cause depression. However, in a group of volunteers who were formerly depressed but now recovered and no longer on medication, the depletion of these neurotransmitters caused a transient but striking relapse in symptoms. This chemically induced depression was accompanied by changes in activity of the neural circuitry involved in processing emotional information (summarised by Cowen & Harmer, 2009). It appears that individuals who have been depressed in the past are left with a metabolic "scar" that leaves them vulnerable to subsequent drops in levels of serotonin and NA, and it has been suggested that this may be a side effect of an overactive stress response (Gerhardt, 2015).

The excessive research put into what is a tenuous and partial role for serotonin in depression appears extremely misplaced when compared with work that still needs to be done on separation distress as a source of depression (Solms, 2012) or in social psychiatry (Blazer, 2005). One study showed that serotonin levels in the brains of untreated depressed people were actually double those of non-depressed controls (Murphy, 2013). Watt and Panksepp (2009), in a review of the evidence, conclude that serotonin may play a role in depression for some people but not others, and that serotonergic hypofunction increases the risk for mood dysregulation in general (including anxiety and impulse control disorders), not just depression. Indeed, serotonin's role as an all-purpose modulator of moods and emotions may explain why SSRIs work only partially or temporarily in most cases of depression (Solms, 2012).

Hemisphere imbalance

The left hemisphere of the brain is more active than the right in most people in the developed world (McGilchrist, 2010). The left brain is responsible for analytic, abstract thought and focused attention in known situations, whereas the right copes with the animate and concrete and with novel situations, is holistic, has broad attention and embraces context. In communication, the left is verbal, while the right communicates nonverbally through tone of voice, rhythm, and body language (ibid.). Schore (2010) has suggested that the left is the location of the conscious mind, and the right of the unconscious.

The left frontal region mediates positive feelings, exploration, and sociability, while the right frontal region is responsible for vigilance concerning danger, and is associated with withdrawal and negative affect, including fear, anxiety, and depression (Cozolino, 2010; Siegel, 2012). Bias towards right hemisphere activation is related to high levels of stress hormones, anxiety, and depressed mood; but the polarity between the hemispheres is specifically linked to the most recently evolved frontal lobes of the brain, with the right frontal region having a depressive stance compared with the left frontal lobe or the right parieto-occipital cortex (McGilchrist, 2010). Depressed people and people who experience more negative affect have "a sluggish left frontal brain, incapable of managing when a storm of negative feelings erupts in the right frontal brain" (Gerhardt, 2015, p. 144). Depression appears to be linked not only to decreased left frontal and increased right frontal activity, but also to reduced activity in the right posterior region, the part of the brain involved in threat monitoring (McGilchrist, 2010). But McGilchrist warns, echoing Jaak Panksepp, that these studies are probably imaging the areas associated with the *cognitive* content of an affective state rather than the affect itself, and indeed cognition—a left cortex property—is impaired during depressive episodes. Depression associated with right posterior hypoactivity has "more of indifference or apathy—a global vague lifelessness—in contrast to the anxious, disturbed depression" of left frontal hypoactivity (McGilchrist, 2010, p. 64), which fits the description of most or all of the memoir writers.

Stress initially activates the left prefrontal cortex, but when prolonged or uncontrollable the right prefrontal cortex is activated. Depressed people, however, may lack this buffering capacity of the left frontal lobe. The hemispheric imbalance associated with vulnerability towards depression is a stable state that appears to be laid down in infancy: babies of depressed mothers lack the left hemisphere predominance even at times when they appear to be happy, and a high proportion of them go on to become victims of depression themselves (Gerhardt, 2015).

Role of prefrontal cortex in responding to stress

Stress is experienced not simply because of *exposure* to adverse events, but also because of how we *appraise* the event and cope with it. The ventral medial prefrontal cortex (vmPFC) plays a role in mediating our resistance or vulnerability to such circumstances. The raphe nuclei in the brain stem provide virtually all of the serotonergic innervation of forebrain and limbic structures. A subpopulation of these 5-HT neurons, arising from discrete regions of the raphe nuclei, are stress-responsive and play an important role in anxiety and/or depression. This has been demonstrated for a variety of stressors that increase 5-HT metabolism or release in the medial prefrontal cortex, hippocampus, amygdala, and nucleus accumbens (in Maier et al., 2009).

The raphe nuclei in the brain stem are activated by both controllable and uncontrollable stress, but are inhibited by the vmPFC if the stressor is controllable. Likewise, there is a top–down regulation of amygdala activity by the vmPFC during *voluntary* reduction of negative affect in humans (for instance, when viewing frightening pictures, one may regard the situation as fake or imagine the outcome as different from that shown) (in Maier et al., 2009). Thus the higher and more evolved brain structure (prefrontal cortex) will inhibit the lower more primitive structures (brainstem or midbrain) when such behavioural coping is an option. This is a helpful resource for the recovering client as long as the cortex is not used simply to repress rather than acknowledge and regulate affect.

The separation distress system

The separation distress system (Chapter Five) is sensitised by the release of prolactin and oxytocin hormones prior to childbirth, which may be one explanation of why women are more prone to depression than men. The attachment and separation system is mediated by opioids which are powerful antidepressants, and it is only because of their addictive properties that they are not the first choice in the fight against depression (Solms, 2012).

Kindling

First episodes of depression are more linked to major life stress than later relapses. The kindling effect refers to changes in the brain that make further depressive episodes more likely after an initial severe depression caused by stressful life events. Each additional episode reduces the threshold for further attacks (Kendler et al., 2000), but it is not clear whether recurrent episodes become independent of stress, or if individuals become more sensitised to stress (Monroe & Harkness, 2005). Kindling could reflect damage to the stress response system or might constitute an adaptation or fine-tuning of "the depression threshold based on experiences in the social environment" (Nesse, 2009, p. 26). Gilbert (2007) points out that the neural pathways of learned fear don't ever disappear. When we learn that a situation perceived as threatening is actually safe, new pathways are formed (e.g., in the frontal cortex). These regulate, but don't eliminate, the old ones (subcortical): if the new pathways are later compromised, the old fears return.

Nature vs. nurture—genetic and environmental influences

One important question for its treatment and prevention is to what degree depression is genetically predetermined and to what extent caused by upbringing and adult environment. While it is clear that we have all evolved to have genes that contribute to mood, the question for the geneticist is to what degree one individual differs from another in her genetic predisposition to depression. Some human characteristics (phenotypes) are determined by single genes (e.g., ABO blood group), others by the effects of a large number of genes acting together (e.g., height). Depression and virtually all psychological characteristics (e.g., personality types) and psychiatric disorders (e.g., schizophrenia) have been found to be influenced by a large number of genes of small individual effect acting together. This has made it very difficult to identify depression genes. However, the nature *vs.* nurture contributions can be disentangled by twin and adoption studies, which produce a calculation of heritability (h^2). This is the proportion of phenotypic variance that is attributable to genotypic variance, where variance is a statistical estimate of the average degree to which individuals within a population differ from each other. (Populations where almost everyone was depressed or nobody was depressed would have very low levels of variance). Environmental influences comprise all the sources of variation that do not arise from genetics; they include: the impact of life's experiences, upbringing, diet, education, cultural influences, etc.

The figures that follow are more reliable for depression than for anxiety disorders, where the research is under-powered. The heritability for major depression has been estimated at thirty-seven to thirty-eight per cent while most anxiety disorders have a heritability of twenty to forty per cent (Flint et al., 2010; Plomin et al., 2013; see Table 6.3). The

Table 6.3. Percentage of variance attributed to genetic and environmental influences (Data all taken from Plomin et al., 2013).

Disorder	*Heritability of liability (%)*	*Environment (%)*
Major depressive disorder	37–38	62–63
More severe depression	70	30
Bipolar disorder	89–93	7–11
Generalised anxiety disorder	0, 20, 27	73–100
Panic disorder	30	70
Phobias	30, 40–60	40–70
Obsessive compulsive disorder	40	60
Posttraumatic stress disorder	40	60
Seasonal affective disorder	30	70

heritability for bipolar disorder (BPD) is much higher—in the region of ninety per cent. In a study of identical twins discordant (one affected, one not) for this condition, the children of the unaffected twin had the same risk (ten per cent) for BPD as the offspring of the affected twin. Family studies are beginning to show overlap in symptoms between BPD and schizophrenia, and a twin study has shown genetic overlap between them, including a common association with the neuregulin and dysbindin genes.

One of the most interesting findings of behavioural genetics has been the discovery of the substantial overlap between the genes contributing to different psychological disorders (Plomin et al., 2013). There is a correlation of 1.0 (i.e., one hundred per cent) between the genes contributing to major depression disorder (MDD) and generalised anxiety disorder (GAD). This means that exactly the same combination of gene variants generates vulnerability to depression or anxiety, and that which disorder will develop depends on the environmental conditions. However there is substantial overlap in the environmental factors as well, with a correlation of 0.5 between the conditions that generate MDD *vs.* GAD. There is also considerable genetic overlap between the different anxiety disorders, with differences largely caused by environmental factors. These data tell us that depression and anxiety are two manifestations of a (genetically) single trait of emotional dysregulation; whichever mood is experienced depends on the particular environmental trigger.

The same kind of multivariate statistical analysis that revealed the genetic identity of depression and anxiety also showed overlap between genes contributing to alcohol and drug abuse, antisocial behaviour, and conduct disorder. The results suggest two broad genetic categories of psychiatric disorder: internalising (depression, anxiety, and phobias) and externalising (substance addiction and antisocial behaviours) disorders. The former are more common in women and the latter in men, not due to genetic differences, but because of dissimilar social influences, for example, in what constitutes acceptable behaviour in males and females. The internalising disorders can be subdivided into those characterised by anxious/misery factors (MDD and GAD) versus fear factors (phobias), with panic disorder incorporating both features. The characteristic of neuroticism (one of the five OCEAN personality traits) overlaps genetically with internalising disorders, and there is a high correlation (r = 0.5) between neuroticism and major depression. Neuroticism is a stable and enduring personality trait, and childhood neuroticism predicts greater sensitivity to stressful life events in adulthood (Geschwind et al., 2009).

A different kind of methodology—genome-wide association studies—has also revealed the sharing of common genetic variation between psychiatric disorders, particularly schizophrenia, bipolar disorder, and major depression (Gratten et al., 2014).

These major genetic overlaps between supposedly distinct psychiatric disorders raise questions about the validity of current diagnostic schemes. They go a large way towards explaining the comorbidity of what have been considered to be separate disorders: patients with one disorder have nearly a fifty per cent chance of developing another within a twelve month period.

Heritability and what it does and doesn't tell you

Heritability refers to the genetic contribution to differences in a *population*, not to the phenotype of an *individual*. Thus the heritability figure for depression cited above does not mean that, for a presenting client, thirty-seven per cent of their depression is due to their genes. Rather, anything between zero per cent and one hundred per cent of the cause of the *individual's* depression might be due to genes.

High heritability within a group does not necessarily imply that average differences between groups are due to genetic differences. For example, we cannot assume that the average difference between an extreme group (such as the severely depressed) and the rest of the population is due to genetic factors.

Heritability applies to a particular population at a given time in a specific environment. Changes in the environmental variance will change the heritability value. For example, if the environmental variance increases (e.g., due to a greater gap between rich and poor), the heritability will decrease without any change in the genetic makeup of the population.

High heritability does not mean that environmental interventions cannot have a significant impact. Even for a condition such as phenylketonuria, which is entirely caused by a mutation in a single gene ($h^2 = 1$ or 100%), a diet low in phenylalanine protects against the phenotype of mental retardation.

It is clear that the heritability concept is entirely unsuited to express the genetic contribution to a psychological trait in human beings. There are, in addition, major methodological problems in the twin and adoption studies used to calculate heritability, which means that the genetic contributions to psychological and psychiatric traits is probably lower than has been estimated (Joseph, 2003). Furthermore, the recent finding that some epigenetic modifications are inherited implies that the genetic element in heritability estimates has been misleadingly boosted by an environmental contribution.

Identifying depression genes

If Joseph is correct about psychiatric conditions lacking a substantial genetic cause, this would explain why it has proved so hard to identify gene variants (alleles) associated with psychopathologies. However, it must be said that it is inherently difficult to identify the small-effect genes that contribute to multigene traits, and the genetic effect might be something non-specific, such as the tendency towards greater social sensitivity.

Because of the polygenic nature of psychological traits and psychiatric disorders and because of the difficulty with defining these conditions, research to discover genes that play a role in depression has been bedevilled by false positive results from underpowered studies.

Depression and neuroticism have been reported to be associated with a variant of the serotonin transporter gene (*5-HTT*). The serotonin transporter is involved in reuptake of serotonin into the neurons, where it is degraded or reused. The expectation was that individuals with more transporter would have less available serotonin and would be more prone to depression. In fact the opposite was found. Caspi et al. (2003) claimed that people who carried two copies of the short allele of the gene and therefore produced less transporter were more prone to depression in the face of adverse life events. However, a 2005 meta-analysis of more than 100,000 people found no association with neuroticism or depression (in Plomin et al., 2013). Furthermore, Flint et al. (2010) reviewed fourteen studies and only one showed a possible link between depression and *5-HTT* gene variants. They concluded that the finding was due to a chance association in an underpowered study. Another meta-analysis published in 2011 found strong evidence for an interaction between stress and the *5-HTT* gene in generating risk for depression (in Plomin et al., 2013), so it is hard to draw any firm conclusion at this stage.

The enzyme catechol-O-methyltransferase (COMT) degrades dopamine, which is associated with positive affect. A less active variant of the *COMT* gene , which leads to higher levels of prefrontal dopamine, increases the ability to respond positively to daily life events, a capacity that was found to provide resilience against depression. Furthermore, those degrading less dopamine also had faster and better responses to antidepressant medication (Geschwind et al., 2009).

MDD, BPD, and schizophrenia are all associated with a variant of the methylenetetrahydrofolate reductase gene (Plomin et al., 2013).

The candidate genes for bipolar disorder that replicate best are those coding for neuregulin (multifaceted role in the development of the nervous system) and dysbindin (expressed throughout the brain). These genes are also associated with schizophrenia (Plomin et al., 2013).

Rather than further attempting to associate gene variants with psychopathologies, efforts are now being put into identifying genes involved in endophenotypes—measures of brain function that lie between DNA and the psychological trait. When gene associations are sought to emotional regulation instead of to depression per se, there is a link to alleles of *COMT*, the monoamine oxidase A gene (*MAOA*), and the serotonin transporter polymorphism (Flint et al., 2010). Likewise, a less active variant of the gene coding for brain-derived neurotrophic factor (BDNF) generated a larger noradrenaline response to social stress than the more active form (Geschwind et al., 2009).

Another approach is genome-wide association studies (GWAS) (Flint et al., 2010) in which variations in the genome (polymorphisms) are linked to a given characteristic. A promising start has been made by utilising the vast amount of genetic information obtained by consumer genomics companies. A recent study examined the genomes of more than 300,000 people of European descent of whom about one quarter had suffered from MDD (Hyde et al., 2016). This revealed fifteen single nucleotide polymorphisms associated with MDD, some in loci that are rich in genes related to neurodevelopment. A previous study referred to in this paper found two loci linked with depression among the Han Chinese, though not among Europeans. These seventeen regions of the genome form the basis for a more refined hunt for individual genes involved in MDD; however, it will take considerable further work to identify the relevant genes and determine their functions.

Genotype-environment interaction

The definition of heritability assumes—contrary to common sense—that genotype and environment have independent effects. However, this is frequently not the case, and genotype-environment interaction (genetic susceptibility to environment) has been documented for a number of psychological traits. For example, severe stressful life events were found to have a greater depressing effect for individuals at genetic risk for depression (Kendler et al., 1995). The point to emphasise is the complexity of depression's aetiology: a large number of genes and multiple distal and proximal environmental causes may interact to trigger an episode.

Most studies of gene-environment interaction are under-powered (Plomin et al., 2013), and there is much controversy over the link between a variant of the *5-HTT* gene and depression (above). However, taking the endophenotype route, it was found that children's avoidance of angry faces was linked to this allele, but only when the mother was very critical. Likewise, children's hyperactivity was influenced by the interaction between the particular *MAOA* allele and early life stress. (*MAOA* is also associated with antisocial behaviour in people who suffered severe maltreatment in childhood) (references in Plomin et al., 2013).

Gene x gene x environment interactions have also been reported: variants of the genes coding for the serotonin transporter (5-HTT) and the brain-derived neurotrophic factor (involved in synapse formation and neuroplasticity) interact with each other and with childhood maltreatment and the presence or absence of social support to influence the risk for depression (Geschwind et al., 2009).

Experiments demonstrating gene x environment interaction provide an important argument against genetic determinism.

Genotype-environment correlation

One of the more thought-provoking findings of genetics research is that our genotype contributes to the kind of environment we experience in life. This can happen in three ways: (1) passively, in that the environment created by our families correlates with our genetic propensities; (2) by our genetic makeup contributing to the kinds of reactions we evoke; or (3) by our actively creating an environment comfortable for our personalities or other genetic proclivities. A known example cannot be supplied here because the precise ways in which genotype-environment correlation might play out in depression have not yet been delineated. However—without in any way condoning the behaviour or blaming the victim—one might speculate that certain personality types (which are *partly* genetically determined) are more prone to being bullied, thus generating acute social stress in both childhood and adulthood. This of course might be just one in a large number of ways in which our genotype could influence the constitution of our environment and make us more vulnerable to depression.

Epigenetics—the environment in our genes

While all of the tissues and cells in an individual contain exactly the same DNA sequence and therefore the same collection of genes, very different sets of genes are *expressed* in different tissues. Gene expression also varies depending on developmental stage or in response to changes in the environment. It can be switched on or off by a process known as epigenetics. Thus, specific genes can be silenced or activated in various ways, such as by the addition of methyl groups to the DNA or by an alteration in the tightness of localised packaging of the DNA round its core of histone proteins. These epigenetic marks are often tissue-specific and may provide the mechanism for gene-environment interactions alluded to above (Zhang & Meaney, 2010). Identical twins show an increasing degree of discordance in epigenetic marks over time (Spector, 2012), showing how the differences in their life experience can gradually override their genetic identity.

Until recently it was thought that an individual's epigenome was established during foetal development; but while this period is still viewed as critical, it is now clear that the epigenome can change in response to the environment throughout an individual's lifetime. Likewise, it was believed that epigenetic changes to a parent's DNA were lost during the production of eggs and sperm, so that environmentally induced changes were not passed on to the next generation. We now know that this is not the case for at least some epigenetic changes, which can be passed on through multiple generations. Thus, changes in our diet, behaviour, our exposure to trauma or environmental toxins can affect the mental and physical health of our descendants as well as ourselves. Likewise, the environment of our parents, grandparents, and more distant generations is currently having an impact on those of us alive today. We cannot rule out the possibility that the epidemic of depression is partly caused by trauma experienced by our ancestors, perhaps during the two world wars. It may take several generations to overcome the impact of war, poverty, dislocation, slavery, or abuse, and it is distressing to contemplate how future generations will be carrying the legacy of our current environmental, economic, and political crises (see Watters, 2006 for a general introduction to this topic). Of course, the converse of this is that under reparative environmental conditions, epigenetic changes can be reversed.

As we have seen, depression is generated by multiple stressful events, whose impact is mediated by the glucocorticoid hormone cortisol. An increased level of glucocorticoid receptors (GR) in the brain results in enhanced feedback to the adrenal glands, which shuts down cortisol production and is therefore associated with a reduction in stress (see section on the HPA cascade). In rats, better mothering (measured by the patterns of licking, nursing, and retrieval of pups) renders the infants more resilient to stress, with improved learning capacity and with the females becoming better mothers themselves. This is not in itself surprising. But what was exciting was the finding by Michael Meaney and colleagues that maternal attention decreased methylation of the GR gene in the hippocampus, thereby increasing GR expression and downregulating the stress response (Weaver et al., 2004). (In addition, over 900 genes in the pups were differentially expressed as a result of maternal care.) Furthermore, environmental enrichment or impoverishment could reverse the effects associated with the variations in maternal care (Zhang et al., 2006). The researchers were also able to reverse the epigenetic signal by injecting the mood stabilising drug trichostatin A into the brains of adult rats.

Meaney and colleagues went on to examine the brains of humans exposed to maltreatment in childhood who later took their own lives. They discovered the same pattern as in rats: there were epigenetic changes in the GR gene in the hippocampus that intensify the stress response (McGowan et al., 2009). These suicide victims also displayed lower levels of gene expression for genes involved in neuronal health and plasticity, including those involved in stress resilience. The same group of researchers have found that adults who report a poor relationship with their mothers have smaller hippocampi than average (McGowan et al., 2011; Zhang & Meaney, 2010).

There is increasing evidence linking depression to alterations in gene expression associated with DNA methylation and histone acetylation (Sun et al., 2013). There is a decrease in brain-derived neurotrophic factor (BDNF) in the hippocampus of patients suffering from depression. Treatment of depression by inducing repeated electroconvulsive seizures (ECS) brings about histone acetylation in several genes including BDNF in the hippocampus, changes that correlated with expression of these genes after ECS. Epigenetic alterations have been observed for other neurotrophic factors in the hippocampus and in other parts of the brain including the orbitofrontal cortex. Some genome-wide studies have been carried out on the epigenetics of depression, but a great deal more work is needed to explore the functional significance of these modified genes.

Mice subjected to chronic and unpredictable separation from their mothers exhibited depressive-like behaviours which were linked to epigenetic changes in the genome. Crucially and astonishingly, the impact of this early stress was transmitted epigenetically to the offspring of the stressed males over generations despite a normal rearing environment for the subsequent generations (Franklin et al., 2010). Thus mice who had never themselves experienced abnormal levels of stress behaved as if they had because of inheriting modified genes from their fathers (This inheritance of acquired characteristics confounds the central dogma of genetics and to some degree validates Lamarck's long-discredited thinking).

Parental trauma is associated with greater risk for PTSD, depression, and anxiety disorders in subsequent generations. Pregnant women who developed PTSD after exposure to the 9/11 attacks subsequently gave birth to children who showed an increased distress response to novel stimuli (Yehuda et al., 2005). Since cortisol crosses the placenta (Gerhardt, 2015), the inheritance of stress by the children is not in itself evidence of epigenetic transmission. But the group's subsequent discovery was major—the revelation that epigenetic modification can be passed on to offspring conceived well after the environmental event that triggered the changes. What was found for mice by Franklin et al. (2010) has now been extended to humans.

Trauma results in epigenetic changes not only in exposed adults, but also in their offspring who had not yet been conceived at the time of the trauma and who did not themselves experience childhood adversity (Yehuda et al., 2016). Working with peripheral blood samples from Holocaust survivors and their offspring, the researchers studied a gene, *FKBP5*, which decreases glucocorticoid binding to its receptor. Expression of this gene has been shown to be altered in both PTSD and major depression. The team compared differential methylation in the Holocaust survivors compared to non-exposed demographically matched Jewish controls. They found epigenetic tags (methylation groups) on the same part of the gene in both the Holocaust survivors and their offspring, but not in any of the control group or their children.

The genetic studies summarised above indicate that most of the cause of depression is environmental rather than due to gene variants that confer vulnerability. Now the work in epigenetics—though still preliminary—implies that we must look beyond our own lifetimes and into the lives of our parents and grandparents (and possibly even further back) to find these potential environmental causes. While it has been possible in some cases to reverse epigenetic changes, a great deal more research is required before we know what kinds of environmental support would bring this about and whether there is a time window when we are more plastic to change. The implications for therapy are both daunting and exciting.

The enteric nervous system and gut microbiota

There are 100 million neurons in the enteric nervous system, and indeed it may be regarded as our first brain, inherited from primitive ancestors who had a digestive tract but no brain as such. We know that emotions influence the stomach, but we are now finding that the stomach influences our emotions as well. Of the body's serotonin, ninety-five per cent is found in the gastrointestinal (GI) tract with the remainder found in the brain, and the serotonin in the bloodstream and gut is made in the enteric nervous system (ENS) (Kim & Camilleri, 2000). The capacity to be happy and resistant to depression and anxiety is influenced by messages from the stomach to the brain. The gut and the brain communicate in both directions via the ANS, the enteric nervous system, the endocrine system, and the immune system. In addition, it is now becoming clear that part of the bottom–up regulation of the brain by the gut comes from the gut microbes themselves. They may be regarded as a third brain. Each of these modes of two-way communication between intestine and brain is implicated in mood and anxiety disorders (Foster & Neufeld, 2013).

We are born with a sterile gut and become colonised by commensal intestinal microbes immediately after birth. Host genetics plays an important role in the composition of the bacterial community, though not the viral community, and the mode of birth delivery (vaginal *vs.* caesarean section) influences the microbes encountered and therefore established (Clemente et al., 2012). As the infant grows, and with the introduction of solid foods, the range of microbiota increases, until the diversity and types stabilise in adults—if diet, health, and environment remain constant and the individual has not been subjected to antibiotic treatments. Maternal deprivation induces gut permeability in rats (Barreau et al., 2007), and the physiological consequences can be alleviated by probiotic treatment of the pups (Eutamene et al., 2007 and references in Dantzer et al., 2009, p. 133).

There are ten to one hundred times more bacterial cells (10^{14}–10^{15}) in the gut than human cells in the entire body; this includes as many as 1,000 different species, among which the two most prominent phyla are Firmicutes and Bacteroidetes (Foster & Neufeld, 2013). Thus our own 25,000 genes are outnumbered by over 500,000 different bacterial genes in our intestines and faeces (Spector, 2012). The nature of our individual combination of gut bacterial and other microbial species (our microbiota)—and indeed the degree to which the microbial genes are environmentally activated or deactivated—impacts on our physical (e.g., bowel and liver diseases, obesity, diabetes, cardiovascular diseases, and cancer) and mental (e.g., autism, depression, and anxiety) health in ways that only now are being revealed (Clemente et al., 2012; Cryan & Dinan, 2014; Foster & Neufeld, 2013; Spector, 2012). There are three distinct groups, called enterotypes, which are not related to race or place of birth (Arumugam et al., 2011) but which correlate with diet. A high animal-fat diet has a *Bacteroides*-dominated enterotype, whereas a carbohydrate-rich diet is associated with the *Prevotella*-dominated enterotype, and a change in diet results in a rapid shift in microbiota within a day (Clemente et al., 2012). Gut microbiota are involved in digestion, as well as energy harvest and storage, and they aid in the maturation of the immune system (ibid.).

Intestinal bacteria—including commensal, probiotic, and pathogenic species—can activate neural pathways and signalling systems and play a role in the cause, prevention, and treatment of stress, anxiety, and depression (Cryan & Dinan, 2014; Dash et al., 2015; Foster & Neufeld, 2013). As we have seen, stress, trauma, and depression are associated with dysregulation of the HPA axis. Beginning in 2004, several studies have shown that mice raised in a germ-free environment (which therefore have an undeveloped immune system) have exaggerated HPA reactivity and enhanced stress reactivity compared to mice whose intestines had been colonised by commensal microbes in the usual way. Not only do microbes modulate the stress response, but the converse is also true. Neonatal stress in rats leads to long-term changes in the diversity and composition of intestinal microbiota which may add to long-term stress reactivity. However, treatment with probiotics (*Lactobacillus* species) during the early stress period normalised the levels of stress hormone. Stress increases intestinal permeability, which may allow bacteria access to immune cells (causing inflammation) and cells of the ENS through which they can influence the central nervous system (CNS). Food-borne pathogenic bacteria were also shown to affect stress circuits of CNS function directly through activation of vagal nerve pathways.

Furthermore, microbiota can influence the CNS via triggering sensory neurons of the ENS (Foster & Neufeld, 2013). Early-life stress influences the gut microflora, which in turn impact on the programming of the stress response. On the other hand, the adult gut microbiome seems to be more stable and resilient and begins recovery immediately after disruption (Dash et al., 2015).

Numerous studies have now shown that the microbiota profile influences anxiety-like and depressive-like behaviour in mice and rats (Foster & Neufeld, 2013). Unexpectedly, the absence of microbiota actually reduced anxiety-like behaviour (cf. HPA results above) and reconstitution of gut microbiota normalised anxiety behaviour, but only when applied early in life. Mice and rats showed decreased anxiety-like and depressive-like behaviours when fed with probiotics—*Lactobacillus rhamnosus* in one study and *Bifidobacterium infantis* in another.

In further studies on mice, the presence of pathogenic bacteria (at subpathogenic doses) in the GI tract increased anxiety-like behaviour even in the absence of a systemic immune response (ibid.). In experiments where there was also GI inflammation there were marked increases in anxiety, while treatment with the probiotic *Bifidobacterium longum* normalised the anxious behaviour. These studies and others correlate increased inflammation with a rise in anxious behaviour.

In the limited studies on humans, there is evidence that probiotics have antidepressive and anxiolytic effects similar to those observed in rodents (ibid.). Healthy subjects given a mixture of *Lactobacillus helveticus* and *Bifidobacterium longum* for a month reported significantly less anxiety, depression, and stress as well as better coping compared with the placebo group. In another piece of research, patients with chronic fatigue syndrome (who had an altered gut microbial profile) were given *Lactobacillus casei* for two months and then found to have fewer anxiety symptoms than the control group.

Foster and Neufeld (2013) concluded their review of the literature by exploring some of the pathways of communication between the gut and the brain. Reduced expression of brain-derived neurotrophic factor and dysfunctions in signalling by the neurotransmitters GABA and serotonin play a role in anxiety and depression. The profile of gut microbiota have been shown to influence each of these systems, but the work is still at a very early stage.

These results show that the profile of gut microbiota plays a role in anxiety and depression. Any factors that affect the microbial profile such as stress, diet, ageing, or antibiotic treatment have the potential to influence our susceptibility to anxiety and depression (ibid.). Depression is linked with diet: a "healthy diet" and a "Mediterranean diet" correlating with a lower risk of depression, while increased intake of sugar- and fat-rich foods is associated with poor mental health (Dash et al., 2015). Diets low in nondigestible fibre reduce microbial diversity and support fewer bacteria that protect against pathogens. Diets high in complex carbohydrates, plant-based foods, fruit, vegetables, and fermented food increase microbial diversity and the presence of anti-inflammatory bacteria, and promote the production of anti-inflammatory metabolites and good health. Inflammation has been linked with depression and is one consequence of intestinal permeability (leaky gut), which is promoted by high fat diets. Less healthy diets higher in fat and lower in fibre were characterised by more Bacteroidetes and Actinobacteria species. Conversely, diets high in fibre and low in fat were found to be associated with Firmicutes and Proteobacteria. The ratio between these groups of bacteria is important in generating pro- and anti-inflammatory balance in the intestine.

From studies of dietary change, Dash et al. (2015) conclude that a long-term alteration in diet may be needed to support lasting and significant improvements in gut health, and that different individuals may have different responses to changes in diet. Microbiota have evolved to increase their own fitness rather than the health of the host, and it is now being suggested that they may affect our eating behaviour towards that end: they make us eat foods that allow them to dominate the intestinal flora! Depressed individuals often crave foods high in fat and sugar, but the long-term effect will only worsen the depressive symptoms. On the other hand, dietary improvement has been found to prevent depression, and increasing microbial diversity may have the additional impact of limiting bacterial control over our food cravings.

Research on gut microbiota, diet, and depression is still in its infancy: the exact combinations of species that promote health have not yet been comprehensively identified, any more than the precise manner in which they interact with the enterotype, genetic makeup, diet, or life history of the individual. Beyond questions about the profile of gut microbiota lies another area for future research concerning the modification of microbial genes in response to environmental changes and how microbial gene expression influences our mood.

Summary

Stress, whether acute or chronic, and particularly that which threatens the attachment system, is a strong predictor of depression. This is particularly so if the individual has experienced an adverse childhood through abuse or neglect. While our reactions to stress are unconscious and instinctive, the manner in which we consciously evaluate it affects our capacity to ameliorate its effects. Stress leads to dysregulation of the HPA axis as well as affecting the immune system, including triggering an inflammatory response.

Most of the causes of stress and depression are environmental. However, our genetic makeup plays a role in our susceptibility, with some genotypes being more vulnerable to adverse environmental conditions than others. Alarmingly, stress and trauma are passed on from generation to generation, not only through parenting, but also through environmentally generated modifications that affect expression of key genes in the stress-response pathway.

Finally, the profile of microbes in the intestinal system is altered by diet and stress and in turn can generate stress and depression. A healthy diet and consumption of probiotics can help in the prevention and treatment of depression.

Since most (at least sixty-three per cent) of the variance in depression within a population comes from variation in *environment*, we can therefore look for probable causes of depression by examining experiential accounts (Chapters One to Three) and by correlating the incidence with changes in society, the subject of the next chapter.

PART III

A DEPRESSIVE SOCIETY? THE IMPACT ON THE SELF, RELATIONSHIPS, AND MEANING

CHAPTER SEVEN

A non-facilitating environment? The role of contemporary society and culture

We are living in depressed times. The epidemic is rising globally (Everyday Health, 2013): the incidence doubled in the 1990s (Plomin et al., 2013), and is increasing by twenty per cent per year (www.healthline.com). Major depression affects more than fifteen per cent of people in their lifetime (twenty per cent in developed countries—Cruwys et al., 2014), and is hitting people at ever younger ages. In the UK, rates of emotional distress have doubled between people born in 1946 and 1970 (James, 2008). Worldwide, those in the eighteen to twenty-year-old cohort are already more likely to have experienced depression than those in the sixty-plus age group, although they have been alive less than a third of the time (Rottenberg, 2014), and the prevalence has more than doubled between the early 1990s and the early 2000s (Plomin et al., 2013). While social disadvantage increases the likelihood of depression, it is on the rise amongst the apparently privileged classes as well. Anxiety disorders have a massive lifetime prevalence of twenty-nine per cent and can lead to other disorders such as depression and alcoholism (ibid.). Depression is in fact today the leading cause of disability worldwide, beating heart disease, traffic accidents, and cerebrovascular disease (World Health Organization, 2012). There may be a rise in reporting and diagnosis, but equally something must be changing in our culture on a global scale to vastly increase the frequency of this debilitating condition.

We saw in Chapter Six that the major causes of depression and anxiety lie in environmental influences rather than in genetic predisposition. Furthermore, since genes evolve very slowly, the rapid rise in depression must be attributed to changes in the socio-cultural environment, possibly supported by increases in the frequency of reporting. While I will be emphasising the many stresses and losses of modern urban life, I should acknowledge that, in many ways, life in the developed world has never been better. In the English-speaking parts of the globe, and in most of Europe, we have been at peace for decades; despite the diseases of civilisation, we have never had better physical health; we have unparalleled material well-being; and women experience unprecedented freedom. We are educated and free to express ourselves. The home environment has improved for children, who are in general treated with respect and thereby develop confidence and self-esteem unknown to previous generations. So in many ways it is hard to make sense of the dramatic and ongoing rise in anxiety and depression: "Never before have we in the West had it so good, and never have we felt so bad" (Verhaeghe, 2014, p. 108).

Perhaps one explanation lies in the fact that the history of the Western world is dominated by discontent—a discontent which, we seem to imagine, can be overcome by progress and improvement, personal, political, and economic. Progress under neo-liberal capitalism—and earlier under the planned economies of communist regimes—is expressed in terms of constant expansion, growth, and innovation. However, the doctrine of progress long predates the twentieth century, and its origins can be seen in the aspiration towards perfectibility in Christianity, and even before that in the notion of the Platonic ideal world of Forms. Perfectibility is a linear notion that devalues the cyclic nature and inherent balance of organismic life in favour of ceaseless and addictive striving (see many of the memoirs) towards a fantasy of perfection. The tool of this striving is the domination of both inner and outer nature. The "dialectic of enlightenment" and of progress is that human beings "pay for the increase of their power with alienation from that towards which they exercise their power" (Horkheimer & Adorno, quoted in Ingram, 1990, p. 62).

Imagination and flexibility are adaptive features, but they also give rise to discontent, according to Anthony Storr. Indeed, discontent is itself adaptive because of the depressing truth that "it is always the dissatisfied who triumph", and the most discontented of all—Western man—has been the most "successful" (Storr, 1989, p. 64). Less restless indigenous societies have been wiped out by genocide and displacement at the hands of predatory colonial powers. However, this Western thirst for endless "improvement" may be reaching burnout, as individuals are being forced to discover that their biological predispositions cannot match the aspirations of their will. Our bodies and nervous systems have evolved for stone-age conditions but are being asked to cope with space-age living.

Human beings are not infinitely adaptable, and object relations theorists have insisted that we come into the world with innate archetypal expectations and capacities. But not all situations are equally facilitative and any premature or excessive adaptation by the child to the parental environment (i.e., compliance) will arrest his development. We are thrown not just into a family but also into a pre-given social and cultural field. We enter this field not as blank slates and infinitely malleable but with archetypal needs for acceptance, holding, mirroring, value, and meaning. The socio-cultural field, like the family environment, can be evaluated according to whether and how it meets our needs and facilitates our flourishing or not. This chapter will argue that the rapidly changing, technologised, competitive, commodifying, atomising, and alienating culture of the present day, far from sustaining the individual, is itself a source of stress and deprivation that frustrates human development—as exemplified by the burnout phenomenon charted in our memoirs.

It has been claimed that postmodern, technologised culture is "less a remedy for alienation than a major source of it" (Labanyi, 2002, p. 33) because it fails to provide the conditions necessary for healthy human development. Applying Winnicott's insights into the maternal function (1989, 1990) to assess society and culture as a facilitating environment, Labanyi points out that we have "a triple crisis of mirroring, holding and object-presenting … The culture deluges us with manipulative and distorted images; … relentless change destroys the capacity to *be*, which is the precondition of healthy growth; and because of 'information' overload, the world decidedly does *not* reach us in 'manageable doses'" (2002, p. 34).

Psychotherapists are beginning to gather anecdotal evidence of the impact of the social environment on our well-being. In a therapy journal editorial some years ago I summarised the findings of the contributors: "Dramatic changes in society, such as developments in technology, globalisation, community and family instability, and the encroachment of market values into the personal sphere give rise to new clinical issues in the therapy room" (Dowds, 2008, p. 3). Clients are alienated from self and other and manifest problems of narcissism, domination by the id, somatic performative symptoms, emptiness, shallowness, and lack of meaning (Dowds, 2008; Staunton, 2008; Verhaeghe, 2008). We live in an age of anxiety where "we have lost our foundations and chaos reigns. … Western society is now characterised by instability, supersaturation and isolation", declares Blazer (2005, p. 136). Meanwhile psychiatry, apparently in a state of wilful blindness, continues to focus on genes and serotonin, having left the study of social psychiatry untenanted since the 1970s after its heyday in the 1960s (Blazer, 2005). Research is focused on neuroscience and the development of profitable antidepressant drugs, while there is very little investigation of the socio-cultural changes that might make sense of the pandemic.

Some twenty-first-century case studies

James has an Irish father and Chilean mother who met through their work for the United Nations. He was born in Geneva and educated at an international school there. He grew up speaking English, Spanish, French, and German and can move with ease from one language and one country to another. After attending university in Spain (having followed an ex-girlfriend there) and spending a year travelling round the world, he returned to what he regarded as his home in Switzerland. James is now twenty-five and suffers from low-level depression. He can adapt to almost any country but doesn't truly belong in any of them. His grandparents have left him sufficiently well-off that he doesn't have to work, and he dabbles in writing poetry. He is intensely lonely because his school friends have scattered all over the world, some pursuing postgraduate studies, some still travelling, and others having got jobs abroad. He is over-dependent on his parents and deeply ashamed that "nobody wants to spend time with me". His main source of contact is through social media, but staying in touch with his 800 "friends" there seems increasingly pointless.

Shelley's family returned to Dublin from London when she was twelve. She is now twenty-four, she feels she doesn't fit in, and has been depressed since her early teens. She has attempted suicide several times and only her shrinking from pain or fear of becoming disabled keeps her from trying again. She believes that her parents hate her, and worse still that her mother singles her out for dislike while demonstratively showing love to her siblings. She was bullied at work and left a sales job in a shop because of a false accusation against her that she thought everybody believed. She binge-drank and took hard drugs in her teens, but her fear of prison (being surrounded by others, particularly violent others) helped her to come off them. She is agoraphobic and fears people, but also needs them. Having had a bad experience with antidepressants she refuses to try another kind. In therapy, as she grows less anxious (less agoraphobic), she becomes more depressed and speaks of suicide. Shelley briefly tries things: jobs, friendships, boyfriends, antidepressants, therapy; but soon her fragile hope turns to despair and she leaves them. She is afraid to hope since she is convinced that she will be let down. Her attachment style is highly avoidant, overlaying a deep grief from feeling rejected: she leaves others before they leave or expel her. This is also expressed in her therapy: she punishes me for holiday breaks by not turning up for her next session. Shelley hates herself and believes that others can't stand being with her. She has no interests, no motivation, and experiences her life as meaningless. She insists that there is nothing to live for and that she has never for a moment felt grateful that her suicide attempts were foiled. She has some values—she is exceptionally honest and believes in treating others well—but is far too anxious to fight for what she believes. At the same time, she is constantly raging about injustice. She has nobody she trusts or loves and nothing she wants except to be loved—and, according to her, she has no power over that.

Isolde is thirty, spoilt, and narcissistic. She is married to a high-earning husband who is "good" to her and they have a six-year-old child. Isolde covers up her emptiness with an obsessive focus on her appearance, which manifests in body makeovers and a shopping addiction. She mixes with the highly competitive yummy-mummy set, where a Miss World contest is daily played out at the school gates. She has a part-time administrative job in a design studio, no interests, is highly judgemental of others (e.g., for not bothering to dress up), and is also acutely sensitive to their judgements. Her parenting is mainly focused on her daughter not letting her down, and the child is already showing signs of resisting all attempts at prettification and control. Isolde has been attacked and vilified on Facebook for having an affair with a friend's husband and is deeply distressed by this. She has few values beyond the appearance of fitting in, and is highly indignant if anybody accuses her of unacceptable behaviour.

These young people have grown up in a vacuous culture with a striking absence of ideals, meaning, or genuine affiliation with others, where roots are shallow and unstable, and where people's capacity for contact and absorption is being eroded by superficial and accelerated technologies. Education today has become far more instrumental than it was some decades ago. Certainly, in the 1970s and 1980s we did hope a degree would help us to get a well-paid job; but universities then still offered a rich intellectual, cultural, and social environment. Now they are brands focused on funding, marketing, competition for the best students and selling jobs-oriented courses. Students are likely to work much harder at their course work, to do work placements outside the university, and to have little time or energy for, or—crucially—interest in, broader intellectual and critical inquiry. Today, despite the proliferation of book clubs, fewer people read, especially those who have grown up in the internet era. Pew and Gallup polls show that twenty-three per cent of Americans didn't read a single book in 2014, whereas in 1978 the figure was only eight per cent. Only twenty-eight per cent read eleven or more books in 2014, whereas forty-two per cent did in 1978. Over-reliance on technology damages our capacity for depth and immersion, together with the accompanying nourishment, empathy, stress release, and experience of flow. One study discovered that reading on an iPad resulted in a less empathic and less transported experience than reading a printed book (Mangen & Kuiken, 2014).

Narcissism, obsession with looks and style, and commodification of the self increasingly characterise the twenty-first century individual. Such "chameleon" people "seem to lack interiority—in the sense of ongoing reflection on not just goals but on their deepest values, motivation and sources of meaning. They care about presentation instead of authenticity, skills instead of content, the *appearance* of success instead of achievement" (Dowds, 2008, p. 10). In response to her father asking her what she wants to do, Marina in the novel *The Emperor's Children*, answers "I want … to do something important" (Messud, 2006, p. 90). She fears being ordinary, but has no idea what actually matters to her. She is thirty and has never had a job because, like James above, she is too proud to start at the bottom and work her way up. If the lifeworld is the source of our identity, "the world experienced as a lived environment: my world, our world, endowed with my and our meanings, lived from within, layered with our interpretations", today we live with "the triumph of lifestyle over lifeworld" (Myerson, 2003, p. 17). Style and self-promotion have replaced an integrated identity. Erich Fromm, with the prophetic powers typical of the Frankfurt School, referred to aspects of this over sixty years ago when he noticed that in the USA the relationship of man towards himself had taken on a "marketing" orientation: "His aim is to sell himself successfully on the market. … Human qualities like friendliness, courtesy, kindness, are transformed into commodities, into assets of the 'personality package', conducive to a higher price on the personality market" (Fromm, 1990 p. 142). Friends and lovers are likewise commodified and expendable since there is no deeper tie to them than to anything that can be bought for a few dollars. Fromm equated depression with the boredom that results, and characterised the 1950s American as "a passive, empty, isolated person for whom life has no meaning and who is profoundly alienated and bored" (Fromm, 1995, p. 69). He is instrumentalised by himself and others and lacks the responsibility and initiative that are essential to moral development (James, 2008).

What I am illustrating here are aspects of the empty condition of the late twentieth and early twenty-first centuries—a condition fostered by late capitalism and materialism, intensified by technologically driven superficiality, masked by ideology, and justified by postmodern theorising. Each of these forces on its own undermines identity, values, depth, coherence, and stability. Taken together, their impact is devastating.

It is not always possible to separate the socio-cultural environment neatly into material (economy, technology) and immaterial (cultural), or objective (structural and environmental factors) and subjective (experiential and psychological) dimensions. Reality is not like that, but rather a complex interpenetration of these levels, and the following analysis will reflect this.

Material changes

Neoliberalism, hypercapitalism, and social fragmentation

Since the 1980s, with the deregulation of the financial system by Thatcher and Reagan, corporations have become dominated by shareholder profit at the expense of any responsibility towards the societies in which they operate. They display loyalty neither to their country of origin nor to their employees. One consequence has been a globalised division of labour, with manufacturing being relocated to developing countries with lower costs and less regulation, while service jobs (banking, computing, advertising, public relations) multiply in the West. The impact on mental health in the West ranges from the depression in old working-class communities degraded into sinks for an unemployed underclass, to the alienation and stress (with underlying depression) experienced by those doing virtual work—sitting at a computer screen all day without the satisfaction of either completion or a material end-product.

Unregulated capitalism has given rise to widespread social, political, and cultural destruction. In the words of Terry Eagleton:

> A judicious apologist for market forces would point to their role in the rapid accumulation of wealth, as well as the general advance of global civilisation, while acknowledging that this has involved not only poverty and inequality but a crassly instrumentalist rationality, ruthless acquisitiveness, economic instability, selfish individualism, destructive military adventures, the withering of social and civic bonds, pervasive cultural banality, and the philistine erasure of the past. (2015, p. 16)

The role of finance is no longer to reinvest profits to expand manufacturing; rather it has sidelined the productive sector altogether in favour of speculation and corporate gambling, often via automated mathematical algorithms (e.g., high-velocity trading). The social costs are catastrophic: high-functioning and profitable companies can be eliminated by vulture capital with huge job losses; global corporations can be worth more than entire states and can dictate to them; the economies of whole countries can be brought down by ratings agencies. Hypercapitalism is opaque and answerable to no one, and has undermined the very foundations of democratic government.

George Monbiot (2016) traces the origins of neoliberalism, not to random forces but to a planned system imposed on much of the world once Keynesian policies began to fail and after Reagan and Thatcher came to power. Its reality was masked by an ideology of freedom, but it was freedom for the rich alone, and brutal policies were often imposed precisely when people's attention was distracted by national crises (Klein, 2008). We are now familiar with the consequences: financial and corporate irresponsibility if not criminality; weakening of democracy; attacks on trade unions; privatisation of public services; increasing inequality, including a "precariat" who work and live without predictability or security; assaults on the environment; and recurrent financial meltdowns. The psychoanalyst Paul Verhaeghe suggests that culture and individual identity used to be determined by politics, religion, the economy, and the arts; now "the only thing that still counts is the economy, and here the neo-liberal economic narrative has taken over" (2014, p. 112). The shocking example of Enron's "Rank and Yank appraisal system" shows the ruthlessness of neo-liberalism: the employees with the highest production figures get bonuses, while the lowest ranking get fired. Psychologically, we have internalised this Darwinian belief system: it alters the way we view ourselves and each other. Our view of society is dominated by individualism, egotism, and competition in place of systemic thinking, altruism, and co-operation. This spawns a nightmare and delusional world of winners and losers, where the rich actually believe they have earned their wealth and the poor blame themselves for their inadequacies. Inevitably, this is having a devastating emotional impact, with epidemics of depression, performance and social anxiety, bullying and self-harm; our very identity is being shaped into a twisted form by this competitive individualism (ibid.). We will return in the next chapter to the relationship between depression and the development of the self in the twenty-first century.

Our current conditions of sink or swim leave us trapped in helplessness—one of the first triggers of depression to be identified. There is no longer any belief that the system can be changed through activism or national politics. Those caught up in the corporate world are treated with scant respect and with little consideration for their needs or aspirations. It appears to be impossible to change the working environment (with its exploitation and instrumental ethos) from within, so the options are to leave, or to hand over your life in exchange for a well-paid but probably precarious job. It is impossible to know who to blame other than the next rung in the chain of command. Workers in the nineteenth century were treated no better, but they may not have felt the same degree of resentment or sense of being trapped, perhaps because they lacked education and accepted their place in the scheme of things. Furthermore they knew who the masters were, so they had a real target for whatever rage or blame they felt, as well as a sense of solidarity. What Marx said about the working class in terms of exploitation and alienation now increasingly applies to the middle class. A central tenet of modernity was that we individuals have power over our lives. We can no longer fool ourselves that this is still the case—and perhaps it never was true: "Real power always resided with networks. … These groupings—corporations, religions, states—are now part of a vast network of interconnected information flows" (Runciman, 2016). What has really changed is that the networks of power are now so vast, complex, delocalised, and even dematerialised that resisting them is becoming harder all the time. Add to that our inability to envisage the future, and we can begin to understand how an increasing number of people feel trapped in helplessness and hopelessness. Our sense of powerlessness may also contribute to the rise in narcissism, and this in turn has its own negative impact. We have expectations and make demands on society, but have little sense of our own obligations anymore. This selfishness is a recipe for discontent, frustration, and anger, and ironically makes us unaware of the part of the bucket that is full as we become fixated on the empty half.

The gap between rich and poor continues to increase alongside decreasing social mobility (comparing UK birth cohorts of 1958 and 1970—Pearson, 2016). It is striking that income inequality has been shown to be detrimental to the mental, physical, and social health of not just the lower end of the socioeconomic scale but also the better-off sectors (Wilkinson & Pickett, 2010). In countries with high inequality, social relationships overall are more aggressive and less trusting, and there is less participation in community life (Wilkinson, 2005). The lower level of control over one's working life is a prominent stress factor in more unequal societies, and the powerlessness and helplessness experienced are known to provoke depression, anxiety, and anger (Verhaeghe, 2014). Inequality and selfish capitalism have an even more insidious and long-term effect than just their impact on adults. The countries that most espouse these policies also provide least financial support for babies and their parents (Gerhardt, 2011; Wilkinson & Pickett, 2010). The result is infants being kept for long hours in overcrowded crèches while parents struggle with two jobs in inflexible working conditions. The effect of such circumstances on a child's emotional and moral development makes it inevitable that countries that underinvest in parenting will suffer social problems when these infants reach maturity. The Anglophone countries, New Zealand, Australia, USA, and Britain, invest least in supporting parents and have the worst social problems, while Sweden, Norway, and Denmark are at the other end of the scale and have the best childhood mental health (Gerhardt, 2011).

Never have we seemed so close to what Žižek calls "living in the end times" (2011). As Blazer says: "Hints of catastrophe haunt our times. People busy themselves with survival strategies" (2005, p. 151). Global warming, pollution, destruction of natural habitats, and extinction of other species as the human population grows to pestilential numbers are wreaking havoc on the natural environment. Gains in human rights, especially for women and minorities, that have been hard-won in the twentieth century, are being eroded or reversed in the twenty-first century. Hatred of women and threats against us are thriving both online and in material form (the Taliban, Islamic State, and American Christian fundamentalism are only the most extreme manifestations), and in the continued corroding misogyny directed at women in the public sphere . There is a terrifying rise in fascistic populism where sectors of the population with genuine grievances are manipulated into blaming racial minorities and immigrants instead of the forces that are actually responsible for their plight. We have never been more aware of the horrors of war and the problems of refugees, economic migrants, and people trafficking, but what's different about wars today is that the main casualties killed or wounded are civilians—seventy-five per cent today compared with five per cent during World War One.

A combination of selfish individualism, neo-liberal capitalism, and much greater mobility/globalisation has fragmented communities and destabilised individuals. Under globalisation "the very notion of identity is fluid and thus problematic, while 'home' is always provisional and, ultimately, empty of real meaning" (Labanyi, 2008, p. 26). Young people can expect to lose their friends as they decamp to universities or jobs in far-flung parts of the country or the world. If they are lucky enough to have a career, they are unlikely to have stable, permanent, pensionable, full-time jobs. They are more likely to have part-time work with perhaps a zero hour contract in a non-unionised work force that meets the market's demand for flexibility. Families too are more unstable, with generations living far apart, parents frequently separated and fathers often absent. The problem is, however, not just one of geographical separation but, much worse, one of loss of fraternity, loss of the experience of communities pulling together for mutual support, whether a neighbourhood or a trade union. When we do identify with a group it is usually a trivial tribal identity with a band or football team, where being a follower is nothing more than a form of extended narcissism rather than an expression of solidarity for a common cause.

Poverty and urban dwelling are predictive of depression, but social cohesion protects against mental illness. Social capital refers to social intercourse between individuals and families who make up a social unit, and the absence of such support at an individual and community level creates vulnerability to depression (Blazer, 2005). Disadvantaged neighbourhoods have higher rates of depression and substance abuse. Such disadvantage is determined by lower socioeconomic status, racial, or ethnic heterogeneity, and residential mobility, all of which militate against residents cooperating to realise common goals and solve problems. They thus generate stress and helplessness in coping with issues such as campaigning for neighbourhood facilities or combatting antisocial or criminal behaviour.

The collapse of community in the USA has been captured by Robert Putnam (2000) in his poignant image of "bowling alone". Showing that Americans have become more disengaged from political and civic organisations, he attributes the decline in social capital to technologically driven individualising of our leisure time via television and the internet. However, others have found that civic participation has not declined in Canada, Holland, and the UK (Andersen et al., 2006), and that in the USA it may simply have taken on different forms (Lemann, 1996). "Depression is a disease of loneliness", claims Andrew Solomon (2014, p. 214), and far more people than ever before are living alone, without the support of family or community. It is not so much belonging to social groups as identifying with them that predicts better health, including providing protection against depression (Cruwys et al., 2014). Yet it makes sense that in our individualistic age, we tend to resist such incorporation, a topic to which we will return in Chapter Nine.

Materialism

It has been estimated that "three-quarters of the hundreds of diseases listed in the DSM are found almost exclusively in the USA and in [industrialised] Westernised elites, whether Asian or European" (James, 2008, p. 39). Oliver James has grouped together various forms of so-called "mental illness" (depression, anxiety, substance abuse, and impulse disorder) using the umbrella term "emotional distress" and has discovered that the incidence in English-speaking nations is twice as high (twenty-three per cent) as among continental western Europeans (eleven point five per cent). The Anglophone countries have high levels of what James calls "relative materialism": addictive consumption far beyond the meeting of our actual needs. He hypothesises that "what does the damage is the combination of inequality with widespread relative materialism, and that comes from Selfish [unregulated, neo-liberal] Capitalism stoking up both aspirations and the expectation that they can be fulfilled" (ibid., p. 149).

Selfish Capitalism (SC) can be defined by four characteristics: (1) a company's success is judged by share price rather than its contribution to the real economy or society; (2) the privatisation of collective goods; (3) minimal financial and labour regulation; (4) the belief that consumption and market forces can meet virtually all human needs. It is evident that in SC relative materialism has been encouraged to run riot; some claim it has been deliberately engineered as a way of buying off class dissent: available credit instead of decent jobs and wages. At a material level, the most significant outcome has been a transfer of wealth and power from the public to the private sphere and from middle income earners to the rich. At an ideological level, the impact has been even greater, generating societies dominated by Darwinian competitive individualism. SC is the dominant force in English-speaking economies that have followed the lead of Reagan and Thatcher in the 1980s; by contrast, other developed nations on mainland Western Europe and Japan have maintained more human-centred economic systems, such as the social market economy.

What impact has relative materialism had on the populations of SC-dominated countries? James cites the research of Tim Kasser and his colleagues who found that people with materialist aspirations (for money, fame, and glamorous physical and social image) were more prone to depression, anxiety, narcissism, unhappiness, and physical symptoms, and more likely to use drugs of solace (Kasser, 2002). The correlation between materialism and reduced life satisfaction has been replicated by other researchers in a wide range of countries. Kasser endorses the principle that people have fundamental needs (see also Chapter Eleven) for security, competence, connection, autonomy, and authenticity, and James goes on to show that SC has a detrimental effect on our capacity to satisfy many of these needs, creating a non-facilitating environment indeed. Kasser showed that insecurity triggered, for example, by reminders of death or by self-doubt generates materialism. So while our most fundamental physical need (for security) underlies materialism, crucially, in its relative, addictive form, materialism has a detrimental effect on our capacity to satisfy our other needs. "Putting a high value on wealth, status and image leads … materialists to devalue intimate relationships and involvement in the community" (James, 2008, p. 66).

Materialist ideology—when people become commodified

Materialists have been shown to have more short-term and negative relationships—not surprisingly, since they tend to be manipulative (of self and other), exploitative, competitive, and superficial. They tend to place a low value on self-expression and autonomy and thus often feel alienated and bored. Indeed they may not be sufficiently in touch with any self that might be expressed. Compared to non-materialists, they have lower self-esteem (as well as defences against feeling it). Because their values come from outside themselves, they not only have overly high expectations of themselves but their self-esteem depends on the judgements of others.

Materialists are more likely to have been deprived of love and to have divorced parents; indeed siblings may vary in their materialist tendencies depending on how their parents relate to them (James, 2008). However, materialism is not just a defence against insecurity and lack of love but also a sign of inadequate development of the self, which manifests in low levels of authenticity, autonomy, and the capacity to form satisfying relationships. In other words, people turn to materialism to distract from their inner emptiness. It is important to remind ourselves here that materialism refers not just to addictive chasing after material goods but also to the pursuit of a particular image, turning oneself and others into commodities, objects to be manipulated, discarded, or replaced. If your friend is a "loser", unfriend him; if you don't like your appearance, get a makeover. Life is not lived but *performed,* because judged from the outside: How do I rank in the popularity ratings? I have to post that selfie from the pub/party/holiday to let everyone know what a great time I am having—code for "I am a winner" and, therefore, "I have value". What is being lost is the concept of an inner self who makes decisions, guides my actions, and which can be nourished only by expressing itself authentically: that is, with congruence between inner and outer.

One's very identity and one's life have become brands to be designed and styled in accord with the latest trends and then to be launched on the market (usually social media) and promoted.

When we are fed a diet of advertising that tells us that a desirable life is made up of certain "cool" possessions (particular brands of trainers, shoes, clothes, or the latest model of mobile phone or tablet) or activities ("travel yourself interesting") or extrinsic achievements (becoming famous by going viral on YouTube or appearing on Big Brother, the X Factor, or any of the other talent or "reality" shows), we lose touch with who we really are and with our basic needs. What is lost amid this narcissism is not just authenticity, but also reciprocal relationship, community, altruism, and ethical values. As Ruby Wax puts it, "we" becoming "I" may be one of the major causes of depression (2014).

Speed and surface: the age of information and communications technology

The loss of an environment that can facilitate a cohesive and rooted sense of self has been greatly hastened by the twenty-first century revolution in information and communications technology. One of the most distressing consequences of the digital age is the absence of boundaries between self and others and the erosion of privacy: "The border between the internal and external world has disappeared, and the external world dominates", observes Verhaeghe (2014, p. 147). In an age of location services, it is no longer possible to escape into seclusion. For many people it is unthinkable, even on holiday, to leave "contact" behind and switch off texting, email, and social media. What Laurence Scott (2015) has called the 4D universe not only decentres our world, it simultaneously recentres it. This recentering, is, I would argue, narcissistic and alienating, as we reduce ourselves to the sum of our online data: to our self-chosen preferences and the "likes" conferred by our "friends". The digital world in addition reduces our capacity for sustained attention; exacerbates narcissism and generates a public (false) self that is performed for an audience; and has made bullying and abuse easy and acceptable (Scott, 2015). Self-viewing starts early, with infants being entertained with videos of themselves: "an experience of self-awareness unknown in the history of human existence" (Smith, 2013, p. 274). If innocence is the absence of self-regarding, it is eradicated at a very early age.

The efficiency and speed of the text message, the email, or the tweet is replacing the tricky but rich, emotionally suffused communication of face-to-face embodied contact. Unlike messy human contact, our self-presentation can be controlled and edited via our phones and tablets. We relate to our mobile devices in class, in work meetings, at social engagements, on the train and bus, during the interval at the theatre or concert, while waiting at the checkout, while boarding the plane. As Sherry Turkle (2011) points out, many young people are now phobic about both solitude and unedited conversation: they are unable to connect either to themselves or to others because they fill every potentially empty moment with being wired. There is thus no space left for connection with self or other, and this will inevitably degrade and atrophy the self. Wilson (2015) claims that due to the "woolly comforts of social media", many of his generation (he is in his twenties) have learned to avoid rather than engage with face-to-face confrontation. The outcome is to infantilise and disempower, which generates anxiety along with its alter ego, depression.

For every practical benefit of computer technology we can find a psychological downside. With the efficiency comes a superficiality and disembodiment of contact, and along with this a speed to which our nervous systems are not adapted. We receive a reply in minutes rather than weeks; there is no longer any down-time for rest, digestion, or consideration. With portability comes a constant intrusion into our inner life: a peaceful walk in nature may as well be a walk on a treadmill in a noisy and smelly gym if my entire attention is on the latest text/email/tweet/Facebook posting/move in a computer game, etc. We no longer engage with the outer material world but with the virtual world of text or image. In the face of its insistent presence we become addictively reliant on the unremitting but superficial stimulus and are unable to rest within ourselves. Indeed the disconnection from our embodied selves (what is described above as our inner nature) is associated with an alienation from the environment (outer nature), as Staunton (2008) has pointed out. She found that re-embodiment (through body therapy) caused people to re-open to their dreams and feelings, and reawakened their capacity to open to the world around them with enhanced sensory experience and spiritual awareness. It is this interdependence of the real world and the real (embodied) self that is disrupted by virtual media, which then triggers alienation, restlessness and, ultimately, depression.

The reductionism of technology screens out everything that is humanly important, rich, and nourishing, leaving us simply with speed and efficiency, as encapsulated in Woody Allen's quip: "I took a speed-reading course and read *War and Peace* in twenty minutes. It involves Russia". Knowledge and understanding are downgraded to information bytes. The ease of fact finding online is certainly convenient, but anything that is so easily accessed is not placed in a bigger picture: the resulting factoids lack the contextualisation of a slow accretion of knowledge, where they hang on a structure already formed. They equally lack the context that connects the virtual experience to our real-life relationship with the world. Another problem with such easy access to information is that we are forced to scan vast amounts of data and filter out everything except the single grain of gold we are seeking in what becomes a highly goal-directed procedure. The excessive choice available for the most trivial decisions leads to anxiety ("Did I choose the right hotel out of 700?"), countered with despair ("What does it matter anyhow?"). This leaves us with a numbed indifference in the face of the infinite information and choices available.

The training of our attention and thinking into a left-brain, speedy, narrow, procedural, practical focus makes it difficult for us to access a softer, more receptive right-brain attention. When we spend more and more time interacting with technology (and bureaucracy), it becomes impossible to access the slowness and broad focus needed for receptivity and a perception of the world as sacred. The world is thus distanced and decathected and, in the process, disenchanted. The sociologist Hartmut Rosa (2015) has linked our accelerating way of life to alienation, but believes that slowing down is not sufficient in itself: what we must do is to be available to moments of "resonance" within an open and reciprocal relationship with the world. In burnout we lose all capacity for such resonance so that life is experienced as arid and meaningless: this is depression. We will return to how meaning depends on connection in Chapter Ten.

Babies accumulate sensory impressions in a chaotic way, but then immediately begin to organise them and build up associations, meaning, memory, and identity (a process that is reversed in Alzheimer's disease). Teenagers hyperstimulated by video games will find it hard to organise and integrate knowledge and experience in this meaning-creating manner, argues Susan Greenfield (2009). They will live in the eternal present of disorganised, unprocessed, and therefore ethically empty and meaningless (because unexperienced) experience. What gives meaning to experience is "the drawing together of fragments of experience, the relating of them to memory and emotion, and the ability to feel them concretely and immediately" (McGilchrist, 1995). What Henry James says of the creative artist is surely a prescription for all human beings:

> Experience is never limited, and it is never complete; it is an immense sensibility, a kind of huge spider-web of the finest silken threads suspended in the chamber of consciousness, and catching every air-borne particle in its tissue. It is the very atmosphere of the mind; and when the mind is imaginative … it takes to itself the faintest hints of life, it converts the very pulses of the air into revelations. (1987, p. 194)

This captures our human capacity for resonance at its highest pitch.

Our current technological change is so radical and fast that we are *not* going to be able to adapt to it, argues economist Andrew Keen (2015). Social and political change have always been needed to realise the opportunities created by technological development (e.g., child labour was abolished after the industrial revolution, but only because of political action), but technological change in the twenty-first century is far too fast and globalised for national politics to stay abreast of it, whether to build on opportunities or limit the damage wrought. We are living in what Zygmunt Bauman (2008) has called the liquid modern world, which is in a state of permanent revolution. This makes it impossible or inadvisable to commit to anything—to a relationship, community, job, or institution. Such a state of flux inevitably creates superficiality of experience and of contact, "the silence that lies on the other side of the roar of messages" (Myerson, 2003, p. 179).

Cultural changes

Nihilism and cultural and moral impoverishment

Societies, and the personal identities they produce, may range from culturally full to empty; open to closed; and stable to unstable (Verhaeghe, 2014). The contemporary developed world falls into the empty, open, and unstable permutation. Thus we have impoverished cultural resources producing stereotyped identities (empty); we are constantly adjusting to the latest hype (open); and identity is at the same time unstable, which causes "a constant seesaw of emotions" (ibid., p. 33).

Addressing our impoverished cultural condition, the Peruvian novelist Mario Vargas Llosa (2015) strikes an elegiac tone: we are abandoning a high culture that cultivated truth-seeking, subtlety, and substance in favour of easily accessible, shallow, sensation-seeking. And he is not just talking about popular culture here; he includes the contemporary art scene as well, damning its "cheap stunts" as "boring, farcical and bleak". Vargas Llosa champions depth and beauty, modesty, ritual, and mystery—in life as in art. A counter-example is sex brutalised by online pornography: this is a negation of love, a sport without feeling or relationship, mere gratification but with an undercurrent of threat and exploitation.

Writing in 1944, Horkheimer and Adorno (2007) had already warned against cultural impoverishment, contrasting the richness and profundity of high culture with the seductive narcosis of popular culture, which manipulates the populace into docile passivity. The danger of what they called "the culture industry"—to differentiate, say, Hollywood and Walt Disney from the authentic grass-roots culture of the people—is that its purpose is to generate false needs that can be met only by the products of capitalism. It thereby cuts people off from their true needs—for freedom, creativity, and genuine fulfilment—and merely encourages passive acceptance (or consumption) of the status quo. Popular films and television have neither authenticity nor integrity in characters, plot, and values. Thus soaps manipulate our emotions by extrinsic, contrived plotting to keep us addictively watching. Most popular culture acts against emotional regulation and exploits an addictive need for uppers (the amphetamines of violent horror films or pornography) or downers (the tranquillising soma of *Downton Abbey*). It has been fashionable for critics and academics in the (unapologetically neo-liberal) English-speaking world to curry populist favour by self-hatingly damning as "elitist" the very high culture that shaped them. In fact, people are cut off from high culture, not for reasons of education or money (rock concerts and football matches often cost more), but because they haven't cultivated the receptive attention that would lead to the discovery that what is more demanding is also more rewarding.

From a psychological perspective, it is clear that in its depth, complexity, and critical capacities high culture grapples with existential truths. It displays subtle, sensitive insight as it engages patiently with the minutiae of intra- and inter-personal contact and awareness. It portrays contrasting meanings and views of life without lapsing into the rhetoric or splitting that lead to caricature and stereotyping. There is a stillness and focus, and a lack of brash narcissism in great art. Such artists are willing to endure the confusion of not knowing and the pain of entering alternative worldviews with compassion, and thereby grapple with the full spectrum of humanness. The crucial criterion for culture is whether it facilitates: most crucially, whether it helps us to create value and meaning. Just as with a meaningful life, art has the capacity to organise and process experience within a context of values. For F. R. Leavis (1962, p. 17), great literature was "distinguished by a vital capacity for experience, a kind of reverent openness before life, and a marked moral intensity." Reading such literature cultivates empathy and helps the reader to receive and perceive life with heightened sensitivity and to fashion a meaningful worldview. The contact with others—both characters and author—who have grappled with the same life challenges provides the kind of inspiration, support, mirroring, and depth of insight that is not often available in real life. As Henry James (1987) stressed, life is not a mere aggregate of experiences. Our impressions must be shaped by our individual sensibility in a process that is analogous to psychotherapy: to adapt Freud, where raw experience was, there meaning shall be.

Ideology and manipulation

Among many others, Eliane Glaser (2011) has exposed the lies and manipulations wrought by power blocks such as governments, corporations, PR firms, and advertising agencies. The phony humility, mock consultation, tokenism, and invocation of people-power are revealed as hypocrisy: all serve to conceal the fact that we are a deeply unequal society, becoming more unequal all the time, and that the redistribution of wealth from the poor to the rich appears to be, if not intentional, at least entirely acceptable to our rulers.

We accept this alarming trend without revolution in part because we are blinded by the ideologies of meritocracy and individual responsibility: that talent and achievement are earned rather than gifts of nature, upbringing, private schools, the right connections, and good health. Part of the reason for our "false consciousness" (not knowing what is good for us) is that "we internalise the demands and expectations of society, and … these get bound up with our innermost desires" (Glaser, 2011, pp. 26–27). Or we rationalise to avoid shame or self-loathing, like educated call-girls and lap-dancers who claim their money-making activities are "empowering". The job of ideology is, if not to conceal, at the very least to spin what is negative into positive. While the public is bought off with sops such as token blacks, the poor, or women being celebrated, the "role-model model diverts attention from exploring the real root-and-branch reasons why people from ethnic minorities [and other disadvantaged groups] may not simply follow the good examples offered to them. [We need] more attention to the bottom of the hierarchy, not the top" (ibid., p. 61).

Glaser is concerned with the degradation of politics and the material outcome of this world of manifest injustice, illusions, and lies. But what are the psychological implications? It is hard not to react to the post-truth culture with rage, but this quickly gives way to resigned or cynical apathy as soon as we recognise our powerlessness. This is the classic learned helplessness that slides into withdrawal and chronic low-level depression. A virtual reality is created by lies and spin in the social sphere just as surely as it is in the cloud-world of information technology. We are losing touch with concrete reality and the grounding that would enable us to engage meaningfully with the world and each other.

A meaningless world: the age of postmodernism

The classic definition of postmodernism is an "incredulity towards metanarratives" (Lyotard, quoted in Blazer, 2005, p. 153). As such, it represents a move towards greater freedom, fluidity, and a more nuanced notion of truth; yet it is also clear that human beings flounder in the absence of grounded certitudes. We no longer trust blindly or believe in the legitimacy of authority, whether in the form of politicians, the judiciary, police force, church, or the professions. What do we believe? Who can we trust? Who—if anyone—is in charge? What lies in the future? Does mankind *have* a future? Where do I belong? Who can I identify with? Is there anybody or anything I can rely on? Does anything really matter? Even—is anything real?

Central to postmodernism is the chipping away at the sources from which we derive meaning. It claims there are no absolute values, we have no allegiances and no purpose. Beliefs are seen as relative and thereby trivialised or undermined. Nothing is more than its surface appearance, so "no one thing is more important or more real than another" (Frosh, 1991, p. 179): E. L. James is as good as Henry James. Intellectuals, the media, politics have all been taken over by the idea, disseminated by the vogue for French theory, that representation is the only reality. Consequently, those who deal with image (rock-stars, TV chefs) are given more credence than those who (should) deal with substance (novelists, thinkers, politicians). In a similar fashion, the tool, as fetishised style accessory, has eclipsed the work that can be done with it.

Because history has been neutered and rebranded as heritage, we find ourselves living in an eternal present where we have forgotten the lessons of the past and have little optimism about the future. This eternal present forecloses the capacity to envisage change. Disagreeing with Lyotard's emphasis on the eclipse of metanarratives, Fredric Jameson argues that we are no more at the end of narratives than at the end of history: that postmodernism is better understood as "the recruitment of the entire world into the same big story, namely the development of global capitalism" (Kunkel, 2014, p. 60). As we look around us, the best we can hope for seems to hang on to what we have.

Most relevant of all to the subject of depression is the loss of identity that is part of the postmodern condition. Tree Staunton has noted such loss in the clients she is seeing: "In the consulting room today we see fragmentation, dissociation and loss of real identity in the extreme, or mere lostness, numbness and lack of inner direction; there is a desperate search for meaning in a world where the rules are no longer clear, and society no longer offers structures to support the flailing ego" (2008, p. 15). The case of Jeff Foster is typical: "lost, wandering in the wilderness of modern Western life". He was highly educated intellectually, but knew nothing emotionally or spiritually: "I didn't know what I wanted, who I was, where I belonged, where I was heading. I felt overwhelmed, and so disconnected, from others, from my body, from my job, so confused" (Foster, 2015, p. 200). After his girlfriend, his "savior", broke up with him, he became suicidally depressed. It was only when he embarked on a spiritual journey and learned to be present to life without the burden of himself—that is, being dominated by his ego—that he was able to break through his depression.

When we liberate ourselves from constraining social customs and beliefs we also lose order and predictability. We become confused and disoriented and have no place or role in the world. I have already alluded to the impact of globalisation on identity. Labanyi expands on the reason for this: "given that our self is not an essence but a product of relationship, it can be neither static nor singular. Thus as we encounter, and move on from, different people and situations over a life span, our self has to keep updating itself" (2008, p. 27). With the exponential increase in the numbers we meet actually and virtually, our self is stretched very thin, being socially chameleon-like but lacking in depth, rootedness, or authenticity.

In postmodernist theory the self is "a commodity, signifying nothing" (Frosh, 1991, p. 179). Consonant with this, psychotherapy tends to be viewed in our culture, above all in the media, with scepticism if not contempt: as mere self-indulgence. For in this ideology, there is no such thing as a self to be healed or repaired. However the negation of the self is a recipe not for liberation but for psychosis (Frosh, 1991; Sass, 1992). Frosh insists: "just because something is constructed with difficulty and mishap along the way, it does not mean that it does not exist. The achievement of some sense of self may be an end rather than a beginning" (1991, p. 181). However this is not easy in a non-facilitating environment: conditions "supplied by contemporary culture are not conducive to the formation of a deep and integrated sense of secure being, a self that is more than a collection of chameleon images" (ibid., p. 63).

The only healthy way forward is to engage in "the struggle towards the construction of an autonomous and honest mode of personal being, even if this can never be an absolute phenomenon" (ibid., p. 180). The struggle can be won only provisionally, for the self requires "unremitting protection and nurture" (ibid., p. 187), while at the same time it must ceaselessly adapt to ongoing social change. The links between current socio-cultural conditions, a weak sense of self, and depression will be explored in more detail in the next chapter.

Stress

We discovered in Chapter Five that a combination of different stresses generates depression, so it is not surprising that the more disadvantaged and disempowered groups within the population have higher incidences of depression. Within developed nations, lower social class, female gender, young age, immigrant status, low educational achievement, urban dwelling, and illness all increase emotional distress (Blazer, 2005; James, 2008; Radloff, 1985; Solomon, 2014). The effects are striking: for example, poor women are up to nine times more likely to suffer anxiety and depression than rich men. The link between low social status and depression may be due to social causation because of being exposed to a greater number of and more severe environmental stressors (unemployment, poverty, poor health, threatening neighbourhood, etc.). In addition, the social selection hypothesis proposes that those of lower social status are more vulnerable to the effects of stress due to lack of supportive social resources, fewer personal resources, and less effective coping responses (Billings & Moos, 1985). Radloff points out that the risk factors (including illness) all contribute to actual helplessness or the perception of a lack of control.

A major contribution to stress comes from patterns of nurture within the family. Lyons-Ruth's research (1992) connected depression to poverty and social exclusion. She found that mothers who couldn't care for their children (often with disorganised attachment), who appeared to be neglectful, apathetic, or angry, frequently had large numbers of depressive symptoms, often chronic and low-level. Their coping capacity was burnt out. It wasn't only current poverty-related problems that caused the poor parenting, but rather the kind of relationship these women had with their own mothers in childhood—though that of course was likewise made more difficult by poverty and disempowerment. Thus poverty causes problems at the time; but, more importantly, it becomes a negative replicator in generating poor parenting, stress, and depression down through the generations. Environmental and developmental factors work together.

While the stress of social exclusion may cause mothers to ignore or lash out at their children, sometimes it is the pressure of wealth that is the problem. Girls from wealthy backgrounds have a high risk of depression, probably because of "over-controlling, perfectionist mothering" (James, 2008, p. 28). Families can be a source of stress when they are less cohesive and expressive and contain more conflict and criticism. However, the unmarried are overall more vulnerable to depression because of lack of support. Families can provide support both emotionally and materially; but when they find themselves unsuccessful in controlling an individual's distress they can withdraw support and become avoidant or actively hostile (Billings & Moos, 1985)—as appeared to be the case for my client Shelley.

While being unemployed predicts depression more than the most stressful job, nevertheless the workplace can be a powerful stressor—as many of our memoirists have shown—and the length of the working week is correlated with poor mental health (Blazer, 2005). This can be compounded by the interconnected stresses of home and work demands. A paradigm of the consequences of "selfish capitalism" can be seen in Australia, where non-mortgage debt trebled in the decade between 1995 and 2004. As a result Australians ended up working the longest hours in the developed world to pay off their debts. Alongside this, there was an increase in emotional distress for both sexes, with the frequency for women doubling between 1997 and 2001 (James, 2008). In most of the developed world there has been a large growth in the proportion of mothers working to service family debt. This has led to a huge rise in stress for these women, and also for the fathers and children in these families.

Longitudinal studies have shown that workplace stress predicts depression (Blazer, 2005). Health care workers, especially direct care staff and women, have worse mental health than the rest of the population. In general, relational conflict and poor social support in the workplace predict depression and burnout (which has similar symptoms to depression). A high level of job demands arises from a heavy mental workload, being impeded in completing tasks, and being subjected to conflicting demands. Job control refers to the freedom to make decisions about how best to perform the work. Jobs that generate most stress are those with high demand and little control. There is an increased risk of depression and anxiety amongst people who experience low control at work or at home, and this was particularly true of women in the low or medium grades of work (ibid.).

Social support buffers the effects of depression and helps provide resources for effective coping with stress. Support within the workplace that counteracts depression comes from being highly involved in the job, and having cohesive relationships and supportive supervisors who encourage innovation and participation in decision-making (Billings & Moos, 1985).

Gender imbalance in stress and depression

The incidence of depression is two-fold higher in women than in men overall, but there are other differences between the genders hidden within this statistic. Men have reported more stress from work and financial problems, whereas women report more health and family-related stressors. Women's overall greater frequency of depression might be partly caused by lower social status, but perhaps also by other factors such as greater sensitivity to the interpersonal emotional field: they are more likely to blame themselves, and receive less support from husbands than they give in return. Indeed, amongst the widowed and the never-married heading their own households, women actually have a lower rate of depression than men (Radloff, 1985). Marriage is not as protective against depression for women as it is for men, but depression in women is reduced by having an intimate and confiding relationship with a male partner (Billings & Moos, 1985). That the higher incidence of depression amongst women is not attributable to biological factors is suggested by the fact that there is no female disadvantage in some circumstances (above) and no gender difference in certain cultures, including several Scandinavian countries, the Amish, and English Jews (James, 2008).

Studies of childrearing practices show that the actions of girls—whether positive achievements or bad behaviour—elicit less response and fewer consequences than those of boys, in terms of either reward or punishment (Radloff, 1985). Females are also less listened to and have less influence on group decisions. In women non-assertiveness was preferred, while the reverse was true of men; and women were less likely to take credit for success than men. Finally, work produced by women was rated as less significant and less rewarded than comparable work by men. Radloff concludes that women are trained in helplessness and discouraged from solving problems. This may be a significant cause of their greater susceptibility to depression than men.

Three decades after Radloff's article, female assertiveness is still disliked. At the same time, women in authority in the workplace are expected to be driven and effective. Such a double bind is immensely stressful and has only become more intense since Simone de Beauvoir observed in 1949: "In women … there is … a conflict between her autonomous existence and her objective self, her 'being-the other'; she is taught that … she must try to please, she must make herself object; she should therefore renounce her autonomy" (1972, p. 308). Women still put the other first—whether men, children, or friends—but equally are expected to get the job done, though without displaying their power.

Women nowadays have the autonomy and boosted self-esteem that accompany economic independence, but working mothers carry the stress of doing two jobs. Where a father is present he may *help*, but the endless tedious detail of remembering and holding household maintenance and children's school, social, and extra-curricular activities is almost always carried by the mother. Nevertheless, it is undoubtedly true that having children is stressful for both parents in today's economic and social conditions (see accounts of Kelly, Rice-Oxley, and Merritt); and it is not surprising that, for both men and women, those with grown-up children no longer living with them were less depressed than others (Radloff, 1985). For stay-at-home mothers, "the work of early parenting, in particular, has become more isolated and denigrated since the 1960s" (Gerhardt, 2011, p. 339); and since isolation and poor-self-esteem are linked to depression, it is to be expected that parenting, and mothering in particular, play a role in generating depression.

It is of course possible that men are just as depressed as women, but that men's depression is under-reported, or under-diagnosed because of manifesting somatically (Chapter Three) or being expressed through different behaviours. When externalising symptoms (anger/aggression, substance abuse, risk-taking) are considered in addition to more traditional ways of diagnosing depression, the frequency was found to be equal in the two genders (Martin et al., 2013).

Summary: stress and loss in an unstable, instrumentalising, and boundary-invading world

Our current society is inherently more stressful than in the past: too much change, speed, and aggressive competitiveness; too little stability and social support. The struggling self is being instrumentalised, while at the same time its protective boundaries are being eroded by technology-mediated threats to privacy. Our values are becoming Darwinian, with contempt for losers, (transient) adulation of winners, and little willingness to listen or to mirror others in their difference. The atrophy of social values and ideals causes people to retreat into self-absorption. With social media, television, and print media feeding and exacerbating the narcissistic trend, the self has itself become little more than an arena for performance motivated by the hope of applause, rather than a site for mutual interaction and communication of felt and authentic meaning.

Democratic national governments are becoming increasingly powerless and irrelevant. Many of the most fundamental decisions that influence our work and home lives are increasingly made by faceless, unaccountable global corporations, which operate solely for shareholders. There is no forum for discussion of corporate decisions that have a social impact; or if there is a consultation process, it is often no more than a cynical pretence designed to absorb dissent until the protest dies down. It is clear that nobody is listening, and the message is that human beings do not matter; this leaves us in states of anxiety, depression, or impotent rage that is easily harnessed by far-right populist movements.

Loss may be viewed as a specific kind of stress. Our society has become so unstable that loss (of spouse, family, built environment, natural environment, jobs, home, country) is constant and unavoidable. This ongoing instability generates insecure attachment, thus making us more vulnerable to the effects of further loss. In particular, our culture causes, and selects for, avoidant attachment (see Chapter Nine), since the individual without close ties or who is unempathic to the feelings of others is seen as useful in the globalised and unstable workplace: he will move to another branch or another country at a moment's notice, and will moreover be defended against the pain wrought on others by algorithm- and market-driven decisions.

While struggling to organise this chapter, I was asked by a friend: "What's your real beef with current society?" The one-word answer that came out of my mouth was "loss". It can seem as if the list of contemporary ills is endless, but for me they boil down to loss: of a meaningful way of life, a tolerable pace of living, a humane and beautiful environment, cultural depth, richness and cohesion, trust in the ethicality of those in power, and a belief that things will keep getting better. We are swept along by a tsunami of change—two years ago, at the time of writing (2016), ISIS had scarcely been heard of; one year ago, the EU seemed relatively stable; and Trump in the White House was inconceivable—and so our grieving can never be resolved because further losses keep on piling up. But a sense of loss is to be expected for a member, like myself, of the Baby Boomer generation. For generation X and even more so for the current generation of young adults (Millennials or generation Y), I believe the one-word issue is, rather: stress. Life is so demanding and feels so meaningless that many fail or refuse to get on the treadmill; alternatively, like so many of the memoirists surveyed here, they become so exhausted trying to stay on it that an increasing number suffer chronic stress, anxiety, and depression. It then takes only a small trigger to provoke a major depressive episode against this background of underlying low mood. I believe that loss affects the younger generations too, but that they may be largely unconscious of what it is they lack. I am thinking of the loss of what some have not known but is nevertheless an inherent part of our animal heritage, such as our embeddedness in nature (see Chapter Ten). In our era of globalised, homeless monads all linked up but deprived of real face-to-face relationships, isolation and loneliness exacerbate stress and loss.

However, despite the gravity of our current situation, we need to bear in mind that despair is performative (Eagleton, 2015). If we allow ourselves to succumb to pessimism or cynicism, nothing is more certain than that things will continue on the same disastrous course.

* * *

We live in an era of constant change, instability, unpredictability, and powerlessness, which brings with it the inevitable consequences of ongoing stress, loss, and isolation. In the long term, each of these states leads to depression and anxiety, as we saw in Chapter Five. Kasser has defined four fundamental human needs, of which three—those for security, connection, and autonomous and authentic engagement—are undermined in today's socio-cultural environment. A combination of finance capitalism, materialism, and information technology, aided and abetted by the nihilistic posturings of postmodernist culture, have combined to erode meaning, identity, and depth of connection to self and other. We will examine the psychodynamic outcome of these problems in more detail in the next three chapters. Any one of these deficits alone generates a background of chronic low-level depression, which, in the face of acute stress or loss, can deepen into major depression.

CHAPTER EIGHT

Empty (narcissistic), false, or fragmented: disorders of the self in late modernity

The self may be defined as the organising centre of consciousness and affect regulation (Cortright, 2007), or as an "internally organized cluster of attitudes, expectations, meanings, and feelings" (Siegel, 2012, p. 210). The healthy adult self is characterised by cohesion, vitality, and functional harmony (Kohut & Wolf, 1986), and has the integrated functions of: body regulation, attuned communication, emotional balance, fear modulation, response flexibility, insight, empathy, morality, and intuition (Siegel, 2010).

The development of the self occurs inside a sequence of Russian dolls: the womb, the post-birth maternal environment, the family, and the society of a particular time and place. But here the analogy breaks down, because the dolls (or succession of wombs) are not insulated from one another; on the contrary, there is influence in both directions. The societal is already present in the family and affects child-rearing practices; conversely, the way children are brought up will impact on the society of the future. The relative contributions of the family and the societal are changing: it is undeniable that parental influence on child development has gradually been declining relative to the technologically mediated social and cultural world (see also Verhaeghe, 2014). We saw in Chapter Four the kind of consistent attuned caregiving that is needed for a healthy self to develop. In this chapter I will explore how the socio-cultural environment influences the processes of forming the self in childhood and the ongoing reshaping of the self (for good or ill) in adulthood. The psychoanalyst Paul Verhaeghe finds that most of his recent patients suffer from depression and anxiety, but that, unlike in Freud's day, this depression cannot be attributed to specific loss. Indeed his current clients' depression does not usually connect to their life histories. Rather it "arises against a background of a general meaninglessness where the most insignificant drawback is enough to trigger the depression that is *already there*" (Verhaeghe, 2008, p. 5, my italics). I will argue that such underlying depression can be traced back to an empty, false, or fragmented self whose development has been etiolated by the non-facilitating nature of our current socio-cultural environment.

Changes in the nature of the self

It has been claimed that late capitalist society is particularly detrimental to the formation and maintenance of self: "Fragmentary and chaotic family experiences, intrusion by the administered consciousness of the mass media, lack of an organic community—all these features of late capitalist life contribute to a weakened sense of self and to the dissolution of intersubjective relations" (Kovel, 1987, p. 342). Likewise, Frosh, with remarkable prescience, noted that discovery of one's own centre of consciousness has become impossible in the face of "communicational immediacy" as well as the blurring of cultural identity arising from globalisation (1991, p. 187). Finding and being ourselves would require relational depth, slowness, inwardness, and receptivity, states that are the shadow of the postmodern self.

If the nineteenth- and early twentieth-century person was circumscribed by commitment and obligation (i.e., a social self), the new norm is for an asocial self characterised by performance, success, and gratification. In the process we have turned ourselves—and the other—into objects. The new ideal is to be hyper-individual, hyperactive, competitive, decisive, enterprising, and versatile (Bergh, 2015). In our downtime, we self-gratify without pleasure: we shop and travel and feed our oral addictions, but nothing sustaining can reach us because we are trapped in speediness, solipsism, and the performance of an inauthentic, commodified self for ego-strengthening purposes. "Traditional bonds and fixed values no longer make up the basis from which the individual develops" (Bergh, 2015, p. 360). Rather we live in an era of self-definition, where burnout or shame at our own shortcomings (rather than the guilt and inner conflict of the nineteenth century) are the price we pay when—inevitably—some of us fail most of the time and all of us fail some of the time. Alain Ehrenberg encapsulates the problem in the title of his 1998 book *La fatigue d'être soi*, which can be translated as "the weariness of being a self" (Ehrenberg, 2009). He attributes depression to a "state of mind inherent to individualism" (p. xiv). Our own supposed sovereignty has itself become a burden: faced with endless opportunities to realise ourselves, we withdraw, overwhelmed by the lack of limits on *potential* self-expression and personal success. Tellingly, what the suicidally depressed Jeff Foster longed for was "life, the taste of life—to live, really live ... without the burden of 'myself'" (2015, p. 208). Depression is the pain of those "who are unable or unwilling to be interactive [i.e., networked], accessible and presentable" in the manner demanded by market mobilisation (Bergh, 2015, p. 374).

Current research is demonstrating that the self (this chapter) and our relationships (Chapter Nine) are indeed being eroded over time in parallel with the neo-liberal project of deregulating capitalism. Numerous studies (mostly among American college students) examining self-indicators in various birth cohorts within the "same" culture reveal great variations in personality and values, including differences in anxiety, self-esteem, empathy, narcissism, locus of control, belief in a just world, sexual behaviour, and occupation-preference. For example, between the mid-1980s and the 2000s there have been significant increases (thirty per cent rise in average scores between 1979 and 2006) in narcissism in college students in the USA (Twenge & Foster, 2008, 2010; Twenge et al., 2008). Out of more than 400 items on the questionnaire, the one that changed most over time was the response to "I am an important person". In the 1950s only twelve per cent of teenagers agreed, but this had risen to nearly eighty per cent in the late 1980s (Twenge & Campbell, 2009, p. 34). Men score higher than women, but the gender gap was closing in a 2009 study (Twenge & Campbell, 2009). The rise in narcissistic traits continued at least until 2009, but may have levelled off since then according to preliminary data (Twenge, 2014). This could be linked to the worldwide recession, since economic hardship brings about greater altruism: there seems to be an inverse relationship between wealth and concern for others.

Narcissistic individuals are materialistic, entitled, and aggressive when insulted or ignored; they have inflated views of themselves and rate themselves as high in self-esteem with a correspondingly low interest or trust in others, whom they view in utilitarian terms—Donald Trump springs to mind. Narcissists tend to be extraverted and seek attention and glory, but have little interest in deep or reciprocal relationships. However, there are also introverted narcissists who feel extra special (the misunderstood genius), as well as communal types who regard themselves as particularly nurturing or empathic. What all three types have in common is an inflated ego, which causes them to believe they are better than ordinary mortals (Malkin, 2015). As we will see, that kind of high self-esteem comes from positive but inaccurate mirroring and is therefore superficial and unstable in the face of adult reality. The lack of realism in self-perception is evident from the statistics: for example, more than two-thirds of high school students expect to be in the top twenty per cent of performance in their jobs (Twenge & Campbell, 2009)!

Twenge and her colleagues used the narcissistic personality inventory (NPI) for most of their work. This is not an instrument for measuring narcissistic personality disorder (NPD, which is considered a pathology), and is therefore a useful measure for a continuous scale of narcissism in the general population. However, in addition to increases in NPI scores, there is *also* a rise in the incidence of NPD. Lifetime rates among young people (in their twenties) are three times that of older people (over sixty-five) despite the younger group having had only a third of the time to develop the disorder (Twenge & Campbell, 2009).

Correlating with these changes are increases in: individualism (Twenge, 2014); self-esteem (Twenge & Campbell, 2001); positive self-views (Twenge & Campbell, 2008); agentic traits (e.g., sense of importance, power, or physical attractiveness, Twenge, 1997); and materialistic values (Schor, 2004) amongst young adults. These studies all report an intensification of individualism, whether directly or indirectly measured. One of the consequences of this social change is a higher level of anxiety, which is at least partly caused by social atomisation (Twenge, 2000) as will be discussed in the next chapter. A comparison between high school and college students between 1938 and 2007 using the Minnesota Multiphasic Personality Scale showed that recent students scored more highly on multiple scales of psychopathology, including seven times more for hypomania (unrealistically high positive self-appraisal, over-activity, and low self-control) and five times more for psychopathic deviation (Twenge et al., 2010; Twenge, 2014).

Depression and youth suicide figures have risen in parallel with narcissism statistics. Where only one to two per cent of Americans born before 1915 experienced major depression during their lifetimes, today the figure is at least ten times higher and this is counting only the more severe forms of depression that have warranted medication or long-term therapy. The numbers on antidepressants have doubled between 1996 and 2008 (Twenge, 2014).

The steady increase in the frequency of depression and anxiety is associated with the weak self that arises under conditions of diminishing attuned intimacy in the developed urban world. This is an inevitable outcome of increasing competitive individualism and the erosion of family and social cohesion. In the 1990s Elizabeth Wurtzel put her depression in context by recognising herself as part of a generation of Americans in "a world that seems to be perilously lacking in the basic guarantees that our parents expected: a marriage that would last, employment that was secure, sex that wasn't deadly" (Wurtzel, 1996, pp. 301–302). More than two decades later, we have gone a lot further down this road. Both narcissism and insecure attachment (see next chapter) are disorders of the self and relationship that arise in a poor parental and/or societal facilitating environment and that leave the individual with little resilience against depression and anxiety.

Narcissism: a disturbance in self-formation

It is axiomatic that the earlier the block in development of the self, the more serious are the consequences (Hedges, 1994; Kohut & Wolf, 1986). In the psychoses, notably schizophrenia, fragments of the self fail to cohere in a stable manner because of the absence of even minimally effective early mirroring (minus four to plus four months according to Hedges). In borderline states, there is chronic functional chaos in the self. The mother blocks the child's strivings towards separation between four and twenty-four months (Hedges, 1994) and pulls him back into "archaic merger" (Kohut & Wolf, 1986, p. 179). The self remains chaotic but, in contrast to the psychoses, the problem is covered by protective defences. However any loss of the sense of self-continuity will produce profound anxiety.

The distortion of the self is generally believed to be less severe in the case of narcissistic personality disorders (NPDs). Kohut recognised that NPDs reflect the frustration and distortion of basic needs in self-formation that can be fulfilled only by a certain kind of relationship (Lessem, 2005). He focused on two clusters of developmental needs that are important in early life: the need to be seen and valued through positive mirroring, out of which ambitions arise; and the need for "calmness, infallibility and omnipotence" (Kohut & Wolfe, 1986, p. 177) through an idealised powerful adult, from whom we form our ideals. The adults who meet these two needs and are used by the child for these functions are the mirroring selfobject (often the mother and later relationships) and the idealising selfobject (often the father and then society at large). The baby internalises grandiosity and omnipotence during its first months of life, while idealisation and identification are later developments of the young child: "If all goes well, the selfobjects are internalised so that the self has a strong core which then enables it to appreciate the externality of others, and to relate to them in an empathic and meaningful way" (Frosh, 1991, p. 102). The baby needs the mirroring selfobject first, and somewhat later the idealising selfobject comes into play. NPDs emerge from a developmental block at the interface between these needs, at the cusp between focus on the (immature) self and focus on the other: either the needs for positive but accurate mirroring have not been adequately met so the child has not acquired the resources to move on (ibid.), or an idealising selfobject is not available to draw the individual outwards to a world beyond themselves (Elliott, 2002).

Where the mother is sufficiently attuned to the baby's needs, the infant experiences a fantasy of power and fulfilment, what Winnicott (1990) called the illusion of omnipotence. But as the child becomes capable of crawling away from mother, as she allows herself to be less reliable and as his needs become more complex, he begins to realise that mother is a separate person with her own agenda who does not always meet his needs at the moment he experiences them. With this gradual withdrawal of perfect adaptation, the child begins to form a theory of mind—that mother's mind is separate from his own. If all goes well, he will come to "the extremely difficult realisation that something other than oneself is real", which is Iris Murdoch's definition of love (1997, p. 215). Sometimes the child responds with rage and envy to the dawning awareness of his own helplessness and his dependence on an unreliable mother (Cooper, 1986). This may arise because his grandiosity needs have been met with disapproval or rejection in the first place, so that he feels threatened with annihilation of the developing self. "The narcissist's struggle for continued being, the struggle against exposure to real dependency and intimacy and hence further rejection, is a life-and-death one, a desperate struggle for survival of the self" (Frosh, 1991, p. 103). The narcissist copes by avoiding dependency and manipulating others, but remains fixated at an early stage of development. Clinical theorists such as Winnicott and Kohut, as well as those with a more societal orientation like Lasch and Frosh, agree that this maternal failure can be traced to social conditions. In a rapidly changing and increasingly alienating world, the parents' own selfhood will be undermined. In coping with their own ongoing loss and emptiness they naturally find it difficult "to offer a stable and still point around which the personality of a child can be formed" (Frosh, 1991, p. 103). The result is an individual unable "to genuinely love anything, whether self or other" (ibid., p. 104) because his own need for validation was not supported.

The loss of the blissful experience of unity and omnipotence is a painful necessity in the socialisation of the child and his internalisation of the other: learning that mother is a separate person prefigures the realisation that other people have their own reality that is quite distinct from the child's needs and desires. In the absence of this socialisation, relationships remain exploitative and therefore non-reciprocal and deeply unsatisfying. The weak sense of self here arises from the absence of a genuinely collective sense of self. An individualistic society is one in which parents and teachers don't demand responsibility towards others from the child; "society" is simply a matter of every man for himself. This tendency is exacerbated by small family size: in a family of ten it would be impossible for the children to be narcissists, whereas in a nuclear family of one or two, and especially with a mother who feels guilty about not being perfect, the parents may run themselves ragged in their worship of the child and their failure to set limits. We will return to the role of the social environment in the rise in narcissism later in this chapter.

Another view of the genesis of narcissism has been elaborated by Kernberg, who sees it in somewhat Kleinian terms as the consequence of the failure of the parents to contain the infant's destructiveness: a failure in affect regulation. He contrasts narcissistic pathology (secondary narcissism), characterised by an absence of trust or emotional warmth, with the normal (primary) narcissism of the young child that is accompanied by loving relationships with others and a genuine if unreliable capacity for dependency and sharing alongside a greater sense of realism. Kernberg focuses on rage as the core of the condition and views narcissism as a disturbed and distorted self rather than one whose growth has been stunted. Here the parental failure is in containing the infant's aggressive demands because the parents "fear, deny, avoid or repudiate them" (Frosh, 1991, p. 111). A splitting defence against the rage comes into play, with alternating swings between paranoid and idealising states.

NPDs are characterised by a poorly established sense of self where the ego feels empty, ineffective, and helpless, and relationships are superficial, manipulative, and exploitative. Since the narcissistic ego has a weak centre of identity, there is little capacity for feeling or empathy, for recognising the otherness of others or being concerned about their needs. The American novelist Richard Ford has picked up on this emptiness in Donald Trump, "who, I believe, is an actual human. … *Thinking* about Mr Trump, trying to fix on the there that's supposedly there, is like wanting to figure out what basic design a kaleidoscope *really contains* down there inside its hollow paper tube. There isn't one" (2016). Among the memoir writers, Elizabeth Wurtzel is the most obvious candidate for narcissism. Betrayed and abandoned by her father, enmeshed with her hysterical mother, and part of a subculture of meaningless sex, drugs and wildly irregular living (e.g., going without sleep and food for days), Wurtzel swung back and forth between frenzied activity and empty depression (1996). The former seems to have been a desperate attempt to fill the empty self, or the hole that she characterised as her depression. Her self-destructive acting-out, her sense of entitlement, exploitation of other people's emotional resources, and constant need for reassurance are all characteristic of narcissism. While relying on the help of others is common to many depressed people, when they emerge from the depression the non-narcissists are once again capable of seeing the other and of being aware of the pressure they have put on their loved ones.

One of the possible side-effects of narcissism is paranoia, where you are the centre of not just positive attention, but also threatening surveillance and hate messages. One client had typical features of narcissism such as a marked sense of entitlement and skill at manipulation (he beat me down to one third of my usual fee) and was furious whenever others put their own legitimate needs ahead of his. But in his mind, he was also the centre of negative attention: he believed that CCTV cameras had been hidden in his workplace to monitor him and that messages on public websites were targeted at him personally in order to humiliate him.

The narcissistic character is dependent on others for approval and admiration—or better still envy—but hates his dependency and is filled with rage at himself and the others on whom he depends. (I discovered this to my cost with a narcissistic member of a therapy group when I cut off some of her longer ramblings and thus refused her the homage that she demanded.) The narcissist longs for self-esteem but pursues it from the outside, looking for validation from those perceived to be powerful. He is trapped in a web of appearances and compensates for an impoverished inner life with external glitter, through wealth, celebrity, or by aligning himself with the achievements of others (Rustin & Rustin, 2009).

Social media and reality television have encouraged the replacement of an authentic inner-directed self by a performing self that feels alive only when being seen and applauded by others. In Murakami's novel *After Dark* we observe a Japanese model, Eri Asai, who has gone into a deep sleep for several months. We see a television screen in her bedroom that flickers into action, eventually showing the room in which the young woman lies asleep. Over the course of the novel the girl is sometimes on screen and sometimes in her "real" room. At one stage she wakes but cannot get out of the room. When on screen she appears to be struggling to get out, but her cries cannot be heard. Elsewhere in the night-time city a friend is talking about Eri Asai to her sister. He senses that when he talks to the model she is a million miles away as if he isn't there: "no matter what I say, it doesn't reach her. … She's not listening to anything I say—not *really*. The longer we talk, the more clearly I can see what's happening. So then the words that come out of *her* mouth stop making it all the way to me" (Murakami, 2008, p. 125). Likewise, the reader never gets to meet Eri Asai as a speaking or relating character; all we see is the *image* of her beautiful sleeping face. Here is a striking picture of the consequences of narcissism: the performing self in the shape of the girl's career as a model, her de-realisation and lack of presence to herself (asleep) or the other (can't hear), the consequences for relationship (she is cut off from others and they from her), and her becoming trapped in this place.

Depression and the empty self of narcissism

Even if the narcissist does achieve some recognition and success, the experience ultimately lacks meaning because what he really needs eludes him: a true centre of self and identity. Without this, he is alienated from himself and others. He has a "deep, but also deeply concealed, experience of diffuse depression" (Levin, 1987b, p. 505). "A mask of omnipotence and aggression [conceals] a profound sense of despair and helplessness" (ibid., p. 503). That the self-absorption of the narcissistic character is associated with underlying depression is to be expected: as I have argued elsewhere, meaning depends on the capacity for connection (Dowds, 2017) and the narcissist lacks connection to others and also, except at a superficial egoic level, to himself.

Kohut has argued that anxiety, depression, and irritability are characteristics of a fragile self structure arising from the fear that the self may collapse, and that this "disintegration anxiety" underlies all psychopathology (Lessem, 2005). Sometimes these feelings are covered over with the grandiosity defence, but for many NPD individuals the grandiose fantasies are unconscious, and they are "aware primarily only of shyness, feelings of unworthiness, fears of competition, and fears of exhibiting themselves" (Cooper, 1986, p. 129). For Alice Miller the grandiosity of NPD is a defence against depression, and "depression is the defence against real pain over the loss of the self" (1986, p. 328). Miller has pointed out that "one is free from depression when self-esteem is based on the authenticity of one's own feelings and not on the possession of certain qualities" (ibid., p. 329). Unconditional love will generate authenticity, whereas a false or adaptive self prone to depression is a consequence of blindness to, dismissal or rejection of, innate propensities alongside a pressure to exhibit particular qualities favoured by the parents that may be alien to the child.

Let us compare a healthy sense of self to a narcissistic personality disorder or false self (Table 8.1 is based on Miller, 1986). The former has "the unquestioned *certainty* that the feelings and wishes [he] experiences are a *part of* [his] *self*" (ibid., p. 325), which results in him having inner freedom, vitality, resilience, and stability. Such an individual has been brought up knowing that his feelings and impulses are real and acceptable; he has not been shamed for being himself and knows that he does not need permission to be express himself (e.g., to be different). With this feeling of comfort in his own skin, he need not fear control by others and is capable of love. A strong and integrated self, according to Siegel (2012), has the characteristics of flow: that is, it is flexible, adaptive, coherent, energised, and stable.

Miller's view of NPD is similar to Winnicott's false self (1990). It is generated by a carer who fails to mirror accurately and respond

Table 8.1. Comparison between a strong and weak sense of self.

Healthy (true) self	*NPD or false self*
Parents and child independent of each other	Fear of loss of love leading to conformism
Self separate from others	Over-sensitivity to others' reactions to them
No need to please others	Perfectionism
Autonomy	Controlled by others because of dependence of fragile self-esteem on others' approval and validation
Capacity to experience and express ordinary impulses	Readiness to feel shame and guilt
Aggression integrated (neither denied nor inappropriately expressed)	Aggression split off and therefore not neutralised
No splitting of good from bad	Denial of rejected feelings
Awareness of needs	Restlessness/inability to be present
Capacity to meet own needs	Envy of the healthy
Possible to love others	Others used to meet narcissistic needs

empathically to the child's needs during the first months of life. (But see above for other theories of the genesis of narcissism.) This is because the mother foregrounds her own narcissistic needs that the child is expected to fulfil. Because the child picks up that his anxiety, aggression, neediness, incompetence, or independent impulses upset mother, he gradually learns to repress his needs and libido. In later years he may become depressed because of experiencing a chronic inner emptiness in place of the true self that never developed. He has learnt to deny his own feelings and fears loss of love if he begins to behave autonomously.

If the parental shortcoming is a deficit in respect and admiration, the older child and adult may strive to compensate for the parent's failure or humiliation and go on to great success, often in a highly visible field. But such success—while crucial to keep despair and self-loathing at bay—will not meet the narcissist's real needs to develop his true self, and so will only be a thin and futile veneer over emptiness and aching lack. For the grandiose narcissist, admiration is mistaken for love because that elision of the two is all he has ever known. If/when his gifts appear to let him down—a bad review or anxious self-doubt—or decline with age, a severe depression can ensue.

The narcissistic offspring of inadequate parents lack not only parts of the self but also one or more selfobjects. The depressive person lives with the constant fear of losing the selfobject, but he needs to "accept the truth that this loss or this unavailability has *already happened* in the past, and that *no effort* whatsoever *can ever change this fact*" (Miller, 1986, p. 346, original italics). Thus the depressed individual must grieve the loss of the parents he never had and relinquish the expectation that others can meet his fundamental needs. The considerable therapeutic challenge is how to support clients through this very difficult process without their depression deepening.

Role of the socio-cultural environment in the rise of narcissism

According to Lasch (1978), Frosh (1991), and Elliott (2002), narcissistically disturbed individuals are merely displaying extreme versions of the normal contemporary alienated character, where the self has been restructured as a consumer "who measures everything in terms of market attractiveness and the approval of others" (Elliott, 2002, p. 63). As I have said elsewhere: "Identity-formation is thin and precarious in the face of rapacious capitalism, globalisation, technologisation, loss of awareness of history and decline of tradition. The depthless and detached self thrives in an environment that rewards manipulation of self and others and demands flexibility and ruthlessness in the service of competitiveness" (Dowds, 2008, p. 12).

The philosopher David Michael Levin has argued that we live in an age of *self*-destroying nihilism that began in the era of Descartes and has been escalating since then and which is eroding the foundations of the self. This process is generating wholesale loss: "of grounding, centeredness, balance, identity, wholeness, meaning, purpose, energy, heart, reality, and a sense of Being" (Levin, 1987a, pp. 27–28). Levin sees nihilism as a consequence of the will to power and a reduction of the self to a wilful ego that fulfils itself through domination and mastery: this is secondary narcissism—or NPD. We become alienated by separating the ego from others and the environment and thereby objectifying everything around us, including the self (Levin, 1987a; 1987b). Capitalism has created a society where competitiveness has destroyed human interconnectedness and all sense of social responsibility, and the authentic self cannot develop in such a dehumanised and hyper-individualised culture (Levin, 1987a). A nihilistic culture fosters the development of NPDs and, conversely, a high prevalence of narcissists creates a nihilistic society. Our culture both facilitates and replicates the parenting deficits that generate narcissistic pathology: "There is little opportunity to enter the stillness needed to achieve a deep state of being and connectedness with self, while equally the over-'gratifying' and objectifying culture frustrates ... cathexis of the other" (Dowds, 2008, p. 12).

Immersed in these profoundly adverse social conditions, we have the choices to respond with fight or flight. Variants of the aggressive response include "anger, rage, hatred, envy, vengeance, contempt, condescension and physical attack"; while withdrawal may be expressed as "sadness, fear, shame, embarrassment, humiliation ... and depression" (Lessem, 2005, p. 192). The epidemic of depression is proof of the increase in the withdrawal response, while the aggression is manifest in the hate speech of the tabloid press, social and other media, in high school shootings in the USA, terrorist attacks, sexism, racism, contempt for the weak, the old, or the poor, online bullying, etc. As we saw in Chapters Six and Seven, there is a higher incidence of the withdrawal defence (culminating in internalising disorders) amongst women and of the aggressive response (the extremes being externalising disorders) amongst men.

In an instrumentalising environment emptied of values, the parent or society fails to provide a wider context of social relations into which the child can separate out of the symbiotic state (Elliott, 2002). When individuals experience others (individuals, governments, corporations, or institutions) as being indifferent or threatening to them, as in today's alienated world, they "can become absorbed largely in themselves, and withdraw feeling and attention" from them (Rustin & Rustin, 2009, p. 209). This is the kind of narcissism epitomised by the children of the Nazi generation in post-war Germany: since the parental generation was tainted by their complicity and could not be loved or respected, their children turned inwards either as an escape, or to work through the family conflicts they had internalised (Labanyi, 1989). Such people are not just disconnected but depoliticised: "narcissistic withdrawal is in part a despairing response to the way in which the public domain has already been expropriated, or at the very least log-jammed, by corporate interests and their lobbyists" (Labanyi, 2008, pp. 28–29). I can't change society but at least I can rebrand myself (like Isolde in Chapter Seven).

The Rustins elaborate two defences that arise from such withdrawal. In hyper-individualism the narcissist is indifferent to others except in their role as admirers—as we see in the hunger of today's youth for celebrity. Miller quotes from a client speaking about her narcissistic and famous mother: "the deeper the hole in my mother's heart was, the bigger the jewels in her crown needed to be" (1986, p. 335). In the other defence, that of pseudo-collectivism, the individual identifies with the collective to borrow strength or support for a fragile sense of individual identity. The collective may be a pop group, football team, neighbourhood gang, religious cult, or terrorist cell. Any identity is better than none, even if, like Shelley (Chapter Seven), the identity depends merely on which are your drugs of choice.

It is important to realise that even adults with a relatively healthy self can be seduced into narcissism under cultural pressure. James Salter's novel *Solo Faces* concerns a rock-climber, a loner who climbs entirely for the intrinsic satisfactions of challenging himself and entering into spiritual communion with the mountains and the snow and ice. But then he becomes famous for carrying out a daring rescue of some trapped and injured mountaineers. His life changes as he becomes feted in the media and the salons of Paris; they expect him not to do anything ordinary any more. His motivation becomes contaminated by the competitive, hero-worshipping society whose values he can no longer keep at a distance. In despair, he blurts out to an acquaintance: "Do you want to know what I'm really interested in? It's disgusting. Making people envious—that's it. That's all it is. I wasn't always that way. There may have been a tendency but not much. I was stronger" (Salter, 2008, p. 170). Few individuals can resist the pull of the herd, which is why so many people in our culture are destroyed by fame. It's a Faustian pact: what you gain in glory or notoriety, you lose in self-determination.

For good or ill, "new object relations can develop throughout the lifetime, and are not wholly determined by early experience" (Rustin & Rustin, 2009, p. 215). This is why, on the one hand, relational psychotherapy works. Yet this same mechanism leaves the psyche (like Salter's hero) wide open to being invaded, colonised, and even reshaped by toxic inputs such as advertising, spin, or other ways of promoting ideologies, even those that betray or exploit us. Moreover these subsequent negative introjects will inevitably resonate with early developmental deficits, tending to favour defensive and regressive self-identifications. The crucial point is that the infant's early experiences of helplessness and dependency are retained in the psyche and nervous system and are therefore always available to be reactivated by subsequent experiences of insecurity in adult life. This is why threats to cultural identity can be experienced as threats to one's very survival and can evoke correspondingly primitive reactions. Thus a social context of extreme instability and increasing inequality will tend to provoke violent responses such as populism. By contrast, "a psychologically secure social condition [is] one in which individuals believe that their wider environment ensures their physical security, is relatively predictable and mild in its impact on them" (ibid., p. 224). The word "believe" underlines that this is in part a matter of perception, which can therefore be reoriented towards the negative by, for instance, "project fear" and other ideologies. Indeed it is "when the elementary foundations of trust in others and in the wider society become eroded that pathological identifications of a narcissistic type come into existence" (ibid., p. 225).

The irony is that in our society narcissism is itself being instrumentalised. Indeed, the Rustins perceive "an attack on the very idea of dependency and relationship" in our current atomised, dog-eat-dog ethos. In such a context, narcissism—which is precisely a defence against relationship—is "desirable in itself. ... Possessive, competitive individualism [has been] promoted ... as for the general good" (ibid., p. 230). A key neo-liberal creed is indeed that there is no such thing as society, and that safety nets such as welfare provided by the state merely stifle initiative. Solidarity and empathy are seen as barriers to economic growth. The task is for all of us to become entrepreneurs—which includes being entrepreneurs of our own selves (as brands). The stress and all the attendant consequences that such a culture generates does not need to be emphasised.

Our privacy is under siege in the contemporary world—by media intrusion, reality TV, a culture of public confession, and, most wide-reaching of all, social media that expose the trivial but often significant details of lives to an indifferent or hostile, but always superficial, gaze. This loss of privacy further threatens the fragile sense of self by eroding our self-containing boundaries (Cohen, 2013).

To summarise, our non-facilitating society contributes to the rise in narcissism and depression in at least four ways:

1. In a materialistic and competitive society that does not respect us and which we cannot respect, we lack an idealising selfobject that would help us to bring meaning to our lives.
2. In a culture that is so diverse, we lack a mirroring selfobject. Instead of being mirrored in who we are, we are presented with a supermarket display of all the things we could be. How do we choose when we have no basis for choice?
3. In a culture that is so commodified and trivialised, we lack mirroring for what actually matters to us.
4. In a political, economic, and climatic context that is so unstable, unjust, unequal, and insecure, we retreat to a narcissistic position to escape our anxiety.

When narcissism meets reality—and loneliness

A thought experiment: a society in which "pain is exceptional and avoidable, and pleasure the normal state of being—[where] everything can be monitored and predicted, and [where] if, very occasionally, something goes wrong, it must always be someone's fault" (Verhaeghe, 2014, p. 158). In fact this is what our current society is telling us, generating an army of narcissists who take legal action if their grades are not to their satisfaction, who divorce their less than perfect spouse, leave their political party to become an independent, or vote to leave the European Union to take back control. This inability to compromise or find common cause is leading to serious political fracturing (in the USA and many European countries), where often valid anger is exploited by populist politicians and divisions are deepened. The spectres of 1930s fascism begin to haunt us again.

In a social psychologist's view of the rise in narcissism and depression, Twenge (2014) attributes the self-entitlement of "generation me" (born in the 1980s and 1990s) to the "self-esteem movement" in schools and homes. Children are shielded from all pain and unhappiness, rewarded merely for participating, and mistakes aren't always corrected for fear of hurting their feelings. The result is a tribe of junior narcissists, with inflated egos and little capacity to deal with adversity. And yet, while being coddled by adults, young people are being bullied by each other, as is inevitable in a culture where they are brought up to believe that "I am the only one who matters". For Frosh:

> Narcissism has its cultural roots in [a] tantalising cycle of excitement and deflation: the constant stream of apparently met, but actually frustrated desires leads to a denial both of the pain of genuine loss and of the struggle involved in achieving reparation, recognition and renewal. Narcissism … reflects, above all, the terrifying emptiness produced by the denial of reality. (1991, p. 125)

When they enter the workplace, young people today meet the opposite extreme from what their childhood promised: harsh criticism, ruthless competitiveness, and high expectations (e.g., that they will work for free as "interns" for the privilege of gaining experience). As Twenge shows, this generation has been brought up with the greatest self-importance and sense of entitlement ever. But they have come to maturity at a time when the gap between rich and poor is ever escalating and where even those with good jobs will struggle to pay the bills. In the USA, it now takes two college-graduate earners to achieve the same standard of living as one high-school-educated person in the past (ibid.). Twenge proposes that it is partly this mismatch between expectations and reality that generates depression and anxiety in the current generation of young adults, though one could equally argue that the reality described is inherently depressing. Instead of a gradual introduction to the reality principle as children, they are having a shockingly abrupt awakening as young adults. I see this gap between expectations and opportunities in a client with a PhD in history whose only way of earning a living is in a career he despises, financial services.

Young Americans are merely the leading edge of an ongoing increase in narcissism and individualism in the developed urban world. The individual's needs trump group needs, we increasingly distrust others, are cynical about government and institutions of power (as the epidemic of populism shows) and see other people as opponents to beat, as mere service-providers or those to blame when they let us down. This is the toxic art of the deal: me first. Core values have changed from the early 1960s—being "honest, hardworking, industrious, loyal, and caring about others"—to in the present day—"whatever makes you happy" (Twenge, 2014, p. 13). With the freedom of such a stance comes the downside of loneliness and the pressure of standing alone. As social beings we need the warmth and security that others can offer, and much of our depression may arise from the coldness and lack of love that characterise a hyper-competitive world.

We can conclude that the depression underlying narcissism arises from isolation from both ourselves and others. The psychodynamic and sociodynamic are reciprocally reinforcing, with poor child-rearing practises creating narcissists, narcissists creating and enabling an individualist society, and individualist caregivers conditioning narcissistic children.

The victim of narcissistic abuse

The underlying depression of the narcissist is only one side of the coin. The other concerns the people with whom they come into contact and who are abused by their manipulation, rage, and hatred. The bullying that signals a weak sense of self is magnetised by perceived weakness in others and contributes to depression in their victims—as described in several of the memoirs, including those by Merritt, Brampton, and Lewis.

Kernberg (1980) identified what he called malignant narcissism, which is characterised by excessive entitlement and self-sufficiency, exploitation, exhibitionism, authoritarianism, and feeling superior. Such people are high-flyers (Icarus before his fall), controlling and predatory, often with malevolent intent. Unlike NPD individuals who have been neglected in childhood, the malignant narcissists have also been brutalised and humiliated (Louis de Canonville, 2015).

All forms of control may be used by the malignant narcissist, including intimidation, isolation, coercion, economic power, physical and sexual abuse (ibid.). The resulting environment leaves the victim in a state of helplessness, panic, and chaos, and sometimes with PTSD. They may suffer low self-esteem, depression, suicidal ideation, and somatic symptoms, as well as shame, humiliation, and self-blame where they have been conditioned to take responsibility for the narcissist's behaviour. Victims often repeat the pattern of childhood narcissistic abuse in their adult relationships and have been taught to stand in the shadows of their narcissistic aggressor so as not to upstage them. The victim can feel inferior and guilty for talking about the abuser, even to the extent of protecting them in a form of Stockholm syndrome.

Other common distortions in self formation

The narcissistic self—together with its extreme in narcissistic personality disorder—is only one form of inadequately established self. Three other common distortions of self-organisation are the false (over-adapted) self, the fused self, and the fragmented self. Each leaves individuals with an underlying depression or anxiety because they lack the resilience and creativity of an authentic, autonomous, and cohesive self, which is characterised by what Carl Rogers (1967) called an "internal locus of evaluation". While the narcissistic self is viewed by Miller (1986) as a form of false self, it can be more accurately described as an empty self for which the individual compensates with an inflated ego. The term false self is more usually used in the Winnicottian sense to apply to the result of complying with the expectations of others, and individuals with a false self are often perceived as "nice" people, though often irritatingly so.

True self, false self: the intersubjective integration or frustration of authenticity and adaptation

The true self is facilitated when the child is directed by her own sense of aliveness, where she has the capacity to get in touch with and express her deepest needs, feelings, and impulses. However, there is also the child who is not rejected or ill-treated, who may have parents deeply concerned for her welfare but who nevertheless grows up feeling that love is conditional upon being who her parents want her to be, thus making her believe that her "instinctive drives and spontaneous impulses are wrong" (Storr, 1989, p. 95). Winnicott writes poignantly of the patient who "has come near the end of a long analysis *to the beginning of her life*. She contains no true experience, she has no past. She starts with fifty years of wasted life, but at last she feels real, and therefore she now wants to live" (1990, p. 148). This woman with a false self feels unreal and that her life is futile and meaningless. The false (or adaptive) self arises when the child is over-adapted to the needs of the parent. He does what the parent explicitly or implicitly wants. In the case of the pre-verbal infant, he looks into mother's eyes and sees, not himself—as would be the case for an adequately mirrored baby—but mother and *her* needs and demands (Winnicott, 1989). This is the "good child" who picks up from a look that mother is tired, depressed, disapproving—and behaves according to what will least upset her. Such people who learn to placate the parent will tend to develop a depressive personality (Storr, 1989).

The conformist is obedient to the demands of society and differs strikingly from the narcissist: far from craving attention, she has little ego.

She is similar to the narcissist in having an external locus of evaluation, but looks to the other for permission rather than attention. Both have underlying depression because of being out of touch with their authentic organismic drives. Some people display a false self only in the company of others, while connecting with the true self when alone. Not surprisingly, they have a particular need for solitude (ibid.) because their relationships with others are fraught with stress and inner conflict.

Conformism to parental or societal demands is not a new or even exaggerated phenomenon, and in the past such people could sometimes live quite happily within a conservative community. However, they were not exposed to the current wide range of different value-systems that might question or threaten their own. The problem for the conformist—with his inherently weak sense of self—when he encounters other values is that he has no backing for his supposed beliefs in his real feelings, needs, or drives (Miller, 1986). He is thus vulnerable to becoming the pawn of more ruthless interests and ideologies, as we see in the ease with which young people can be "radicalised" into terrorist groups. Such an adolescent conforms to the new ideals just as he complied with the demands of his parents or social group previously.

Winnicott's essay on the true and false self was written in 1960, at a time when obedience to the requirements of family, school, and authority structures was still the norm. However, compliance with authority is today notable mainly for its absence, so most Western youth are not especially at risk of replacing one form of explicit authority (e.g., parental) with another such as religious cults or terrorist leaders. So in what way is the false self a more general problem in contemporary society? My contention is that while we may refuse to comply with overt authority, we are often unaware of the covert messages in advertising and the media. In a desperate desire to be seen as cool and successful, young people are highly vulnerable to being manipulated by the messages and ideologies promulgated by consumer capitalism, such as materialism, competitiveness, or self-commodification. This conformism to media-inspired commandments generates depression just as surely as being over-obedient to one's parents or other legitimate authorities. One such was the writer Mary Loudon who, after therapy, confessed: "I have lost the frantic desire to please which found expression in the hot spur of quivering ambition. I'm not sorry, for the depressions have more or less entirely disappeared along with it" (1996, p. 73). While most people experience "some degree of conflict between inner desires and outer realities", for adolescents in particular, the emotional imbalance can lead to "depression, anxiety, uncontrolled rage, a feeling of meaninglessness and disconnection (as in a 'false self'), loss of motivation, and interpersonal difficulties" (Siegel, 2012, p. 354).

A primary need being frustrated in contemporary society is that for authenticity, and I have connected the rise of the conformist herd self to the destabilisation and uprootedness of the twenty-first century (Dowds, 2008). Instead of possessing genuine roots, we adapt transiently to one group after another, in each case adopting the values—or more often merely the style—of that group. In 1955, Fromm was already referring to "the alienated personality who is for sale", who has lost almost all sense of self. We compensate by acquiring what he called a secondary sense of self, by "being approved of, worthwhile, successful, useful" (Fromm, 1990 pp. 142–143). This is a particular marketing version of Winnicott's false self. Nowadays, the marketed self is increasingly widespread and even more alienated at work or play, as it answers the demands, not just of a more ruthlessly competitive deregulated capitalism, but of globalisation and technologically driven change.

Kathryn Hughes (2016) has admitted to working on a book "for an embarrassing number of years. Let's say seven, because it sounds just about respectable and even slightly biblical in its heroic capacity for endurance. And I can honestly say that every day has been hell." How much does her struggle reflect the difficulty of accessing and realising her creative vision and how much was she battling her organismic impulses in order to live up to an introjected ego ideal? The truth is we can never fully distinguish the authentic from the adaptive self—we must go beyond the misleading dichotomy of the true and false self, and indeed the notion of the self as a fixed entity. The self "can never be finished .... It is always in the process of constructing itself, giving play to both its elemental impulses and its relationally derived identities, inside a framework held in place by reflection on both" (Seigel, 2005, p. 151). This beautifully captures the layered complexity. First, that experiencing is a creative process: fluid, reciprocal, and open-ended. Second, the self process is both personal and relational, even in adulthood. Third, this process is organised and ceaselessly updated by mentalizing self and others.

We all have needs to follow our own libido, to be true to our organismic drives, to live through first-hand, embodied experiencing, rather than the virtuality of technology or the commodified desires introjected from the media. But we are also social creatures and need somehow to find or create a place for ourselves in the society in which we live. Part of this is about our need for holding: at times we need to let go of responsibility for creating every moment of our lives; sometimes we just want to relax and follow the crowd. Secondly, we have a need to be accepted by others. We gain much of our sense of meaning from identification with social groups, and we help shape and in turn are shaped by their norms. For example, eating behaviours run through groups, and reminding people of one of their social identities (age, gender, political or sports allegiance, etc.) is sufficient to shape how they perceive themselves (e.g., how intelligent or ethical they are or what matters to them) (Cruwys et al., 2014). So my personal self and socially adapted self are in constant tension, each influencing the reality and the perception of the other.

We negotiate this balance between true and adaptive self in every encounter in every moment of our lives. Indeed, the person I take myself to be is as much determined by the mirroring of others as by my understanding of myself. We are intersubjective beings: not just in how we develop, but also in how we interact, behave, and even experience ourselves as mature adults. In an analysis of the novels of Henry James, the philosopher Robert Pippin evokes the complexity of this:

> What one takes oneself to be doing is always in some sense some reflection of what others would take or have taken this sort of action to be, and which formulation I am inclined to act upon, or which gets to be my motive, cannot be simply viewed as a result of my choice, given how much of the "me" doing the deciding is also already some internalization of "who I have been taken to be", or what I have been given by others as a self-understanding. (Pippin, 2001, p. 49)

James highlights "what he calls the 'negotiated' nature of psychological meaning itself, as if it actually exists somewhere 'between' and not 'in' persons" (ibid., p. 64). In this light, authenticity cannot be seen as a purely individual matter but is always relational.

It is certain we will experience a vacuum of meaning in the absence of an authentic self. However, if we compromise too little and refuse to adapt to others, we neglect the relational part of the self and will be lonely; but equally importantly, we will not be able to ground our authentic impulses. Unless stabilised through interactions with others, our feelings, desires, and identifications, no matter how authentic, are merely transitory, changing with each situation. Indeed "our identity-conferring identifications are drawn from, and are answerable to, the shared historical commitments and ideals that make up our communal life-world" (Guignon, 2004, p. 155). Clearly this doesn't mean that we indiscriminately soak up whatever we are exposed to: instead we sift through what we encounter in our family and broader social worlds and integrate what most convinces us or appears to have most value. We must negotiate our need for relationship: not by dominance or submission, but through loving union with the other without losing our own identity (Fromm, 1990). Here we inhabit intersubjective space and can connect with the other without losing the self (see Dowds, 2014, p. 245). This is a reciprocal and co-creative space where the needs of two people can be simultaneously appreciated, where the wonder of the other expands rather than diminishes the wonder of the self.

Adapting too much to others is a major source of depression, as we saw in the majority of the memoirs (Chapter Two), where the authors over-compromised and paid too much attention to what the "world" thinks. One defence against the empty self is constant activity as a way of running away from that realisation. In the absence of a bigger sense of self, the individual identifies with his ego, indeed believes he *is* the ego. Productive activity has a second purpose, that of feeding the ego with career and social success. Many of the depression memoirs register a hollow self and an ambitious and competitive ego that depends for its self-worth on ruthlessly driving itself to ensure success in the working and social environments (This seems to be most extremely true of Rice-Oxley, Kelly, Thompson, Martin, Manning, Wurtzel, Merritt, and Jamison). One of the characteristics of an empty self is a lack of self-awareness and a difficulty in learning the lessons that depression carries. This is particularly the case for Rice-Oxley and, more shockingly, for Manning, who is a clinical psychologist and yet believes that she is "the simple product of effort, will and design" (1994, p. 97) and covers up the hole in herself with constant activity.

The question arises whether we must share assumptions, passions, beliefs, and values in order to create shared meaning in our social groupings. How much does my individual meaning depend on a shared meaning? If I find I can share beliefs with, say, nineteenth-century novelists I will have some support that I am not simply insane, that is, living in a reality occupied only by me. But if I don't share meaning with anybody in my own era I will be profoundly lonely and unsure of myself. This is the dilemma for people living in what they consider a sick society: they don't want to be part of it, but there isn't any significant alternative other than living on a desert island or in a very small clique, perhaps in mere virtual online connection with each other. So compliance isn't the only block to authenticity; atomisation or erosion of shared values and meaning is another.

To conclude: authenticity is not monadic. Such is our formation through relationship, such is our ongoing interdependence with others, that a fully authentic sense of self is intersubjective.

Fragmented self

The false self must become fractured because conforming requires diverse adaptations in different contexts. If empathically attuned responses from the caregivers are insufficient, shame is the inevitable outcome. We react to this with anxiety, and then defend against both unpleasant emotions by keeping much of the authentic self cordoned off, which generates fragmentation. The self that is prone to fragmenting is:

> beset with shame, anxiety, depression, and stress, preoccupied with its own competence, fearful in relationships, and rarely capable of true intimacy, alienated from its own deeper self, committed to an inauthentic life of distraction and entertainment, addictions and pseudo-intimacy, with at best sporadic periods of feeling emotionally nourished by relationships or work. (Cortright, 2007, p. 64)

In humanistic therapy, the separated fragments are referred to as subpersonalities (Rowan, 1990) or as configurations: "a coherent pattern of feelings, thoughts and preferred behavioural responses symbolised or pre-symbolised by the person as reflective of a dimension of existence within the Self" (Mearns & Thorne, 2000, p. 102).

When we split off from our authentic feelings we are left with "massive internal clashes" and depression, as for instance experienced by one survivor of childhood sexual abuse who grew up in a culture where emotions were ignored, repressed or shamed (McLaren, 2015, p. 29). She suffered the first of multiple severe depressive episodes at the age of ten, but it wasn't until her late twenties that she found the courage to ask what her depression was telling her and began to access the anger and other emotions beneath it. The denial of some parts of the self by other parts is facilitated by disembodiment, disconnection between thinking and feeling, and shallow relationships. There is additionally damage to creativity and accessing spirituality (Cortright, 2007).

Fused or confluent self

Occasionally I come across clients who, despite living in loving extended families and supportive communities, are nevertheless crippled with anxiety and depression. Because they are enmeshed with their families, they have never discovered their authenticity or autonomy. The founder of family systems theory, Murray Bowen (1978), defined the functional family as one in which its members are both differentiated from each other as well as flexibly linked together. Emotional separation from the family begins in early adolescence, and the person who remains in a state of fusion is psychologically pre-adolescent. Such people have a hive mentality: they are threatened by variety of opinion or by independent action on the part of other members of the group, and stress spreads through them like electric shock between people holding hands. Here depression arises out of co-dependence: the individual feels guilty about having needs of her own or attempting to meet them because that is deemed "selfish". Since they are bound hand and foot to others, they are powerless to move independently. Indeed they can be so focused on the perceived needs of others that they are completely unaware of their own. My client Marie knew that she felt angry at "having to" do so much for others; but her resentment was simply a source of guilt rather than of awareness that might draw her attention to her own needs. Remaining in fusion is similar to the problems of ambivalent attachment, while the defensive reaction against it—cut-off—has the characteristics of avoidant attachment. Confluence is an archaic defence that is declining in postmodernity, but can still be found in more traditional enmeshed families and communities.

Summary

The vulnerability to depression of a large number of the memoirists could be attributed to a poorly established sense of self. Compensating for the weak self by overachievement generated stress and exhaustion, which was the final trigger for the onset of an episode of major depression. The current socio-cultural environment is both more depressogenic in itself and is at the same time spawning people who are inherently less resilient to depression. Social and cultural changes are both cause and effect of mutations in the nature of the self (Taylor, 1989). Deconstructive intellectual fashions have fostered disenchantment and nihilism, while political, economic, and technological "progress" has contributed to material and psychosocial changes such as social fragmentation, instability, commodification of people, competitive individualism, erosion of privacy, the overvaluing of power and success relative to love and support, and the loss of public ideals. Above all, it is the nature of relationships that has suffered, including those in the public and private spheres, and the parent–child bond. Anything that diminishes the quality and depth of our contact with others has a constricting effect on the development, maintenance, and growth of the self.

Beneath the carapace of the inflated narcissist is a hollow man. Such a person has not had the selfobject experiences that would facilitate the emergence and blossoming of a true self. In his inability to recognise others in their own right, he denies the fact of and his potential for mutual interconnectedness, and is thus cut off from the nourishment and complexity of the web of humanity, as well as from his place in the wider scheme of life, love, nature, the world, and inevitably from his spiritual being. In place of all that, he has only a fragile inflated ego, craving favourable attention and therefore desperately dependent on the unreliable other. The defended egos that compensate for these fragile selves have no more substance than balloons that can be burst with a random, and often unintended, pinprick. Such people are cut off from their organismic impulses and therefore from meaningful living. Other problematic distortions of the self, in addition to the empty narcissistic self, include the compliant false self where life feels futile, and the fragmented self that is a mass of contradictions riven with anxiety about shaming exposure.

The person with a fragile self, whether empty (narcissistic), false, or fragmented, is stressed, anxious, and has an underlying depression. Such compromised individuals are more vulnerable to a non-facilitative, bullying, competitive, non-mirroring, demanding, depriving, or over-impinging human environment, or indeed an impoverishing, alienating (ugly, inhuman, or aggressively urban), and/or over-stimulating material environment.

Depression is primarily a disorder of the self and only secondarily a mood disorder. If this is taken on board, the implications for therapy are immense, for moods cannot be regulated when they are so reliant on unstable and out-of-control extrinsic conditions. Moods can be stabilised only when there is a strong sense of self: (a) with the capacity for depth of experiencing; (b) that is relatively independent of the opinions, judgements, and beliefs of others; and (c) that has the organismic capacity to discern what is nourishing and what is toxic in its environment and choose accordingly.

CHAPTER NINE

Relatedness under threat: anxiety and ambivalence

In Chapter Four, we showed how it is the relational process with the parents that enables the self to develop, and with it the child's capacity for connection, attunement, trust, autonomy, and love. In Chapter Eight, we examined how these relationships and others can go awry and generate disorders or temporary derailments of the self. Now I want to explore other reasons why relationships are vitally important throughout the lifespan. We have seen how their quality is critical for security, self-formation, and our experience of our lives as being meaningful. These early beginnings determine our capacity for relating as adults, and we continue to depend on others—though not to the same degree—for development and maintenance of the self, for meaning, and for feeling safe. The attachment system, which evolved to keep the child safe by remaining close to the parent, is subsequently transferred in later life to a spouse or partner who will also improve our chances of surviving and reproducing. Evidence that a supportive relationship diminishes our perception of threat comes from an experiment on a woman subjected to electric shocks who showed reduced activity in the worry and discomfort neural circuits when her husband held her hand (Coan et al., 2006). Indeed, emotional connection with at least one other person provides resilience and protects individuals against the long-term effects of chronic social risk (Werner, 1993). We have a lifelong need from others for mirroring (Lessem, 2005), to tell us who we are, and we continue even in adulthood to look to others for their emotional response to tell us how we "should" feel and react (Pearmain, 2001). We also derive existential meaning, in the form of love and belonging, from intimate relationships; and as we shall see in the next chapter, the question of meaning is central to depression. These relationships can be with spouse and family, but also friendships in which we share values and interests and can be true to ourselves. A study on married couples who moved to a new home found that they were distressed at losing their old neighbourhood groups despite retaining the intimate relationship with their spouses (Weiss, 1982). Community is important in providing an extended sense of self as part of something larger (Cruwys et al., 2014). The downside of our dependence on relationships is that anything that is so important to us is inevitably bound up with anxiety. For we can lose relationships through fate—disease or accident—or we can be abandoned or rejected. Or, we may find others so difficult to deal with that we deny our need for them.

A longitudinal study, started in 1938 in Harvard University, has followed hundreds of men (Harvard students and boys from Boston's poorest areas) from their teenage years to old age. The current director of this Study of Adult Development says: "the clearest message we get from this 75-year study is this: good relationships keep us happier and healthier. Period" (Robert Waldinger on www.ted.com, 23 December 2015). He contrasts this with the *actual* life goals of the millennial generation, which were to get rich (eighty per cent) and become famous (fifty per cent). Loneliness shortens our lives and makes us less happy and less healthy. However, a highly conflicted marriage is also bad for health, and it is the *quality* (intimacy and stability) of relationships that is important. The main task for younger couples is managing conflict, whereas the most significant factor for older people is mutual support: in a group of elderly couples, higher attachment security was linked with better mood, fewer depressive symptoms, fewer marital conflicts, and greater marital satisfaction (Waldinger et al., 2015).

While we all need relationships, the *amount* of human contact that we can process varies widely, extraverts in particular needing more environmental stimulus to keep the brain aroused than introverts (Cain, 2013; Carter, 2009). Introverts are exhausted by excessive contact, and parents need to be careful about expecting the same degree of participation in after-school activities from an introverted child as from others. Such children may be so worn out by the enforced sociability of school that they need hours alone afterwards to recover (Cain et al., 2016). Anthony Storr points out that "some natures are more inclined toward finding the meaning of life chiefly in interpersonal relationships; others toward finding it in interests, beliefs, or patterns of thought" (1989, p. 74). But the distinction may not be so clear-cut, and at least some of the latter group who are focused on being seen through their achievements may be compensating for not being "embedded in a family and social nexus ... [so that such a person] has to make his mark in individual fashion" (ibid., p. 81). It is important to emphasise that being an introvert is not the same as being avoidant in your attachment style. The former is more sensitive to social and other stimuli; the latter has learned early in life that people are not trustworthy. However, in both cases ambivalence about other people is the understandable result. This in no way negates the importance of relationships, but it certainly complicates them.

A suboptimum upbringing can mean that adult relationships often take away from our sense of self instead of adding to it. "Depending on what you were told when you were assembling your identity, you are either certain of yourself, confident in your dealings with others, and sure of your own superiority; or, conversely, you are timid, ashamed of yourself, and shrink from interaction with others, convinced that they think you worthless" (Verhaeghe, 2014, p. 23). We may learn to feel confident and self-respecting with some people, but not others. Thus the beliefs we introject about the opposite and same sex and about authority stem from the early relationships with parental figures, while the way we interact with peers is formed during our childhood interactions with siblings and other children.

We saw in the last chapter how society contributes to (as well as being affected by) the rise in narcissism and other disorders of the self. Likewise, it impacts on the way we interact with each other. Relationships are riven with insecurity in our fluid world, as well as with uncertainty and concern when they are no longer governed by uniform societal rules, as we will see in the section on social anxiety. The current trends of competitive individualism and addictive consumption underwritten by neo-liberal capitalism are disastrous for lasting relationships (Verhaeghe, 2014). Competing against or cheating on our loved one or refusing to curb drinking, drug-taking, shopping, or gambling is obviously not the best way to generate self-esteem, security, trust, or love on the part of your partner.

Changes in attachment over time

The main way in which the capacity for relationship is assessed is through attachment styles. A recent American meta-analysis showed that between 1988 and 2011, while there was a small increase in insecure attachment overall (fifty-one per cent up to fifty-eight per cent), there was a much greater (approximately fifty per cent) increase in the avoidant (dismissing) style (twelve per cent rising to nineteen per cent) within one generation (Konrath et al., 2014). There have also been decreases in dispositional empathy between the late 1970s and 2009 (Konrath et al., 2011). This matches the attachment data, since dismissing people have lower empathy scores (Diehl et al., 1998). Low empathy in turn is associated with holding a negative view of others (Britton & Fuendeling, 2005).

Konrath et al. (2014) associate the rise in avoidant attachment with the increase in narcissism because the two conditions share the characteristics of self-reliance, low levels of affiliative concern, and the dismissal of close relationships that may threaten self-concept. Nevertheless, the similarities are superficial, for the psychodynamic origins and motivating experiences are quite different. The key questions are: for the avoidant "Am I safe?"; for the narcissist "Am I valued?" The avoidant fears intimacy and prefers to be independent of others, whereas the narcissist needs other people to affirm her. The other doesn't exist in his own right for the narcissist: she remains unsocialised, omnipotent in a world of one. People with attachment disorders, on the other hand, do not negate the other; rather, the avoidantly attached don't trust the other to meet their needs. What the two conditions do have in common is a fragile sense of self and a vulnerability to depression and anxiety. The parallel increases in dismissing (avoidant) attachment and narcissism may well indicate that the current social environment fosters the avoidance of intimacy as a defence for a weakly established self.

The increased frequency of narcissism and avoidant attachment could have emerged from changes in child rearing and/or the adult environment, which promote personality shift in individuals already at risk. In heritability studies, environmental influences were found to account for virtually all of the variance in avoidant/dismissing attachment (ibid. for references). While attachment styles are generally relatively stable over time, the avoidant is less stable than the others. It appears likely therefore that socio-cultural changes exert more influence over this attachment style. Speculating about the reasons for the increase in dismissing attachment, Konrath et al. (2014) hypothesise changes in family values (focus on self rather than other) or family structure (working mothers, divorced parents, and more single mothers, less involvement of an extended family), and/or changes in media content (e.g., competitive reality TV) and usage (social disconnection due to increased digital connection).

Overuse of technology is having significant effects on attachment. Schoolteachers are finding that they have to teach children how to read the human face (Rowson & McGilchrist, 2017). Even young infants are engaging with screens instead of mother's face, thus sidelining the development of self that depends on attunement with the primary caregiver. In addition to deprivation of human contact, excess screen time also generates distraction, overstimulation, and blurring of the distinction between the real and the virtual, all of which sets children up for dissociation from their embodied and relational humanness. This paves the way for replacing attachment needs with, for instance, addiction to internet pornography, as well as for distancing and objectification of others, which is exemplified by how we become numbed to violence in films and video games (Tweedy, 2017). Most importantly, all of this dehumanisation of self and other seeps into real life in the form of hatred, abuse, and physical violence.

Sherry Turkle (2011) warns about the consequences of the dominance of distanced and superficial communication via technological devices. Technology can provide the illusion of belonging without the demands of friendship; but in so far as we fear uncontrolled, unedited exposure to the other we are in reality losing the capacity for intimacy. Real relationships are messy and demanding and require constant practice. The benefit is the depth and richness of contact by which our own self is deepened, extended, and pulled out of aloneness. In our addiction to our devices, we equally shy away from moments of solitude and interiority, during which we might make contact with ourselves and discover our real needs. A downstream effect is that to the extent that we relate from our real self, our relationships can become more authentic and therefore rewarding. If we commit to the effort, there can be a mutually reinforcing feedback loop between a strong sense of self and good relationships that combine intimacy with autonomy.

The character Frank Bascombe and his occasional lover Sally in Richard Ford's novel *Independence Day* are examples of uncommitted, detached monads who come together once a week—if it suits—ask no questions and demand only freedom of each other. Of Sally, Frank reflects: "And whereas in marriage there's the gnashing, cold but also cozy fear that after a while there'll be no *me* left, only *me chemically amalgamated with another*, the proposition with Sally is that there's *just* me. Forever. I alone would go on being responsible for everything that had me in it; no cushiony 'chemistry' or heady synchronicity to fall back on, no *other*, only me and my acts, her and hers, somehow together" (2006, p. 177). But he himself is no better: "A type of 'go' [at life] I could never quite catch the trick of, even in my most halcyon days, when we all were a tidy family in our own substantial house in Haddam. I somehow could never create a sufficiently thick warp and woof, never manufacture enough domestic assumables that we could get on to assuming them" (2006, pp. 283–284). Frank is unable or unwilling to believe strongly enough in anything to commit fully to life or relationships and establish himself in the long term. He is living in an increasingly fragmented and provisional world (late 1980s USA), where people change marriages, location, and career as they might change their clothes. Such a society is markedly lacking in civic trust: over the course of a four-day period, even the blameless, white, middle-class, middle-aged, Frank is twice stopped (by police and a security guard) for supposedly suspicious behaviour. The forces of law and order abuse their power, assume guilt, and provoke people to try to create the violent reaction that would justify unleashing their aggression.

An age of anxiety?

Insecure attachment leaves us in a permanent state of anxiety to varying degrees, and anxiety is a predisposing factor for major depression, suicide attempts, and substance abuse. Indeed, as we have already seen, the same set of genes determines our vulnerability to the apparently different kinds of mood dysregulation, anxiety, and depression (Plomin et al., 2013). Anxiety is also linked to a range of physical disorders, and out of the Big Five personality traits, neuroticism, which is closely linked to anxiety, is the strongest predictor of negative affect (references in Twenge, 2000). If fear is the emotion associated with a known threat, anxiety is a pervading sense of unease about either subliminal or unidentified threats. Anxiety is connected with the expectation of danger; therefore, if we can recognise the threat, it allows us to prepare an appropriate response. Anxiety *disorders* occur, not from experiencing anxiety per se, but rather from negative reactions to it: feeling threatened by the physiological sensations; worrying about worrying; judging anxiety as a sign of weakness; or having a narrow focus of attention in the direction of potential threats (Roemer & Orsillo, 2016).

We appear to be living in an age of anxiety. A meta-analysis comparing cohorts born between 1952 and 1993 showed a large (effect size) increase in trait anxiety (stable individual differences in anxiety-proneness) in both schoolchildren and college students in the USA, with a stronger birth cohort effect in the children's group. Indeed so dramatic was the change, the *average* American child in the 1980s reported more anxiety than child *psychiatric patients* in the 1950s (Twenge, 2000). A more recent study by the same author compared high school and college students between 1938 and 2007 using the Minnesota Multiphasic Personality Inventory. Anxiety had increased again among recent students, and seven times more rated themselves as depressed (Twenge et al., 2010; Twenge, 2014). Twenge (2014) notes that increases in anxiety and depression have now levelled off, but suggests that this may be attributed to the high levels of medication in the USA, where one in ten now take antidepressants. Compared with the 1980s, in 2012 twice as many (thirty per cent of) college students reported feeling "overwhelmed by all I have to do". The increase in stress compared with previous generations in the same age cohorts is showing up in a rise in psychosomatic symptoms associated with depression and anxiety. The slight decrease in the numbers reporting suffering from colds counters the argument that the current generation are just more prone to complaining.

While both anxiety and depression can be precipitated by the experience of loss, only anxiety manifests when loss is threatened (Rholes et al., 1985). The source of anxiety may be unknown to the individual experiencing it, but the cause is ultimately about fear of loss—whether of life, or of physical or psychological well-being. Two-thirds of the time, it is life events that threaten our security that are the triggers for anxiety (study cited by Solomon, 2014, p. 65). The overall level of anxiety in a society rises in the wake of war, violence, or other social crisis. This happened after the first and second world wars, and Salecl (2004) believes we are now inhabiting a new age of anxiety. This could be connected to 9/11 and its aftermath of war and the escalation of terrorism, as well as to growing threats of worldwide economic collapse and climate chaos and its consequences. However, it could be argued that these fears are no worse than those faced in earlier eras such as the world wars, the great Depression, the threat of nuclear Armageddon especially during the cold war, or—going back further—the high incidence of childhood mortality before the age of modern medicine.

Psychologists postulate three socio-cultural factors in anxiety: overall threat; economic conditions; and social connectedness. Twenge (2000) found that the rise in anxiety correlated with preceding decreases in social connectedness and increases in environmental dangers, but that economic factors played little role. She points out that many of the changes in both threat (e.g., crime rate, AIDS cases, index of social health) and social connectedness (e.g., frequency of divorce and people living alone, mistrust of others) stem from the increasing individualism and excessive "freedom" (erosion of social ties, commitments, and obligations) of American society. One measure of diminishing social connectedness is the steady increase in the number of people living alone, and socially isolated young (American) adults rated everyday events as more stressful, despite not suffering more frequent stressors (Cacioppo & Hawkley, 2003). They exhibited a range of lowered physiological repair functions, including blood pressure control associated with passive coping and hypertension, slower wound healing, and poorer sleep efficiency.

The decline in intimate relationships can be traced partly to narcissism and individualism, but also to socio-political and technological forces, such as long working hours and unstable and globalised employment. Here the individual moves from one city or country to another so frequently that she hasn't got the time to establish long-term friendships or close relationships; or perhaps worse, she establishes them only to lose them—repeatedly (The one exception to this trend is that more people in their twenties are living with their parents because they can't afford to move out). Furthermore, "we're malnourished from eating a junk-food diet of instant messages, Facebook posts, email, and phone calls, rather than the healthy food of live, in-person interaction" (Twenge, 2014, p. 150). Loneliness is consistently correlated with poor mental health, with single and divorced people being more likely to suffer from depression (ibid.).

Anxiety and our place in the social order

In *Inhibitions, Symptoms and Anxiety*, Freud (1926d) asserted that anxiety expectations vary according to the person's stage in life (see also Emanuel, 2002; Salecl, 2004). In infancy, he maintained, they were linked with an inability to completely discharge built-up instinctual tension (excitation). Freud's intrapsychic drive and discharge model has long been superseded by an inter-relational model of the person, so that nowadays over-arousal is understood in terms of inadequate affect regulation by the parent rather than incomplete discharge by the baby. The main source of anxiety for slightly older children, Freud believed, is loss of the parent's loving care, what today we would call separation anxiety. For adults, Freud contended, anxiety derived from a punitive superego that had internalised society's rules for keeping the unruly id in check. In the twenty-first century we could argue that the id has been well and truly let out of the box. But despite (or because of) the absence of the clear social prohibitions of the past, we are still beset with anxiety about our place in the social order. What is striking about the stage-dependent forms of anxiety is that all concern the quality of our relationships: sensitive, mentalizing, and supportive relationships in infancy, childhood, and adulthood all serve to calm and regulate us, whereas distanced, unattuned, judgemental, or competitive relationships escalate our anxiety levels.

It goes without saying that the anxiety characteristic of infancy or childhood can persist chronically long after that life stage has passed if the needs of this developmental period (e.g., for affect regulation or mentalizing) have not been adequately met. This is of course true of all developmental steps that were not taken or were blocked. Alternatively, anxiety may recur in acute form in particularly stressful situations that are restimulative and thus induce regression to the earlier state—as when an adult experience of not being seen or held reactivates early relational deprivation. Living with anxiety that comes and goes most days creates an extreme sensitivity to the smallest trigger: the nervous system is only a hair's breadth away from overdrive. Thus a crowded place like a shopping centre or a visit to the hairdresser with the implicit need to make conversation are often quite sufficient to bring on a panic attack. Solomon suggests that panic disorders are really "disorders of scale" (2014, p. 65), where events that are mildly distressing for many people most of the time become unspeakably terrifying.

Identification with social groups

Fears about our physical survival or radical threats to our lifestyle, whether at an individual, nationwide, or species level, don't require a lot of explanation. But what is less obvious is how anxiety can be provoked by social atomisation (see last section). The importance of our place in the social order is shown by studies in military psychiatry (Salecl, 2004). In traditional war, it was recognised that comrades and leaders provided structure and meaning for the individual; therefore men were motivated to fight, not by hatred or ideology, but by the desire to contribute to the success of the group. But the ideology of individualism began to dominate military thinking during the Korean and Vietnam wars, so that individual soldiers were sometimes placed in units for a short time and then redeployed elsewhere. Psychiatrists began to notice the prevalence of anxiety, which was linked to these short-term postings where there was little support from comrades and not much motivation for the existing formations to incorporate transient newcomers. Further evidence comes from the observation that soldiers who suffered breakdowns were found to recover faster when treated near the battlefront close to their mates. In addition, prisoners of war reported feeling sustained by group (family and country) loyalty and idealisation. The widespread trauma experienced by Vietnam veterans was caused not just by the atrocities they perpetrated, witnessed, or suffered themselves, but also by the antipathy they encountered when they returned home. We can conclude that being part of a cohesive group makes us feel safe and provides purpose, which in turn reduces our anxiety by permitting us to identify with something larger than our individual selves.

Our identification with social groupings can be seen in the depression that is experienced after humiliation (due to failure, job loss, etc.) or because of lack of due recognition (Salecl, 2004). Dismissal by the social group can lead to an individual taking his own life, often accompanied by an explanatory suicide note—in the hope that even in death the other will finally recognise him. This kind of despair is more common amongst men, whereas women are more geared towards survival, so that job loss, for example, tends to be experienced less as a humiliation and more as a practical problem to be dealt with.

Individualism, stress, and anxiety

Hyper-individualism creates isolation—a major source of stress, as we have already seen from social psychology statistics as well as from the evidence for the importance of attachment. It also leads to a loss of trust in and empathy for others so that we become more selfish, competitive, and ruthless. One of the economic outcomes is the rapidly widening gap between rich and poor, which threatens not just material security but also social status for the bulk of the population. In a survey of the world's fifty richest countries, almost every social problem was found to be made worse by income inequality (Wilkinson & Pickett, 2010). This included mental illness and distrust of others as well as rates of crime and violence. Crucially, even the rich do worse in highly unequal societies than in more equal ones. The authors propose that status anxiety generates stress and distrust *throughout* the social hierarchy. When people face evaluation from others—as many people do daily in their personal or professional dealings with social media—the stress hormone cortisol is elevated, and this has a direct negative impact on emotional (e.g., trust, mental health) and physical (e.g., obesity, life expectancy) health, and ultimately on societal (e.g., crime, violence, literacy) health as well.

In the face of individualism and social atomisation, we are insecure about our place in the social order—or even unsure that there *is* a social order. Both narcissism and avoidant attachment reinforce each other and deprive the self of the corrective and potentially nourishing experience of the other. Our identities come to rest far more on our own shoulders and derive much less from our being accepted as part of a stable community. Rather than having a resilient and flexible sense of self with an internal locus of evaluation, we are more likely to have a weak self that, while rejecting others, at the same time relies on them for praise and admiration. This not only places our self-esteem in the unreliable hands of others, it also makes it dependent on our achievements. We must *win* in the competitive wars and our achievements must be recognised. Since it is pretty obvious that we can't all be winners, we must cope with being losers most of the time. As long as winning is the predominant value in a society, it is inevitable that we will have high levels of depression and anxiety. According to Verhaeghe, the most common forms of anxiety disorder are performance anxiety and social phobia: "In other words, fear of the other, who is either an evaluator or competitor, and sometimes both at once" (2014, p. 205). This boils down to status anxiety, which—now that in the developed world our material and physical safety needs are well met—is where most anxiety originates. Shame constantly beckons as the social sphere becomes more judgemental (particularly via social media), while at the same time we pretend that we are self-determining and independent.

Individualism is being fed to us as an ideology: the contention that autonomy, personal freedom, and success rest entirely on our own shoulders. But as Axel Honneth points out, such a view of the human represents a profound misunderstanding of who we really are as relational beings (Petherbridge, 2013, and Chapter Eleven). Thus it is not surprising that we feel depressed and anxious in our current individualistic society, where competition and one-upmanship threaten to replace co-operation and group loyalty. We are told that we alone are responsible for our lives and so we do little to maintain community or even family ties. It has been predicted that "in the future almost everything will be a paid-for experience in which traditional reciprocal obligations and expectations—mediated by feelings of faith, empathy and solidarity—will be replaced by contractual relations" (Salecl, 2004, p. 59).

What do others expect of me?

For those of us living in relative economic comfort in a country at peace, our anxieties tend to revolve round our place in the social world. Salecl (2004) quotes a television self-help adviser who named five major anxieties: "There isn't enough (money, love, etc.)"; "They won't like me anymore"; "It's too good to last"; "I will be found out"; "My life doesn't matter (what will I leave behind?)". How we react to our social environment will of course depend on the self-structures and capacity for supportive relationship that have developed in our early years. But gendered expectations play a role here too. Thus, women today are drowning in conflicting commitments—to their children, friends, family, and workplace. Indeed, a self-help book has just been published on exactly this subject: *The Life-Changing Magic of Not Giving a F**k* (Knight, 2015). Women seem to have virtually no time for themselves, nor are most able to be selective so that they only do what they want. They put the other first because of fear of disapprobation and, ultimately, fear of losing the relationship. This apparently trivial, first-world luxury problem has serious consequences that lead to stress, anxiety, and panic attacks, as life becomes more and more unmanageable. Despite often being overextended and overburdened in their working lives, men appear to worry a lot less about offending or letting the other down. It is no accident that Knight's role model for change was a man, Jeff, who "simply could not be bothered to do things he didn't want to do—and yet he was widely liked and respected" (2016, p. 34). Unfortunately, women don't help each other in this respect: they are often charmed by, or at least accepting of, a man's self-love; but they would not extend the same tolerance to other women. Indeed, stress due to overactivity seems to be one of the great curses of modern life in the first world, as we saw from the memoirs.

In the past, people knew exactly what was expected of them by the family, the workplace, the church, and society at large. But nowadays we are beset by social anxiety because we don't know what people expect of us. We live in a double bind where, on the one hand, we are told that we should be ourselves, live a little, have fun, but on the other hand—despite the escalation in individualism—we still care very much about what others think of us. However, in our current era of prioritising individual freedom above social connections and commitments, society at large is not making *explicit* demands of us; rather we are left in a vacuum of unknowing. Advice columns, ads, lifestyle magazines, and television soaps all exhort us to enjoy in a bigger and better way independent of social constraints: better body, sexual pleasure, relationships, career, home, travel itinerary. With this tremendous burden of freedom comes inevitable anxiety and/or guilt about getting it right in the absence of any ground or holding for decision-making. Underlying our anxiety about *how* to make the right decisions is a fear of failure and humiliation. At the same time, we are told that it doesn't matter what other people think, so we must then deal with a sense of inadequacy from knowing that we *do* actually care, as well as the fear that our denied dependence on others will be exposed. People's choices under late capitalism "are very much bound by what they perceive society values as the right choice". We are, paradoxically, "on the one hand addressed as an individual, totally free to create an identity from scratch, but on the other following an arbitrary popular model of who to be, often derived from the life of a celebrity" (Salecl, 2010, p. 44).

The socially isolated individual

Social isolation is a strong risk factor for depression (Cacioppo et al., 2006; Wade & Kendler, 2000), and interpersonal conflict was shown to be the most important stressor for predicting mood fluctuations (Bolger et al., 1989). Thus people—especially those who are poor at managing them—are in a double bind with respect to relationships: we can't live with them or without them. It is perhaps not surprising then that, once depressed, we find it difficult to engage socially, so loss of social connectedness is also a consequence of depression (Hirschfield et al., 2000). Furthermore, low social support predicts poor response to and early withdrawal from treatment (Trivedi et al., 2005). Depression is often triggered by social loss from death, conflict, relationship breakdown, or workplace bullying, and conflict is both the most important predictor of mood fluctuations as well as one that escalates them if it continues (whereas with other stressors there is a possibility of habituation in the short term). Even more than objective social isolation, it is our perception of it that best predicts depression. It is the context and perception of the isolation that is important: "social isolation would be far more likely to engender depression in contexts where it threatened rather than affirmed a contextually meaningful social identity (e.g., as a football fan vs. a mountaineer)" (Cruwys et al., 2014, p. 224). While identifying oneself as part of social groupings is generally a protection against depression, it can work the other way round if the group is a stigmatised one (e.g., a mental health support group) or if it encourages unhealthy behaviours such as self-criticism or self-harm.

It is much less the objective fact of belonging to social groupings than the degree to which we identify with them in terms of shared norms, goals, and aspirations that is critical in shaping behaviour, attitudes, and self-concept, and in protecting us against depression (see Cruwys et al., 2014 for a review of the literature). This identification provides us with shared meaning, support, influence, and belonging. The support element—whether emotional, intellectual, or material—benefits our health to the degree that we perceive the source of the support to be an in-group member, in other words people who matter to us.

The parent–child relationship: parents' problems are society's problems

The impact on children of the relationship with the parents cannot be overstated. Stressful social conditions are inevitably transferred to children via the effects on their parents. While low income and poor housing are among the conditions that place children "at risk", most of the risk factors are, in fact, consequences of the relationship with the parents. These risk factors include: parents who are ambivalent about being parents; parental mental health problems; insecure attachment; and the emotional dysregulation which manifests as antisocial behaviour. A low level of parental education is another risk factor, but this may itself be mediated through relational capacities: in the poor "development of reflection and awareness, which are psychologically protective" for children because they underlie the capacity of the parents to mentalize (Gerhardt, 2011, p. 316).

Mothers experience a sharp increase in stress after having a first child, three times that experienced by the father (Buddelmeyer et al., 2015). Another study has shown that women were less happy while caring for their children (sixteenth out of nineteen tasks) than while engaged in almost any other activity including housework, and just ahead of commuting to and from work and work itself (Kahneman & Krueger, 2006). Rachel Cusk (2002), in *A Life's Work*, has courageously and gruesomely described her experience of the misery of motherhood, to the outrage of many who resist such truth-telling or in some cases have had a genuinely different experience. The likelihood that she is telling a general truth is supported by research that showed that the average drop in happiness in the two years after the birth of a first child is greater than after divorce, unemployment, or, staggeringly, the death of a partner (Grimmond, 2015; Whippman, 2016). One can speculate about the causes, but anxiety, exhaustion, isolation, and the erosion of identity and privacy are some of the consequences of having children in the nuclear family conditions of the socially atomised developed world. The pursuit of perfection generates anxiety and depression, though it may be a defence against them in the first place. Women who tried hardest to be a perfect mother and who held the most absolutist views—in short those who were most "intense" about parenting—were found to be the most unhappy and the most at risk of depression. The most intense mothers experienced depression at a level three times the frequency in the general population (Whippman, 2016). We may conclude that current social conditions in the developed world—including the two-career family and the increasing unsupported isolation of nuclear families or single parents—are not compatible with child-rearing. If this continues, developed world society will rapidly become unviable.

What are the consequences of this crisis of parenting for the next generation? First, they are exposed to the stress and depression of their mothers, which as we saw in Chapter Four are transmitted directly to the children. Second, a large proportion spend their most formative years under conditions of professionalised care, often within the communal conditions of a crèche. Impersonal and unattuned relationships, particularly in the first two years of childhood, make children more likely to become depressed, anxious, stressed, and lacking in empathy and impulse control, amongst many other effects. It is not just individuals but society as a whole that is damaged in a multitude of ways if children do not receive sensitively attuned care in their early years, when they are learning how to regulate emotions and how to interpret the social world. Greenspan and Shanker warn that "societies decline and regress when vast numbers of children are deprived of these co-regulated emotional interactions" (2006, p. 384) on which a secure, resilient, and flexible self depends. The lessons of extensive research are unequivocal. Attunement of carer to child depends on consistency of care and on the carer's own attachment type—how they themselves were parented. Secure attachment depends on good mentalization on the part of the parent, relative, or childcare worker. This can be achieved only if the carer is in a moderate level of arousal of the autonomic nervous system—not over-aroused due to stress, nor under-aroused/too laid-back, (e.g., due to a marijuana habit). It therefore requires a facilitating environment where the carer is not too busy, speedy, exhausted, worried, or concerned with other affairs; nor should she be spaced out on drugs, soap operas, or other soporifics. This is very difficult to achieve in a single-parent family, in a home where both parents work full-time, in a child-care facility where the staff are overburdened, or where a rota of constantly changing strangers look after the children. Secure attachment requires time and attention as well as the capacity for sensitivity and the power to respond appropriately. In a crèche it can happen only where the primary objective is child welfare rather than financial gain, bureaucratic distraction from the real work of care, or fear of the consequences of minor infractions of the regulations. It is evident that, while today's parents are in general more aware of and empathic towards children's needs, the wider social and employment environment is making it very difficult for them to provide consistent attuned care rather than a guilt-laden absence of attention compensated for with excessive "treats" (often bribes) such as screen time, sweets, toys, or electronic gadgets. Time is necessary for parental attunement: "secure attachments are founded on being emotionally available and responding when the other person needs you, not just at some designated moment of 'quality time'" (Gerhardt, 2011, p. 332).

Selfish capitalism, in its worst forms, ensures that both parents must frequently work full-time to pay the mortgage; that the workplace is more ruthless, demanding, and inflexible and less family-friendly; that crèches are expensive, understaffed, and defensively managed; that mothers return to work soon after giving birth. Infants respond to the functional or impersonal care of paid childminders by becoming passive or withdrawing, in comparison to their response to sensitive mothering (Pearmain, 2001). As a result, avoidant attachment becomes the norm. The consequences of the deficiency in sensitive attunement that underpins insecure attachment are manifold: lack of emotional awareness and regulation; an empty sense of self with an absence of genuine self-esteem; need for constant distraction in the absence of a capacity for beingness; selfishness based on insecurity and poor self-esteem; devaluing of relationship; deficits in empathy with consequent poor moral development; an undeveloped capacity for managing conflict or power relations. In other words, such children are handicapped in both managing themselves and negotiating the social world. So selfish capitalism ensures poor emotional development of children; but likewise, those children, once grown, may not want anything other than the empty rewards of materialism because they simply don't recognise, or can't tolerate, the nurturing or satisfaction inherent in personal (or indeed transpersonal) relationships or activities that demand sustained attention or reflection. A risk of poor early care is the "defensive self-sufficiency" of avoidant attachment: people "who turn away from human contact as the greatest good, seeking comfort in the safer pleasures of food, drugs, gambling and passive entertainments" (Gerhardt, 2011, p. 321). In addition, the child who has not had empathy modelled to them cannot develop a finely tuned ethical sense, and therefore may have no problems with the inequality inherent in selfish capitalism. As Gerhardt pessimistically concludes: "Perhaps there is a social momentum which demands our collective detachment from our own feelings and which keeps us focused on the material world" (ibid., p. 322).

As if being out of touch with their feelings isn't enough to lay down the roots of depression and anxiety, infants who have to interact with a group all day (e.g., in a crèche) suffer the kind of stress that makes them more prone to aggression and poor regulation (ibid.), and that predisposes the individual to depression. Furthermore, attunement is not possible if parents only see their children when tired and pressed at the end of the working day, and children whose mothers were stressed or depressed when they were infants are less resilient to maternal stress when older (age four and a half) (Gerhardt, 2015, p. 95). So, babies need consistent, one-to-one, non-stressed, attuned care for the first two years of life. After that, the social contact with their peer group that nurseries provide becomes beneficial for most children (Gerhardt, 2011).

For our society as a whole to thrive, parents above all others need to be supported. This includes practical interventions such as parental leave and state-supported child care as well as family centres for supporting stay-at-home parents with the problems of isolation and self-esteem. Gerhardt isn't proposing that we return to the pre-feminist era where women had no economic power. Rather, she recommends the Scandinavian model, where there are "high rates of maternal employment, but within a flexible system of generous payments that enable parents as a couple to create their own personal formula to combine work and caring for their small children" (2011, p. 322). As a culture we need to start taking feelings seriously, and realise that listening to and respecting a child's feelings—contrary to the beliefs of the "let them cry" brigade—creates the kind of society we say we want. This is a society where impulse-control and empathy have been absorbed from the parents, primarily during the second year of life, which leads to citizens who are thoughtful, compassionate, and realistic. Such adults would bring to parenting, work, and social environments attributes that are neither punitively authoritarian, nor chaotically permissive, but warmly authoritative and able to embrace the needs of everyone involved (Gerhardt, 2011; James, 2003). Investment in early childhood makes sense on the balance sheet as well: it delivers returns over the course of a lifespan many times the original investment, according to the World Health Organization and the New Economic Foundation (cited in Gerhardt, 2011).

Personal constructs and beliefs characteristic of depressed adults

One outcome of our development within the family and the wider social environment is a set of beliefs about ourselves and other people that dominates the way we live as adults. Coming from the perspective of personal construct psychology, Dorothy Rowe has elucidated six implicit beliefs that build "the prison of depression" (2003, p. 17). These are: (1) being certain that you are bad; (2) believing that other people are to be feared and envied; (3) having unhelpful moral or metaphysical beliefs, (e.g., that goodness will be rewarded and that victims of suffering are being punished for badness); (4) being dominated by the past rather than the future, and being certain that nothing will improve; (5) being convinced that it's wrong to be angry; and (6) never forgiving anyone, especially yourself. These internal scripts are what emerge from the shame-based identifications associated with four of the "survival styles" (Heller & LaPierre, 2012) that manifest as a consequence of the thwarting of our most fundamental needs for connection, attunement, trust, and autonomy (Chapter Four).

Shame becomes lodged in an embodied rather than a cognitive or rational way. Kafka's horrific story "In the penal colony" tells of a torture machine that literally inscribes the "criminal's" offence into his back with a needle. The explorer asks the officer: "'Does he know his sentence?' 'No' said the officer … 'There would be no point in telling him. He'll learn it on his body'" (1971, pp. 144–145). Kafka's victim protagonists refuse to let go of their shame-based identifications. They consistently swallow the shame in order to protect the father or authority against attack or blame. Children and even adults are willing to pay a high price to safeguard the attachment relationship: our need for security and psychic structure precede and are more important than the need for self-esteem.

Rowe views depression as a defence against unthinkable anxiety. Our belief systems served us well as children by protecting the attachment bond and therefore allowing us to survive. However, when we form new relationships in adulthood, any beliefs that do not match our novel social environment can be very destructive. When reality conflicts with our old beliefs, our sense of identity and orientation is threatened: Who am I, what can be expected from other people and the world, what is expected of me? Thus if you believe that goodness or hard work will be rewarded but find that your polite, obedient compliance is treated with contempt, suspicion, or abuse, your sense of being a good person can be shattered. Or you believe that success will bring happiness, but instead find it is hollow and doesn't fill the emptiness at the core of your being—perhaps because you are living out of somebody's else's ambition. Or your experience to date tells you that one success leads to another, only to find that the path of achievement has suddenly ended because you are the wrong class, race, age, or gender—like Esther

Greenwood moving into the adult female ghetto of the 1950s (Plath, 1999). So in the confusing limbo between belief and reality, depression can be triggered.

Thus our relational experiences during our early formative years generate specific beliefs, expectations, and patterns of emotional processing and interacting with others, which, in the absence of therapy, carry over into our adult lives. An internal working model of the self as "not good enough" or "bad" is easily triggered by environmental cues in later childhood and adulthood, with the result that the individual is always living on the edge of depression. As Gerhardt says:

> I believe that the core of depression is a fragile sense of self. It is a deep well of inner hopelessness, which brims over periodically when a vulnerable person's stocks of well-being are depleted—whether by a lack of essential nutrients, a lost relationship, a humiliation, an illness, or a burglary. ... such events often ... trigger depression in someone who is already prone to it. (2015, p. 136)

Systems that cause or maintain depression

Cognitive behavioural therapists view depression as an *intra*psychic process: the result of negative thought patterns (maladaptive cognitive structures) and withdrawal from engagement with others (Kovacs & Beck, 1985). However, like everybody else, depressed people are part of a complex dynamic system of relationships and interactions that affect whether depression is likely to develop and be maintained.

Rowe (2003) explores the familial patterns that cause depression and keep it in place. Adult clients frequently believe that they have one perfect parent and one demon, but—as she points out—this is impossible. If one parent was abusive and the other failed to protect the child, then this person is hardly a perfect, much less a good, parent. Removing the angel from his pedestal is part of the work of therapy. As family therapists are well aware, the sick (or bad) person in a family is not the problem, but rather a symptom of a system that involves the interactions between all its members (Nichols, 2013). A wife may protect her husband by not exposing his weakness or anxiety, thus putting herself in the conflicted position of supporting him while maintaining the fiction that he is strong and independent. This double bind alongside the burying of her own truth and autonomy can generate depression: she becomes the weak member of the couple so that her husband can appear strong. Or, "sometimes what the 'well' partner needs is to be needed, and the 'ill' partner obligingly meets this need" (Rowe, 2003, p. 187). A saying of family therapists runs: "The craziest member of the family is the one who refuses to turn up for therapy sessions" (ibid., p. 185), and Rowe points out that this person is the one who has a vested interest in believing in the medical model of depression. If they engaged in therapy, these people would have to examine their own behaviour and acknowledge that their partners' depression is a symptom of the struggle for power between them, where the "well" person is controlling the "sick" person and blocking any change in the relationship.

In Chapter Eight, I referred to fusional families where the members have failed to differentiate as individuals. In one such family, the teenage daughter became the identified patient who suffered from depression and was at risk of suicide. She was overprotected from anything that was too difficult for her emotionally, so naturally she failed to learn how to solve her own problems or how to live independently. At the age of twenty-eight, she had made a short foray away from home, but was so unhappy that her parents encouraged her to come back to them, fearful of the return of her old depression. The daughter was distancing, angry, and manipulative, taunting her mother Marie with work failures and suicide statistics, to which Marie responded with hysteria. When Marie turned up as my client, it became clear that her daughter was trying to emotionally separate from the family, but was fearful of taking this step and was not being helped by her parents' overprotectiveness. In turning to psychotherapy, Marie was finally acknowledging her own depression and anxiety, which came from the absence of an autonomous self. The more she began to differentiate, the easier it was for her daughter to do the same, and the more the depression and anxiety of both began to abate.

Depressive symptoms are perpetuated or deepened partly because of the reactions of other people: "much of what is customarily viewed as cognitive distortion or misperception is characteristic of information flow from the environment" (Coyne, 1985, p. 312). In other words, depressed people don't just *imagine* people don't like them: others in their social world are giving mixed messages, such as pretending/wanting to be supportive, but in reality revealing that they are scared, confused, uncomfortable, embarrassed, bored, impatient, or annoyed. If the depressed person comes across as passive in interaction and needy of reassurance, others may react with irritation, guilt, or defensive aggression. Communication from other people is likely to be incongruent: reassuring in verbal content but rejecting in emotional tone or abandoning behaviour—which only serves to heighten the anxiety and poor self-esteem of the depressed individual. The social space itself changes when even one member is depressed, and the depressed person needs, but probably lacks, the skills to cope with this new environment. The depressed individual may require a great deal of reassurance, but will constantly test or doubt family and friends, "wanting to avoid rejection, yet at the same time fearing acceptance" (ibid., p. 326). It is crucial that they are met with congruence between the verbal and nonverbal message. Otherwise, Coyne concludes, what is eventually created is "a system in which feedback cannot be received, and various attempts to change become system-maintaining" (ibid., p. 328).

Individuals not only take on complementary or antagonistic roles in family or social systems, but also *adapt* to the norms of a group. We identify with particular groups because of sharing their norms and aspirations; but groups also serve to *shape* the individual's behaviour, attitudes, and even perception. A variety of experiments demonstrate that how people rate themselves (e.g., for cognitive deficits) depends heavily on what is or is not made salient for them (e.g., their identity as an older person). Individuals conform to the behaviours within groups, including social withdrawal and suicidality, and there is evidence that depression and suicide run in groups (Cruwys et al., 2014). The norms of groups influence the members' thoughts, feelings, and perceptions.

Thompson's memoir hints at interwoven ways of conceptualising depression that involve both process and systemic thinking. She believes that depression is partly generated by certain character traits, but also that it in turn gives rise to qualities that may then go on to perpetuate the illness. She suggests that "depression tends to foster an array of personality traits which can remain as its permanent legacy: manipulative behaviour, passivity, unremitting self-absorption" (1995, p. 12). She argues against the prevailing therapeutic assumption that these behaviours are the origins of depression; rather she regards them as the outcome of trying to cope with the condition, and accumulating evidence suggests that this is indeed the case (Chapter Five).

Thompson contends that both depression and addiction are rooted in the same cause: psychological denial. This is expressed through emotional withdrawal in the depressive and dishonesty in the addict. Thompson applies the family systems theory of addiction to depression: other people's responses to the patient's behaviours contribute to keeping her sick and helpless—they *enable* the depression, just as the family of the alcoholic frequently enables the drinker. She gives the example of her grandmother, who lived with Thompson's own family and took to her bed for ten years. Through her weakness she manipulated others into performing basic tasks for her, such as washing her hair and clipping her toenails, and refused to acknowledge any strengths she possessed.

Rachel Kelly makes a similar point in her account. Her nanny was hostile to her depression and told her she didn't believe in it as an illness. As far as she was concerned it was simply the result of Kelly's behaviour: "If you lie in bed all day then you'll be depressed" (2014, p. 133). Kelly is honest in acknowledging that her behaviour could affect her mood. "Some days I did just lie in bed when I could have roused myself if I had really tried". However, she goes on to point out that this dualism doesn't get us closer to the truth. "It was a false division to say it was either all about the illness or all about my own behaviour. The truth was a more complicated, nuanced dance between the two" (ibid., p. 134). Nevertheless, there is a clear message for the family and friends of depressed individuals that not only too little but equally too much help can be detrimental.

Anxiety and depression: over- or under-attached

> "Can calm despair and wild unrest
> Be tenants of a single breast …?"
>
> —Tennyson, *In Memoriam*

We have seen that our place in the social world can either protect us against or make us vulnerable to depression and anxiety depending on the quality of our relationships. We saw in Chapter Six that these two mood states represent swings between the two branches of the autonomic nervous system whereby an excess of arousal—anxiety—is balanced out by a corresponding degree of inhibition in the form of depression. In other words, depression can be understood as a defence against anxiety.

We can also view the relationship in existential terms: "One side lies anxiety, the other, depression. Too much meaning or none at all", observes the novelist (and later psychoanalyst) Marie Darrieussecq (2004, p. 18). In our age of scientific rationalism, much of our meaning comes not from a religious or spiritual source but from our relationships and social status. How does this play out for the increasing number of young clients presenting with depression/anxiety? One way of shoring up a fragile sense of self is to provide yourself with a meaning-generating mission. This probably conforms to what is admired by your contemporaries, though there may be an illusion of individual choice. The less the mission has emerged organically from the true self, the more rigid the individual must be about the aims and objectives and the time frame for achieving them. Thus your life becomes a business plan where reaching the targets becomes the structure that holds the fragile self together. Such people may well ask, "How do I know what is real and meaningful for me?" The answer is they will only know through their body responses: "Do I feel right in this situation?" (Gendlin, 1996).

The young clients who are increasingly presenting for therapy are twenty- and thirty-something women who adhere rigidly to the pursuit of a set of goals (four children, a fantasy house) or ambitions (success in career) within a given time frame. They see themselves as pieces on a chessboard to be played as successfully as possible and, above all else, not be eliminated from "the game". Because their self-worth depends on their achievements, they are strung out with anxiety. Anything at all that blocks their trajectory—from problems getting a mortgage, to an unambitious or overly narcissistic boss who doesn't support their career plans, or inner conflicts between relationship and job demands—sends the anxiety rocketing. The whole of their self-esteem is extrinsic and based on achievement, often with the double bind of mutually-exclusive goals. They take one hundred per cent of the blame for any failure or delay in the programme, believing that they alone are responsible for the material outcome of their objectives. There is no flexibility and no resilience in their life plans; indeed no flexibility or resilience is possible with the concept of a plan (as distinct from a general direction).

The later progression for such goal-orientation is seen in Isolde (Chapter Seven), who had achieved all her objectives—husband with good job, two children (one of each), and a large and beautiful home. When there was no longer anything to strive for, the meaning dropped out of her life. She had no values or interests other than the narcissistic kind: how she looked, her ratings on Facebook, and squabbles with her friends were the substance of her counselling—it never deepened into therapy. Her shopping addiction and recovery programme provided a substitute diversion for a while. But the depression that was always lurking because of her inner emptiness—the lack of what Almaas calls a "sense of experiential significance" (2001, p. 227)—threatened to emerge, so she (unconsciously) created another diversion to keep it at bay. This was the drama of an affair, the destruction of her "perfect" life, and a new set of objectives to keep her mind off the real issue. We see this scenario in countless films and TV dramas; it is so common it has become a cliché.

Driven, but anxious, individuals are conceivably better off than the people who take a detached and alienated view of their peers' ambitions with the cold eye of depressive realism (e.g., Shelley in Chapter Seven). They see the emptiness of their age cohort's attempts to convince themselves that life matters. They take the depressive's road of too little meaning: in order to avoid the humiliation of failing they have given up trying. They may fall into drug or alcohol addiction to mask the nihilism, but this usually exacerbates the depression. Depression is a defence against anxiety, and the reason why the anxiety is often worst in the morning is that the armour has been dissolved during sleep (Rowe, 2003). But sometimes the defence works too well and becomes a problem in itself—a deep, dark, and airless pit out of which the suffering individual cannot climb. In a less extreme polarity, there may be a switching back and forth between depression and anxiety, each side of the scale providing a refuge against the other. If I am tormented by anxiety at what my "friends" think about me, I will protect myself by removing all significance and substance from their opinions—nothing matters. I isolate myself physically and/or psychologically and am left with the meaninglessness of depression. But now cut off from the world, I cannot survive or feel good about myself because my self-esteem is externally located, for good as well as ill. So I dip my toe into the social world once again: I feel less depressed because I am getting social validation and no longer judge myself to be such a misfit. But as soon as others' good opinion of me looks uncertain (this may be real or my paranoid projection), my anxiety shoots upwards once more. This is the wretched cycle for people who lack a true self with an internal locus of self-esteem. They are riven with anxiety, floored by depression, or swing back and forth between Scylla and Charybdis. This is currently called a mood disorder; but in reality the mood is only disordered because it is so dependent on others outside of one's control. Such a pattern of placing meaning and self-esteem in the hands of others has all the unreliability of depending on the kindness of strangers. While we need a place in the social world, we also need an internal locus of evaluation independent of others. We need the kindness of an inner source, who understands, accepts, and loves who I am—one who can "call myself beloved", in the words of Raymond Carver.

Fear is about concern for our boundaries, asserts the transpersonal therapist Seymour Boorstein (1997). Our biology drives us to ensure the survival of the individual self, but it equally reminds us that this survival depends on our place in the social group. Thus we are inevitably caught in a bind between letting others in and keeping them out. If we fail in the calibration of that balancing act, we open ourselves too much to others and become anxious, or we close ourselves off and become depressed: too much and too little connection respectively. The more anxious individuals try far too hard to conform to others, the most depressed withdraw into isolation.

It has been suggested, based on the learned helplessness theory of depression, that an expectation of helplessness creates anxiety. When the anticipation turns to certainty, what ensues is a mixture of depression and anxiety (Alloy et al., 1990). Likewise the threat of loss generates anxiety, whereas the reality of loss can provoke depression as well (Rholes et al., 1985). A slightly different spin on this comes from George Brown, who proposed that "depression is a response to past loss, and anxiety is a response to future loss" (quoted in Solomon, 2014, p. 65). Since the past is certain and the future unknown, Brown is really saying the same thing: that depression is about certain loss and anxiety about the imagined possibility of loss. This doesn't contradict the distinction concerning degrees of meaning, and we could put the two definitions together: depression is a consequence of loss of meaning that has already happened, whereas we feel anxiety about possible future loss of meaning because of our excessive attachment to it. At the level of neuroscience, the pleasure (dopamine) and alarm (adrenaline) systems are competing with each other (Chapter Six). When we are depressed, the pleasure system is switched off. This leaves the way free for the alarm system to operate and therefore create anxiety.

Summary

Human beings are social animals in two ways: first, we need intimate relationships to keep us safe, tell us who we are, and to accept and love us for what we are; second, we need the holding environment of a stable and cohesive society to offer connection and containment, as well as a set of humane values that can nourish and motivate us and thus imbue our lives with meaning. With social disconnection we lose not only support and belonging but also the identity that comes from shared meaning, and the power and effectiveness that accompany social influence (Cruwys et al., 2014). These are exactly the resources that are threatened by late twentieth and early twenty-first century capitalism and technology, particularly in the urban developed world. Anxiety and depression arise from the diminished quality of our relationships and from the loss of cohesive communities. Our current socio-cultural conditions are so stressful for adults and so adverse for child rearing that, unless there is a radical change in the non-facilitating environment of our individualistic and competitive culture, it is difficult to imagine any scenario for future generations other than a further escalation in anxiety and depression.

Dysfunctional family relationships can contribute to generating or maintaining depression in an individual who (unconsciously) sacrifices himself to prop up the system. Furthermore, the social environment can exacerbate or maintain the depression through group norms that encourage or reject depressive behaviour.

In the next chapter, we will see that existential meaning can derive not just from connection with self and other but, more fundamentally, from a spiritual dimension that holds our lives in a broader and deeper context.

CHAPTER TEN

Depression and meaninglessness: the loss of connecting and experiencing

The Hitchhikers' Guide to the Galaxy features a supercomputer called Deep Thought, which is investigating the question of the meaning of life, the universe, and everything. It took seven and a half million years.

The answer is forty-two.

The undertaking—and its answer—lampoon the quest of many philosophers and theologians who seek meaning outside themselves, looking for some grand design or ultimate plan in the universe. Even if a seeker were to unreservedly accept such an absolute and extrinsic solution to his existential questioning, the answer wouldn't in any way help the alienated individual to *experience* his life as meaningful. Nor can meaning be achieved by rational argument, if only we think deeply enough. In the words of Freud: "The moment a man questions the meaning and value of life, he is sick ... ; by asking this question one is merely admitting to a store of unsatisfied libido to which something else must have happened, a kind of fermentation leading to sadness and depression" (1960, p. 436). *Thinking* about meaning is guaranteed to drive meaning further and further into the distance because the abstract and instrumental thought process of the left brain disconnects us from our primary process of sensory and emotional engagement with life. What

I am concerned with here is not the different ways of conceptualising absolute meaning, but with the experience of meaninglessness, its origins, and some remedies for it.

Existentialism claims that we create meaning through our actions in the world, like Camus's hero Dr Rieux helping the sick in the city quarantined by the plague. But the beliefs and values that form the foundations of meaning in our lives are not consciously chosen. In reality they derive from the deepest level of our early development and neurobiology and are therefore implicit, as the theologian Graham Ward has argued (2014). Indeed, Allan Schore concludes from the neuroscience evidence that "a preconscious yet fundamental meaning system can operate before a conscious language meaning system" (2003a, p. 147). As we saw in Chapter Four, the infant's meaning-making is implicit: pre-symbolic, affective, and sensorimotor, "involving the interplay of multiple systems at multiple levels of organisation acting in a causally circular manner" (Tronick & Beeghly, 2011, p. 110). Yalom (1980) has pointed out that even the despairing person who writes a suicide note has implicit meaning; otherwise why would he bother to communicate his pain, sorrow, guilt, or anger. This individual has somebody in his life who matters enough to make him want to communicate. What I want to stress is that meaning is not so much created as discovered or excavated from the unconscious. If the motivation to help the sick is an intrinsic value for the individual and therefore implicit, it can provide meaning. However, if it is extrinsic, if this course of action is taken only because others hold it to be virtuous or because it corresponds to my ego ideal and is therefore willed, then it cannot be a source of authentic meaning. Almaas realised that "the search for meaning ... is actually the search for the essence of the self" (2001, p. 228). Thus meaning is not an abstract solution to the purpose of life, nor is it about the right action: finding a profession that suits me, or moving to a house in Tuscany. Rather meaning emerges when we encounter a level of experiencing in which we are in touch with the self.

Most people experience their lives as relatively meaningful, and it is only when there is a break in continuity, when the rail tracks suddenly run out, that they hit a crisis of meaning. They experience this as an interruption in the narrative of their lives, like Gwyneth Lewis: "People in the middle of a depression are beings who live, for a while, *without a story*, which is why it feels as though you've lost your soul" (2002, p. 96, italics added). This may occur when a marriage breaks down, or following bereavement, or after an individual is made redundant or retires, or in Lewis's case when exhaustion forced her to stop everything. For a religious person, loss of faith brings a crisis in meaning, as so harrowingly portrayed in Bergman's *Winter Light*. At a secular level, many lost faith in society itself during the recent recession when so many expectations were threatened or betrayed. We expected banks, governments, and regulators to behave with responsibility and justice; we believed that contracts, such as pension plans, would be honoured; that mortgage payments could be met through hard work; that there would be a safety net for those out of work. For many, the social contract itself was breached. Such damage to trust breaks the continuity of our existence, and challenges the implicit meaning on which our lives are founded. Not all threats to society need cause despair or depression. On the contrary, a threat that unites the populace against an external enemy could decrease rates of depression because of greater social unity. Indeed, negative events are less likely to lead to depression in people who are less self-preoccupied (Sakamoto, 1999). By contrast, it is threats or losses that leave us isolated that generate depression. People who lost their houses in the recession suddenly experienced their aloneness. Trusted friends, neighbours, and even family did not sympathise enough with their plight to take them in off the street, as would happen in a tribal setting. In an atomised society, loss of spouse or job can be devastating because there is no cushioning by a cohesive and supportive community or extended family. We, in postmodern, individualistic cultures, live on a knife-edge where the smallest loss can remove our entire foundation for existential meaning—the equivalent for an indigenous person of being excluded from the tribe.

When we think of the sorts of things that make our lives meaningful, we might come up with helping others, delighting in children, immersing ourselves in beauty, living in harmony with nature, participating in a great project, conducting ourselves honourably under difficult circumstances, or plunging into the joys of mystery or exploration. All of these derive from our sense of *connection* to the great web of being. Meaning comes from "the elaboration of an increasingly intricate ground plan of broad relationships and ramifications" according to Ernest Becker (1985, p. 370). When we experience ourselves, not as *separate from*, but *part of* a cause, the human community, nature, God, or the cosmos, our lives become meaningful (Dowds, 2017). Connection with such an expanded or higher sense of self appears to be essential to our well-being. Viktor Frankl contrasted the mechanistic and reductionist concept of man espoused by the Freudian psychoanalyst (or *shrink*) with the project of the logotherapist, which should be to *stretch* us towards our higher aspirations—our will to meaning (1985). It is connection that brings meaning into our lives, and this capacity develops early—in the womb, as we saw in Chapter Four. Meaning-making for the infant has been shown to be a dyadic affair: he seeks emotional connectedness because of the psychic and somatic *expansion* he experiences as a result (Tronick et al., 1998). Conversely, when connection is lost, meaning drains away: when there is a narrowing of who we are, of belonging, and of what is important to us, this is a wound to our sense of connection. Furthermore, we must have the capacity to *experience* available connection if it is to be any use to us, and excessive speediness, over-impinging stimulus, or appetites over-indulged all damage our ability to experience with depth and presence. Genuine experiencing is the same as being present to one's life.

Our existence lacks direction, meaning, and value if lived only for ourselves: "if we have at the centre of our lives no more than our own projects or self-image to guide us, there will be no ultimate objective grounding to our being in the world—nothing beyond our own finite and contingent selves to serve as an orientation for our lives", declares the philosopher John Cottingham (2015, pp. 126–127), painting a hollow and repellent picture of late modernity. I would argue that, increasingly, the citizens of advanced capitalist societies live in just such a nightmare and suffer widespread underlying depression as a result of their disconnection and shallow experiencing. We are disconnected from ourselves thanks to the narcissism project, where we confuse the ego with the self. We are disconnected from each other in becoming more individualistic and avoidantly attached, and through the mediation of interpersonal contact by technological devices. Finally, we are disconnected from the greater web of being: our place in the natural world and/or the transpersonal. With each disconnection, we suffer further loss as our identity becomes more shrunken and cut off from wider identification. As Stephanie Merritt (2009) discovered, we also suffer a temporal constriction, when we cease to believe in an afterlife and realise that death is the end. Awareness of our mortality, or equally of the wearying emptiness of egoic successes, can trigger such a profound crisis of meaning that everything is called into question. A new level of response is required. Such ultimate meaning depends on engaging the spiritual or transpersonal self: it is this that engenders the capacity for experiencing what Almaas (2001) calls "Essence". Even for those fortunate individuals who have developed a strong and authentic individual self, our society is not conducive to the formation of a transpersonal self with its sense of connectedness to others and the world. To add insult to the injury of disconnection, we don't benefit from the connection that is available when we do not fully experience it: in Gestalt therapy terms that means failing to complete the contact-withdrawal cycle and being left chronically unsatisfied.

Political and cultural impoverishment of meaning

We live in an age of meaningless production (of superfluous baubles and techno-toys), meaningless consumption (ditto), and meaningless, emotionally disconnected sex (Fisher, 2013). Through its inflation of the ego by privileging competitiveness and acquisitiveness, capitalism exerts a commodifying force that normalises spiritual emptiness. Allied to this is the dissemination of toxic and cynical ideologies that buttress power interests, as we saw in Chapter Seven. What I want to examine here is the *psychodynamic* impact of public figures telling lies with impunity, and advertising degrading what is fundamentally important to us.

When things that matter to the self are repeatedly devalued into style accessories for the ego or manipulated by PR or spin, meaning is evacuated from our world. When a woman's magazine says that babies are the new accessory; when a quality newspaper informs us that we should read certain works of literature because celebrities claim to be reading them; when a television ad urges you to "travel yourself interesting", meaning is eroded. The authentic drives of the true self become displaced and hollowed out by the colonised, pressurised, or competitive ego. Our current world is poisoned by such overt and covert messages. When sport is glamorised as the "clash of titans" with team photos shot from below to make the scowling, arms-crossed players look tough and unyielding, we are being brainwashed with a distorted and offensive exaltation of a limited version of masculinity, strength, and heroism, and ultimately of what counts in this competitive world. Every time lies, spin, or PR are presented as the truth, when a mission statement or logo is offered as reality—as innovative, cutting edge, ecological, compassionate, or simply cool—another block is added to the tower of cynicism in which the public sphere is housed. Both the naive and those who knowingly play the game of lies inevitably promote themselves in the same way, both buying into and replicating the manipulation and erosion of truth, reality, and meaning.

The hole in meaning has cultural as well as political and economic origins, and each influence reinforces the other. One attack on meaning comes from relativists, who claim that there is no truth, no rightness, only preferences that have been programmed into us by culture. In denying our biological legacy of innate values and propensities, and evidently alienated from their own bodily felt sense, such postmodernists claim that meaning is either arbitrary, mere bourgeois nostalgia, or indeed that life has no meaning at all (Fisher, 2013). Already in the 1940s, Horkheimer and Adorno (2007) had argued—developing Nietzsche—that Enlightenment thinking was destroying itself by carrying its self-criticism so far that there were no longer any grounds for drawing conclusions about truth, beauty, or meaning, or indeed about anything not testable by scientific means (positivism). They prophesied that: (1) high culture, having deconstructed its own foundations, would collapse; (2) we would regress into infantilism, stupefied by the instant gratification of the culture industry (exemplified by Hollywood cinema and pop music); and (3) that society itself would collapse at its first serious test due to the absence of moral conviction. While our society does indeed lack any apparent intentional direction, we *are* nevertheless going somewhere: drifting unaware "towards refeudalisation, as intensifying wealth concentration is post-hoc justified by a kind of neo-Georgian notion that some people are intrinsically better than others", as Zoe Williams (2015) has observed.

If objective criteria for morality, truth, or beauty are reduced to mere subjective preference, we become infantilised, argues Kit Wilson (2015). For example, if I say "inequality and greed are wrong", I may be told that this is simply my personal prejudice or that I am just an envious loser. "Arguments about the thorniest of ethical dilemmas or the most sublime of artworks are reduced to the level of a toddler's tantrum", concludes Wilson. Evolutionary biologists go further, claiming, even more reductively, that since we are no more than animals we are not therefore to blame for our aggression or promiscuity. This removes any incentive to cultivate virtue or civic responsibility. Wilson fears that, weakened by nihilism and infantilising gratification, we lack the moral and emotional backbone to face threats to our fundamental values such as the corrupt oligarchy of Putin's Russia or Islamist terrorism. "As long as we see ourselves as the spiritless inhabitants of a meaningless world, we will teeter precariously above a precipice of our own making" (Wilson, 2015). Williams, too, makes the same point that our "enemies ... are bound to be stronger because they know who they are" (2015). But I am not so sure that Western Islamists really know who they are. An explanation for the ferocity of their actions is that religious fundamentalism is for them a *borrowed* identity rather than one that is authentic and organic. They protest too much and use brutality to try to convince themselves—like my clients who create the shell of a self in rigid pursuit of their life goals, or the anorexic who, in the absence of genuine meaning, uses control over her eating habits as a substitute (MacLeod, 1996). Such people are simply reacting to the rudderless drifting of Western society, where any identity is better than none.

People will go to extraordinary means to cobble together an identity at any cost. Becker presents an example of older women in rural Ghana who became depressed after a lifetime of rearing a family, caring for a home, and running a business, only to have "the fruit of her labor ... lavished by the husband on a younger bride" (1985, p. 373). Suddenly the sources of meaning have been withdrawn, and to avoid the realisation that perhaps life has no meaning, the woman justifies her worthlessness by hurling "accusations of vile witchcraft" against herself. Becker understands this behaviour as "merely a continuation of the inescapable burden of fashioning a coherent identity to the very end" (ibid.). Loss of identity through loss of a person, a role, or an idea (Brown, 1985) generates—for all of us—anxiety and depression so long as we deny ourselves what is perhaps our deepest need: for authentic meaning in our lives. Such meaning is not top–down but must be accessed and sustained experientially.

Rachel Cusk, in her novel *Outline*, reflects on the relationship between disillusionment and familiarity: "if he could only love what he did not know, and be loved in return on that same basis, then knowledge became an inexorable disenchantment" (2015, p. 175). Such a person will shun stable attachments and seek constant novelty: a perfect adaptation to our current culture. A different character in the same novel is a playwright, Anne, who has lost all motivation to write because of the problem of summing up: "Why go to the trouble to write a great long play about jealousy when *jealousy* just about summed it up?" (ibid., p. 232). Such reductionism leading to nihilism was now invading Anne's own life as well: she "was beginning to question the point of continuing to exist day in day out when *Anne's life* just about covered it" (ibid. p. 233). Both of these characters are suffering from a loss of desire in the absence of anything real or essential towards which their libido could be pulled (rather than directed by the will).

A large proportion of people in the developed world no longer do work that has a meaningful outcome (growing food, caring for others) or even a material product. Instead, gazing at screens all day, their actual work is remote from any product or service, entailing mainly report-writing, futile meetings, public relations, and image management—like these office workers interviewed for *The Guardian* (Tucker, 2016). A project manager summarised her day's work as updating her Gantt chart, chairing a weekly meeting, writing up risks and issues, updating a project plan, and looking at some finance. A charity worker had to develop a job description, edit a funding proposal, put together a proposal for coaching training, and check that volunteers were OK. A PR executive tried to sell a phone book app to "grumpy jaded journalists who hate every PR person", read celebrity gossip as part of his job, and ended the day making a list of thirty "actionable items". Not surprisingly, he was the most cynical of the lot; who wouldn't be, swimming in a medium of lies and spin, his boss bamboozling the client with jargon, claiming they went for "a rifle-shot, as opposed to a scatter-gun, approach"? A magazine editor with a first-class degree in English literature checked Twitter feeds, Facebook updates, and Instagram posts, scrutinised photos of celebrities' thighs, and edited two features. Ending her day with a Twitter-stalk (whatever that is), she noted: "Sadly, the magazine pays 10 times more attention to nail masques than to life-saving smear tests".

Dimensions of meaning

Frankl (1988) proposed three categories of values and meaning: (1) meaning derived from creativity, accomplishment, and giving to the world (not driven by narcissistic motivations); (2) experiential meaning—being open and receptive to nature, art, love, and other encounters with the world; and (3) attitudinal values that manifest in our stance towards limitation and suffering. Thus meaning may be expressed through doing, being, and relating respectively, and Frankl's categories are open enough to be applicable to either a secular or a spiritual worldview. Boorstein (1997) describes three clients who succumbed to depression through life seeming futile or unfulfilling. One, combining harsh self-criticism internalised from a perfectionist mother, with a lack of purpose triggered by recent retirement, is an example of Frankl's first category. Another's despair came from the failure of her marriage against a background of having had a very angry mother. A third had a passive father and angry mother, and his marriage was currently in crisis, leading to a sense of disillusionment with life. The latter two clients may be understood as having difficulties with limitation and suffering in the absence of a developmental or spiritual worldview that might give their pain some value. For example, crisis could be understood as an opportunity for inner growth, or the individual might transcend her own feelings by modelling grace under pressure for the sake of other family members. All three clients were helped by transpersonal therapy (here Buddhist meditation) to let go of rigid mind states and of clinging (what Buddhists call attachment) to what they thought they wanted. They gained acceptance of what *is*, as well as a wider perspective on life so that their disappointments no longer loomed so large.

According to the existential therapist Emmy van Deurzen-Smith (1997), we can derive meaning from each of four dimensions of living: the physical, social, personal/psychological, and spiritual. On the physical level, we gain meaning through a sense of efficacy; on the social, through establishing relationships with others; and in the psychological dimension, through a sense of self-worth and identity. But ultimate meaning lies on the spiritual plane, through finding our place in the wider scheme of things: this is the terrain of the transpersonal self. Unlike the relatively superficial satisfactions of the physical dimension, the other domains of meaning—social, psychological, and spiritual—are much depleted in today's world. The psychological and social have been discussed in the last two chapters, but now we will focus on the spiritual dimension. John Cottingham reminds us that "encounters with the sacred tell us that we are not, and cannot be, creators of value: we can only *respond* to value. ... [in art] we are not creating beauty and goodness, we are simply *transmitting* or *channelling* them" (2015, p. 124). Thus we are relieved of the burden of creating meaning; our only task is to be open to it and experience it fully.

The spiritual dimension

Our spiritual drive expresses the longing to retrieve connection to the great web of being through a sense of unity between subject and object

(Levin, 1988). Indeed, our capacity to flourish is "founded upon a lifelong search for a powerful relationship to the ground of our being, and … whether it takes a religious or secular form, such a search is the ultimate purpose of a well-lived life" (Simon May, quoted in Cottingham, 2015, p. 107). Even those who have developed well psychologically, but fail to connect to Essence or Being, remain stuck with an *individual* sense of meaning dependent on self-expression and self-actualisation. But "because we are relational beings, ultimately meaning comes from connection—to the world and each other" (Dowds, 2017). We become self-preoccupied only when we have *missed* our life's meaning, observed Victor Frankl, while Buber proclaimed that there is a greater value than the salvation of individual souls (Yalom, 1980). Likewise Cottingham (2003) has argued that a meaningful life is an integrated one, where my projects do not exonerate me from my responsibilities to others.

As a society we have substantially lost contact with the meaning that can be found only on the spiritual plane. This may be partly attributed to the cultural trend for deconstructing beliefs, values, and meaning, which, as we have seen, culminates in nihilism. Nevertheless, David Hay (2006), while investigating spirituality in the UK, found that seventy-six per cent of subjects claimed some spiritual experience such as synchronicity, awareness of the presence of God, or of a sacred presence in nature—seventy-six per cent despite only seven point five per cent regularly attending church at the time. Further in-depth interviews revealed the research participants to be uneasy and defensive until they were reassured that there was no hidden agenda to either criticise or convert them. Hay concluded that "officially, God is dead but the ghost of God, Beckett's 'bastard who doesn't exist' is still there" (ibid., p. 247). He reviewed a large twin study exploring whether there was a genetic contribution to self-transcendence: ability to lose oneself in a task, unity with the rest of nature, and concern for the profoundest mysteries of human existence. The concordance was twice as high for identical as for fraternal twins, implying that self-transcendence is substantially determined genetically—thus undermining culturalist critiques of spirituality. By contrast, church attendance was determined solely by the social environment.

The psychologist Michael Jackson has found that spiritual experience typically occurred during times of existential crisis, and that these transcendent experiences brought about an effective and meaningful solution (ibid.). So the capacity for transcendence is adaptive when we are subjected to great terror, loss of meaning, and other acute difficulties. He found that the same process was invoked in schizophrenic patients under stress; but in their case it failed, leading to psychotic episodes. Putting together Jackson's research with his own, Hay concluded that the reason spiritual experience is adaptive is that we become aware of being part of something that transcends ourselves. After feeling abandoned and alone, we return to the fullness of relationship and overcome our alienation. He hypothesises that our spirituality restores us to the relational consciousness that characterises being human and which is crucial for our early development: we are created by and composed of connection. Hay ascribes the cultural destruction of spirituality in the developed world to possessive individualism, and he believes that to heal this trend we must build a spiritual community, because "it is through shared metaphor that social and spiritual capital are built" (ibid., p. 242). Hay's research into "the biology of the human spirit" gives us permission to attend to our spiritual intuitions, and to foster the part of ourselves that can lead us out of the lonely and alienated strivings of individualism, rationalism, materialism, and instrumentalism and into a more still, nourished, and connected future.

Another reason for our diminishing spirituality is developmental: our capacity to access transpersonal meaning is severely curtailed when our narcissistic needs have not been fulfilled. Those who try to grow spiritually without first doing the necessary psychological work are performing a by-pass, where spiritual ideas are used to bolster rather than transcend psychological defences. An obvious example is the reinforcement of avoidant attachment through misunderstanding the Buddhist precept that attachment is at the root of all suffering. (As far as I understand it, the Buddhist concept of attachment refers to *clinging* to people, possessions, ideas, and self-concepts, not to the capacity to form an intimate, interdependent relationship.) Thus a necessary prelude to spiritual work is the psychological work of development of the self. Boorstein, citing Jack Engler, speaks "of the need to become 'somebody' before becoming 'nobody' … which means developing a mature ego, a healthy, balanced, strong, and integrated sense of separate self, before doing the work of lessening one's attachment to it" (1997, p. 31).

The main movement of reparative therapy is backwards: we return to early experiences of wounding to heal them. In contrast, the main movement of spiritual practice is forwards: we transcend and expand our self-identifications. Many practitioners in both fields ignore the complementary approach. This is foolish, because a spiritual by-pass will involve building on compromised foundations: the necessary repair work must be done before the earlier levels of the self can be healthily transcended. Conversely, excessively secular therapists can commit the corresponding error. For there are woundings so fundamental that the very core of the self has been left untenanted (as in narcissism, for example), and which deconstructive therapy alone cannot fill. The individual with narcissistic wounds has a chronic inner emptiness and meaninglessness that derive from the lack of a sense of self and, ultimately, "alienation from [his] spiritual core", according to the self-psychologist and spiritual teacher A. H. Almaas (2001, p. 227). This emptiness is the underlying depression to which Miller, Levin, Frosh, Gerhardt, and Verhaeghe all refer. This sense of a meaningless life is not due to being in the wrong job or marriage or other external condition. Working on these will be worthless, warns Almaas, unless a process of *inner* change—literally *self*-realisation—is engaged. The narcissist who repeatedly experiences boredom and loss of value in his relationships and activities must start to recognise these as merely symptoms of his own inner emptiness. The meaninglessness arises not because a philosophy or narrative is lacking; rather what is missing is "a sense of experiential significance, a sense of profundity and substance in our experience" (ibid.). The spiritual seeker may come to discover Essence—a sense of presence, wholeness, and unity—as something that sometimes happens *to* him as an epiphany. However, Almaas insists, until he experiences himself *as* Essence, he will still be identifying with an empty shell.

The path of soul

Guiding us through the realm of transpersonal practice, Cortright (1997) distinguishes between spirit paths, where meditation can be over-focused on the aware *mind*, and soul paths, which aim at opening the *heart* through a relationship with the personal divine. Rosalind Pearmain is a psychotherapist and practitioner of a heart-focused form of Raj Yoga. Working with her clients' depression, she views the condition as arising from a kind of "inattention to our soul, to our inner depths … the places of feeling … our sources of sensitivity and knowing, the place of the heart" (2001, p. 129). Prayer focuses on and aims to evoke a presence, called God by practitioners of the soul paths, to which or to whom one can relate: "The increasing connection to one's soul is often experienced as a deepening or widening of one's identity not into an insubstantial void but into a powerful, very substantial sense of presence" (Cortright, 1997, p. 136). The crucial point is that, like therapy, the soul paths are based on *relationship* and therefore can lead to a greater capacity for presence, inner deepening, and enhanced feelings of empathy and love with reduced anxiety.

For seventeen years, the distinguished spiritual teacher Catherine Ingram walked the Buddhist (spirit) path until all meaning it had held for her fell away, along with its allied belief systems of karma and reincarnation, and the goal of enlightenment. The problem was an excess of detached awareness, which made her feel joyless, like an observer of life—without embodiment, aliveness, or engagement (Deife, 2004). She fell into a two-year depression in reaction to the loss of all that had constituted her life for two decades and in the knowledge that worldly answers would not meet her needs. She says that Buddhism can be used "as a justification for seeing things clearly"—a kind of depressive realism—and that it kept her in "a habit of being unhappy" (Wolf, 1998). Then, meeting Poonjaji, a teacher in a soul path, she says:

> I went from a sense of no-Self; which was emphasised in Buddhism, to a sense of all-Self. I went from a feeling of emptiness to an experience of fullness. It was a very joyous discovery. I started to feel intimately connected with everything and in love with everything. It was the end of the belief that this "I" is going to get something more, in fact in this clear seeing that you are already in totality. (Ibid.)

She had moved from a spirit path that rejects the world and aims to transcend it to a path of connection that brought a soulful "feeling of intimacy with everything" (ibid.).

Cortright's soul paths include the major religions of Hinduism, Judaism, Christianity, and Islam. But there is another way of living soulfully, indeed with reverence, that does not follow a religious tradition or require a formal spiritual practice. I am thinking of the secular soulful way of life espoused by Thomas Moore and many other Jungians. This could include animistic practices, such as shamanism, as well as informal modes of nature-worship (see later), but also an openness to the built environment and old objects: ruined houses, ancient paths, early photographs—"images of the human countenance from a time when it still wore an air of silence" (Eiland & Jennings, 2014, p. 364)—to anything with what Benjamin called aura. This is a solitary path that requires a sensitive eye and ear, a devotion to the beauty in the everyday. Its hallmark is the capacity to experience a certain radiance, often in the unexpected; it requires the attention of the poet, the ability to slow down enough to return to a child's participative consciousness with the world around. Patrick Kavanagh knew that nothing is barred from love: "The common and banal her heat can know" ("The hospital"). He is a poet of the ordinary, in nature and in human creations: a hospital ward, a bridge, a battered gate. I have written before (Dowds, 2014, Chapter Three) about how the immersive and embodied attention of the right brain can re-enchant the world: how we can all access the poetic soul within. Cherishing the half-light of mystery is an important part of the meaning derived from an enchanted world. Indeed, "To care for the soul, we must observe the full range of all its colourings", Moore cautions (1992, p. 137), and depression can in some cases be a response to too much disenchanting brightness and clarity, which leave no room for mystery.

What exactly have we lost? The ugliness and squalor of the blighted urban landscape is captured in Zadie Smith's London novel *NW*. Nat and Leah go for a walk.

> To their right, a foreclosed shopping arcade and a misconceived office block, empty, every other window broken. To their left, a grassy island nestled beside a dual carriageway. Intended as a green oasis, it is a fly-tipping zone. A waterlogged mattress. An upturned sofa with ripped cushions, foully stained. More eccentric items, suggesting lives abandoned in a hurry: half a scooter, a decapitated Anglepoise, a car door, a hat stand, enough rolled-up lino for a bathroom floor. (2013, p. 68)

Then they spot what they are looking for:

> A little country church, a medieval country church, stranded on this half-acre, in the middle of a roundabout. Out of time, out of place. A force field of serenity surrounds it. A cherry tree at the east window. A low encircling wall marks the ancient boundary … It is eleven thirty in the morning, in another century, another England. (Ibid., p. 69)

The sheer *loss* evoked is almost unbearable. But here too is a recognition of our need for beauty, resonance, and continuity, for an environment we can cathect with personal and transpersonal meanings.

Meditation and prayer: impact on depression

While her Catholic religious faith did not prevent Rachel Kelly becoming depressed in the face of overwhelming stress, prayer was an important comfort to her when she was well enough to concentrate. Initially, her mother read the prayers out loud, but later Rachel herself recited her own favourites: "They temporarily laid my anxiety to rest by fixing me in the present. It was as if the words had become embodied, almost physical in their power, something to hold on to and rub, like prayer beads for the mind" (2014, p. 50). This makes it explicit that the healing force of prayer lay precisely in its capacity to evoke and connect with a presence: something tangible outside the depressed psyche that Kelly could relate to. For Martha Manning (1994), by contrast, Catholic retreats were important in slowing her down and becoming quieter and more grounded within herself, which seem like benefits that could equally be derived from solitary or group meditation.

Oliver James (2007) has noted the protective impact of religion—like a vaccine—against depression, regardless of the particular religion or the gender, class, nationality, or ethnicity of the believer. Solomon (2014), too, acknowledges its prophylactic effect, though on its own it cannot usually pull people out of depression. However, for the believer, it does confer dignity and purpose to pain, as well as faith that you will emerge when God wills it. Of course, religion offers even more than a larger identity and the promise of infinite time. It also provides "a support system, shared values, moral certainties and the opportunity—through confession or prayer—for people to talk about their problems and concerns to someone whose job it [is] to listen and dispense advice" (Merritt, 2009, p. 13). Solomon interviewed an Episcopalian, Maggie Robbins, who used religious ritual to contain her experience and, instead of battling within herself, externalised her battles on to God the Father, Son, and Holy Ghost: "The Church is an exoskeleton for those whose endoskeleton is eaten away by mental illness" (2014, p. 132). In this sense it functions like the holding of a reparative therapist, who both provides and models a self-structure that the client can gradually move into. Robbins finds therapy and religion similar in their use of the unconscious, but opposite in their attitude towards the ego: "In therapy I learn to erect ego boundaries; in church I learn to drop them and become one with the universe, or at least part of the body of Christ" (ibid., p. 131). The capacity to move back and forth between these two states of a boundaried and a dissolved ego may be a fundamental requirement for good mental health. For Robbins, moving away from the delusion of monadic individualism was a very important part of her newly acquired Christian faith.

Harding (2013) believes that the erosion of religion generates loneliness, sadness, and melancholy, and Merritt says that one of the contributing causes to her depression was loss of the faith that had played such an important role in her childhood and adolescence. Her dismay at her new foreshortened perspective (pulled back from a Christian eternity) caused her to be "almost frantic with the need to wring every last drop of experience out of life before the deadline" (2009, p. 73). If we believe that everything ends with death, life can be a very pressurised and stressful experience—though it is this very pressure that can motivate spiritual seeking.

Mindfulness meditation, even in quite early stages of training, can ameliorate anxiety (Roemer & Orsillo, 2016) and reduce the relapse rate for depression (Pedulla, 2016; Piet & Hougaard, 2011). Long-term meditation has been shown to have radical effects on the brains of expert meditators (Brefczynski-Lewis et al., 2007; Hay, 2006; Pavlov et al., 2014). This includes increased blood flow in parts of the brain involved in focusing attention and personal boundaries, which coincides with the dissolution of the separated self into an experience of unity. Here is a state of enhanced connection that is the antidote to the alienation and isolation that cause such profound despair and meaninglessness.

Nature and meaning

> "No outcast he, bewilder'd and depress'd;
> Along his infant veins are interfus'd
> The gravitation and the filial bond
> Of nature, that connect him with the world."
>
> —Wordsworth, *The Prelude*

Wordsworth recognised that when we experience ourselves as part of nature it is not possible to feel the alienation of depression. The pursuit of transpersonal connection through prayer or meditation within the established religions and Buddhism has been criticised because it relies on transcending the body, sexuality, and the earth itself. This ascent model views "spirit exclusively in terms of consciousness, emptiness and form to the exclusion of spirit as life, fullness and process" (Heron, 1998, p. 4). "Transcendent spirituality is detached, hierarchical and is often associated with the ideology of the patriarchy, whereas a non-institutional, immanent spirituality oriented towards wholeness and the body emerges from more feminine experience and values" (Dowds, 2017). A more embodied approach to connection is found in the earth practices, such as traditional shamanism, ecopsychology, or in the rituals of Jung (1983) and some of his followers.

The natural environment, according to the biologist E. O. Wilson, is central to human evolution such that we have an "innate tendency to focus on life and lifelike processes" (1984, p. 1), and research has shown that people experience improved well-being on exposure to natural environments (Gullone, 2000). We have evolved as part of nature for millions of years, but since the Industrial Revolution—far too little time for genetic adaptation—and picking up pace with the growth of the giant metropolis, the abstraction of education and employment and the virtual world of computer technology and social media, we have been losing our place in our earthly home. One of the characters in the novel *The Emperor's Children* does temping work in a New York company "engaged in middle man activity, the procuring of rights—of abstractions—that permitted, elsewhere, the actual trading of information (also abstract) for huge sums of money. ... It was as though the entire office were generating and moving, acquiring and passing on, hypotheticals, a trade in ideas, or hopes, to which value somehow accrued" (Messud, 2006, p. 82). Of course the value referred to is money, which has come to replace any intrinsic meaningful value in the working life of so many. The old self grounded in sensory reality in the natural world has been emptied out and replaced by an obsessive, narcissistic, commodified construct, which identifies "instead with grand self-images that act in fantasy to compensate for [its] terrible sense of inadequacy" (Fisher, 2013, pp. 85–86). In Fisher's view we have four tasks in ecopsychology: psychological, philosophical, practical, and critical, of which the first is to acknowledge that we humans have a significant relationship, not just with other people, but also with the natural world.

As we saw in Chapter Eight, dissociation from the body is both cause and consequence of a fragile sense of self. But since our sensory experience is our most fundamental reality, we shut out not just the rejected feelings, but the full richness and joy of living—a life that is alive—including contact with the earth. We have begun to regard our over-mentalized existence as normal, and "the average person today is lost in a fantasy world of thinking, planning, rehearsing, chewing over unfinished situations from the past, and imagining future triumphs, immersed in the past and future but lost to the present moment" (Cortright, 2007, p. 65). Many of us live in an almost entirely mediated and image-dominated virtual world. It has always been the case that experience was controlled and interpreted through the dominant world-view, for instance, through the lens of Christianity. However this was balanced by a grounding in sensory reality and a knowing that human-kind was part of the natural world, of the greater web of being. Our current alienation from the natural world squeezes us into a straitjacket of restricted identity and myopic ego-centred awareness—or should that be blindness? In our estrangement, we commit untold atrocities against the earth: we plunder, pollute, murder, and torture. We cannot bear to *see*, so we do indeed blind ourselves to the plight of our kin, our fellow animals in the concentration camps of factory-farming and the torture cells of research and industrial laboratories. (If anyone has any doubt that animals feel not only physical pain but also fear, panic, and grief, Panksepp's research will sweep aside any self-justifying claims about the dangers of anthropomorphising (2011)).

Children, and tribal peoples who live in kinship with the land, are instinctive animists. They view animals as "sentient purposive creatures" (Roszak, 1993, p. 299) and feel part of, not separate from, the natural world. This is endorsed by the Buddhist teacher Susan Piver (2015), who is horrified at man's cruelty towards the animal kingdom and finds herself in a struggle between feeling and pushing away the unbearable pain this brings. In general, though, urbanised adults are estranged from Gaia, and such estrangement produces, according to Roszak, an underlying neurosis. In advanced "civilisation" many have forgotten that we humans are animals too and that we evolved in intimate symbiosis with the animal and plant worlds and with seasonal and diurnal rhythms. We have lost touch with our larger eco-identity (Abram, 1997; Fisher, 2013), which I believe contributes to an underlying sadness and depression in modern man. We are in a double bind, because those who have not lost their identification with nature are heartbroken at what humankind is doing to it. Indeed the philosopher Glenn Albrecht coined the term "solastalgia" for "a form of psychic or existential distress caused by environmental change" when studying the misery of communities whose landscapes had been destroyed by mining and drought (Macfarlane, 2016). Christina Baldwin (2015) intersperses lyrical descriptions of her home in Washington State with writing about the destruction wrought by rapacious exploitation and her grief at knowing that the beauty and serenity are coming to an end. Like Piver, she is caught between denial and despair. She is close to giving up, but realises this is *not* clinical depression, however much it feels like it: her sadness is in no way malignant, rather an entirely natural, fully human response. Baldwin concludes: "I didn't want medication; I wanted stamina to endure and learn" (p. 144). In the words of James Hillman, who wasn't afraid to name and shame:

> Of course I am in mourning for the land and water and my fellow beings. If this were not felt, I would be so defended and so in denial, so anesthetised, I would be insane. Yet this condition of mourning and grieving going on in my soul, this level of continuous sadness is a reflection of what is going on in the world and becomes internalized and called "depression", a state altogether in me—my serotonin levels, my personal history, my problem. And the drug industry ... and insurance companies are in general agreement. You must become even more anesthetized. Take Prozac: Depression is a disease and weakens the economy. (Quoted in Fisher, 2013, pp. 12–13)

By and large, the world of psychotherapy is a fellow-traveller within—when not actively an enabler of—the socio-political-cultural world of advanced capitalism, not least in its systematic denial of the non-human world. It views the mature adult as a largely monadic affair, for whom relationships with other people are conceded to be important, but with little need for an expanded identity beyond that. Jung was a shining exception in being acutely aware that man's "contact with nature has gone, and with it has gone the profound emotional energy that this symbolic connection supplied" (quoted in Fisher, 2013, p. 4). Accordingly, Roszak (1993) sees the deepest level of Jung's collective unconscious as an ecological unconscious: this is where our inherent embeddedness in and kinship with the natural world is located.

The psychoanalyst Harold Searles called for the "broadening [of] our focus ... to include man's relationship with his nonhuman environment" (quoted in Fisher, 2013, p. 3). But that was in 1960, and the project of ecopsychology is still developing only very slowly. Yet we are sick, and "our longing for nature is like an invalid's longing for health" (Bate, 2001, p. 73). Indeed, many suffering from depression have found for themselves how much help there can be in nature. Richard Mabey alludes to the old idea of a nature cure, where you let nature take you out of yourself. City dwellers Sally Brampton and Rachel Kelly both found solace in gardening during their depressive episodes; Stephanie Merritt had a moment of calm amid the grandeur and violence of the sea; and Gwyneth Lewis embarked on a sailing trip after her depression had abated. Michael Harding discovered that "staring at lakes" provided a new horizon. He writes lyrically of "snowy mornings in the Leitrim hills ... when the soft snow fell to earth; enveloping the leafless naked bark of birch, weighing down the rusty beech leaf and the handle of a spade, covering and silencing everything" (2013, p. 214). Such profound silence revealed the futility of striving; just being was sufficient.

Indigenous people cannot but be aware of their interconnectedness with the earth and all its life forms (e.g., Abram, 1997; Liedloff, 2004). This is as much a sensory, intuitive, or feeling awareness as a matter of the intellect; it is the implicit knowing of the behaviour of predators and prey, the unthinking capacity to avoid environmental hazards, the felt sense of changes in weather, the location of edible plants or water-holes, or the inbuilt knowledge of when and where to plant and harvest. Liedloff noticed that the children of the Yequana Indians in Venezuela didn't need to be explicitly taught about dangers such as fires and waterfalls, they just *knew*: they had picked up the knowledge from being carried by mother and living in ongoing symbiosis with her movements, sounds, starts and stops as she went about her normal life and work (2004). Not merely connected, she was in a "continuum" with the natural world and the baby was in a continuum with her. Participating in nature like this involves all of the senses to pick up sounds, smells, textures, as well as our currently overused vision. It invokes both broad and narrowly focused attention acting in concert together, like an animal's unblinking focus on prey while all its senses scan for lurking predators. This requires the two sides of the brain, the left as well as our currently underactive right hemisphere (McGilchrist, 2010). Such active engagement with nature brings gratitude and veneration for a nurturing mother as well as respect for a potentially dangerous foe. For the modern urbanite, it is quite hard to believe in our dependence on the earth, much less have our senses and instincts attuned to it. Even less do most people feel *part of* Gaia except, in some cases, as a purely intellectual acknowledgement of this fact.

We are contracted and impoverished by this narrowing of our identity and by our alienation from the planet that is our home. We end up foregrounding what is human, with the non-human as a mere backdrop, if indeed we notice it at all. If however we reverse the relation of figure to ground so that the human and the man-made are mere ground and the landscape and all its inhabitants become the figure for our attention, something changes for us. In trying out such an intersubjective encounter, Deirdre McKibbin says she "was affording the non-human full subjective status and identifying with it" and "this was experienced spiritually" (2007, p. 10). What I believe she means by this is that we experience a shift in the centre of gravity of our identity out of ourselves into the wider world, and that with this comes rest in the arms of something greater than the individual self or human world. There is tremendous relief in entrusting ourselves to being held by mother earth and letting go of the pettiness of the demands of an ego endlessly negotiating or competing with all the other egos in this overpopulated world. We can fall back into our proper place of being a tiny speck in a magnificent universe that will keep functioning without any effort on our part. This affords us a place for experiencing love, worship, and awe for the riches we have been given.

Although this is the kind of fusion that psychoanalysis tends to frown upon, Anita Barrows (1995) proposes a theory that encompasses more than one pole of growth, where we don't simply separate *from* mother but also move *towards* exploration of the world. With its pathologising of merger, she argues, psychoanalysis fails to pay attention to the reality of the broadening of our identification, the organic expansion of our identity. Her ecologically based model takes account of two opposing tendencies: the movement towards shape/coherence and the tendency to yield/dissolve. Taking a developmental perspective, Washburn locates merger not only in infancy but also in the inward and descent phase of "the curve of life" (Jung, 1934, para. 798), as we begin our return to the dynamic ground after the midlife transition (Cortright,

1997). Merger is only a problem when it is imposed by another or when we are unable to reinstate our boundaries (Totton, 2005). Human beings need fusion—temporary and voluntary—to heal our isolation and alienation (Dowds, 2014). Indeed we already spend parts of our daily and life cycles in states of merger: it is where we go in love, sex, or sleep to find restoration (ibid.); it is what happens when we open ourselves to the beauty of nature or music. If we cannot merge through non-destructive means (e.g., loving, trusting sex; unity experiences) we will seek substitutes in alcohol or drugs. When ego defences are relinquished, we have the potential to enter into participative consciousness with nature; then we merge with a much greater home—where for a while we can occupy a mercifully small, almost ego-less, space.

One way in which nature takes us out of ourselves and our petty human self-preoccupation is through its beauty. The philosopher Roger Scruton grasps this in almost explicitly psychodynamic terms: "Beauty makes a claim on us: it is a call to renounce our narcissism and look with reverence on the world" (2011, p. 145). Yet to talk about loving nature or the beauty of a landscape may also reveal our subject-object separation from the earth. Jonathan Bate (2001) notes that we moderns have fallen into self-consciousness about the natural world in a way that a child or an ancient poet would find incomprehensible, because they are still part of nature. Moving into the future, there is a danger that nature will not simply be separate and objectified, but narrowed still further into a two-dimensional image (viewed through a camera lens) or turned into a plaything of the ego in the form of a fashion statement. This is the way to get trapped in meaningless, isolating *re-presentation* by the left brain (McGilchrist, 2010). By contrast, when we are directly *experiencing* we are involved in a right brain, emotionally suffused relationship between earth and body.

We need to *engage* with nature to become part of it: we need to be out there getting wet and cold, building a fire, gathering food, sleeping in the woods; or more radically, like Charles Foster, living as a badger for six weeks, eating worms and road kill, navigating by smell and sleeping in a sett, as he describes in *Being a Beast* (2016). Or like the motherless feral nomad girl Lalla in Le Clézio's novel *Desert* (2011) who spends days alone wandering the North African desert communing with the lizards, snakes, scorpions, praying mantises, and leaf insects, thorn bushes, rocks, caves, earth, sky, and sun, and with a kind of ancestor spirit, the Blue Man, whom she calls al-Ser, the Secret. More domestically, Levin in *Anna Karenina* is only really happy when out in the fields turning hay with the peasants. This gives him respite from his endless and fruitless ruminating on life, death, and meaning: thinking about living is no substitute for living itself. Morris Berman (2000) makes the case that, for nomads and hunter-gatherers, their fluid sensory dialogue with the land obviated the need for religion. Walking the territory was sufficient unto itself: participating in the daily and seasonal cycles, grazing their herds, gathering food, setting up camp, and all the time enjoying the sun or rain on their skin, the prospect of the view over the next hill, the anticipation of rest in a spot that provides for their needs for water and shelter (also Dowds, 2010). Michael Harding (2013) experienced such a welcome loss in goal-directedness and urgency when travelling with a Tibetan lama across the wastes of Mongolia.

Of course, it is impossible to retrieve our old embeddedness in nature, partly for practical reasons. With a world population of seven point four billion and rising, we would destroy the remaining wilderness if we all took to living in the wild, hunting, gathering, burning wood for cooking, and burying our (often non-biodegradable) waste. Most urban dwellers don't have the resources to leave the city; and even if they did, in many cases they would just be fleeing into an agricultural factory-land, privatised and stripped of all the soul of virgin territory. The psychological reasons why we can't go back are just as powerful. We cannot heal the subject-object split just by wishing. We cannot return to the Garden of Eden, since the Fall was, after all, brought about by tasting of the Tree of Knowledge of Good and Evil: we cannot un-know what we know (Labanyi, 2011). But "the recovery of our lost wholeness can only be achieved by tasting and assimilating the fruits of consciousness to the full" (Edinger, 1992, p. 21). Instead of trying to go backwards, we actually need to go further on our path of spiritual development and fully integrate our highly developed cognitive capacities with our original embodied experience: this is equivalent to Wilber's model of "transcend *and* include" (2000, p. 51). But while modern man may only rarely achieve states of participative consciousness with nature, and full integration may, realistically, be beyond most of us, we can heal some of our deprivation by consciously inhabiting and working with nature, as Jung (1983) discovered during his breakdown and as some of our memoir writers found. It is even easier with children, as shown by a case-study of nature-based therapy with a twelve-year-old boy, Joseph (Berger and McLeod, 2006). It was the boy who invited his therapist to go for walks with him and who created a home of sticks and stones under a willow tree on a river bank. Joseph didn't need to be taught any of this: he just knew.

Capacity for experiencing

Merritt's (2009) emphasis on wringing experience from life is telling, though it is an error to believe that it can be willed or rushed. Meaning depends on a capacity to be present and receive and *experience* at depth, as thinkers as diverse as the secular Frankl and the spiritual Almaas have proclaimed. Never have Westerners had so many opportunities for rich and stimulating lives—and so little capacity to actually *experience* them. (This of course explains the current vogue for mindfulness meditation.) We are all familiar with the erosion of this capacity for experiencing, for presence, as we mature into adulthood. The child is wide open to sensuous experience, and can change the ordinary into magical treasures with a poet's power of enchantment. But as we grow older and are more exposed to intractable reality, we become defended against not only unpleasant but also potentially enriching presence to life. What we don't recognise sufficiently is that we defend ourselves, not just against a noxious *quality* of input (e.g., a frightening or disturbing film), but against an excessive *quantity* (e.g., deafening decibels) as well. At a sensory level, our current urban world is just too much—too much noise, too speedy, too crowded, too many images and flashing lights competing for our attention. We calm down the over-arousal by blocking, withdrawing, numbing, or departing.

Our cultural, social, and commercial spaces are as overwhelming as our sensory world: our attention is too divided for us to be truly present. The mobile phone is a major recent contributor to the erosion of the ability to be present to experience. Laurence Scott is in his thirties: he is therefore old enough to remember a predigital world, but young enough to be immersed in social media. Arguing that each moment is now four-dimensional because it exists in multiple places at the same time, he observes "the bleeding away of presence" generated by our "everywhereness" (2015, p. 3). If we are everywhere, we are in reality nowhere, de-localised, and life passes us by.

We can receive and process life best at an optimal level of arousal: neither too much nor too little. If under-stimulated, we may not bother to attend; if overstimulated, we must withdraw and defend ourselves.

Of course the setting differs between individuals and also according to age. There appears to be a bell-shaped curve of optimal arousal, with infants and old people tolerating very little and young people tolerating or even craving much greater amounts before the endurance of high levels of sensory stimulus begins to decline in the middle years.

Overwhelm or jadedness is the result when we do not repel excess stimulus. This generates, as a defence, a withdrawal from experiencing that is an early manifestation of depression. In the privileged world, we live in a society where desire is so constantly and easily satisfied that our problem is, in Lacan's words, "not a signal of a lack, but the absence of the support of lack" (Salecl, 2004, p. 68). Lacan believed that this lack of space for the build-up of desire provokes anxiety within us. It certainly stifles impulse and motivation and leads to a sense of bulimic meaninglessness: a state that is, I would argue, more like depression than anxiety. As with stimulus, we need neither too much nor too little gratification, just the optimum amount.

The capacity to experience depends on connecting to one's own subjective world. But beginning in the 1960s, psychoanalysts began to encounter patients who were estranged from their interiority, a state of self-alienation that Christopher Bollas (1987) called the normotic. In the words of Josh Cohen: "Instead of the inward retreat described by Freud, *into the world of fantasy and hallucination*, the normotic's oxymoronic impulse is an outward retreat into an externalized, *abnormally normal* world from which all ambiguity, strangeness and pain have been expunged, a world reduced to an infinite series of desiccated facts" (2013, p. 196). This kind of person is dominated by operational thinking and, like a robot, manages very well in the world of science, engineering, and computers. He—it is usually a he—is alienated from the imagination, symbolism, and human feelings—in short, from the right hemisphere of the brain—and ascribes so little significance to feelings that he is scarcely aware of suffering. Normotic people are becoming increasingly normal. They fit well into our alienated, science-dominated, and instrumentalising culture, where the robotic human will compliantly accept a left-brain, abstract world that lacks love, respect, beauty, imagination, or existential meaning. They couldn't be better adapted to global techno-capitalism if they were specifically designed for the role. Since they don't even know what they are missing, they are in no danger of becoming troublesome rebels—not as long as they remain normotic, anyway!

Summary

Depression is primarily a disorder of the self and, in particular, of the capacity of the self for connection. The late modern self is increasingly disembedded, narrowed, and disembodied. The self for which we are adapted by evolution is rooted not just in the human community but in the natural world, as well as in a religious worldview. But the twenty-first century self has been curtailed to the individual self—and even that is frequently strangulated down to mere ego. Our cultural and spiritual milieu is inherently depressing because of the dissolution of beliefs, values, and meaning, and the downgrading of embodied primary experience in favour of representation and virtual "reality". With the atomisation of society and the deification of the successful individual monad, separation is valued over connection. Furthermore, our condition as alienated, future-directed, obsessive, and competitive egos in a speedy, overstimulating, and over-gratifying culture militates against any depth of experiencing, of connection, or of living.

Perls viewed meaning as the satisfaction-assimilation phase of the contact-withdrawal cycle; in other words "the meaning of life is that it is to be lived" (in Fisher, 2013, p. 69). By such an understanding we can see that a sense of meaninglessness derives from being out of contact with ourselves, each other, or our environment: to adapt Adorno, such a life cannot be *lived*. To sum up, and to synthesise different categories: we need *presence* if we are to *experience Essence*, and this requires connection.

CHAPTER ELEVEN

Fundamental human needs: a conclusion

This book has argued that depression is not primarily about mood but the self, which is always a work in progress. It has complex causes: as well as possible genetic predisposition, there is an interaction between vulnerabilities arising out of early development (linked to stress) on the one hand, and stress triggers in adulthood on the other. But what is stress? It is not just about overload. It occurs when certain innate human needs are not being met: the fundamental biological, psychological, social, and spiritual requirements that Anthony Stevens has called "archetypal needs". The existence of such needs is not merely hypothetical or speculative. On the contrary, there is substantial evidence from anthropology and ethology that "mental health depends upon the provision of physical and social environments capable of meeting the archetypal needs of the developing individual" (Stevens, 1997, p. 63). Accordingly, psychopathology results when there is "frustration of archetypal intent" (ibid., p. 62). Given that human beings have innate and therefore non-negotiable needs, this gives us a set of criteria to assess how far a particular socio-cultural environment is likely to generate chronic stress and, with it, depression.

Economists (e.g., Skidelsky & Skidelsky, 2013) who place well-being before material gain have developed theories that delineate the multiple necessities of human life. The development economist Manfred Max-Neef (1992) describes our fundamental needs as: subsistence, protection, affection, understanding, participation, leisure, creation, identity, and freedom. He suggests that the first seven of these needs have existed since the origins of our hominid ancestors, whereas the demand for identity appeared at a later stage of evolution, and that for freedom even later. It has subsequently been argued that a tenth need—for transcendence—while not yet universal, will become so in the future (www.alastairmcintosh.com). Studying the downside of American materialism in relation to mental health, Tim Kasser and colleagues claim that humans have four basic needs, which are roughly those that were previously espoused by Maslow (1943). These are to feel: safe and secure; competent; connected to others; and able to be autonomously and authentically engaged in work and play (Kasser, 2002). Their research shows that emotional well-being improves when these needs are met and declines when they are not.

Perhaps the clearest lesson from surveying the memoirs is the danger of sacrificing the requirements of the organism and the self to meet the demands of the ego. Building on my analysis, I went on to show (in Chapters Eight to Ten) that it is our needs for authentic self, relationship, and meaning that are frustrated for many people in contemporary society. I then discovered that these corresponded closely to most of the core needs identified in 1955 by the psychoanalyst and social theorist Erich Fromm: for relationships, human roots, identity, a frame of orientation and devotion, and transcendence. His psychosocial theory of needs both confirms my findings and serves as a systematic overview of the themes of the last three chapters.

Human-specific psychosocial needs

Fromm makes the crucial distinction between man's human-specific *vs.* animal or physiological needs. Because the latter are easily satisfied for most people in the developed world, what we need to pay attention to are our uniquely human needs. These derive from being "torn away from the primary union with nature" (1990, p. 30) and from our having consciousness, reason, and imagination. The central feature of our humanness is that we are aware of our *separateness*—from other people, nature, and the world. Although this capacity is of course acquired during childhood, nevertheless we retain a core self from our period in the womb and early infancy. Because this foundational essence continues through life to seek to maintain a state of fusion or confluence, its primary process unconsciously and vigorously rejects difference (West, 2016), because difference is a reminder of the threat of separateness. An extreme intolerance of difference is apparent in the narcissistic defence.

Our awareness of separateness has several consequences, according to Fromm:

> (a) We need relationships to negotiate the gap between self and other. Our innate isolation and relative helplessness stimulate us to connect with others, but in our current climate of selfish individualism, we are in denial of the extent of our need for relatedness (as distinct from narcissistic exploitation of the other). This denial, claims Fromm, generates an infantile regression that comforts us in our aloneness and that is readily supported by our consumer culture. "An endless menu of regressive fantasies is offered by mass consumer culture ..., fantasies which produce narcissistic pathology and related disturbances. The key feature in this neurotic unfolding of the self is that other people are used instrumentally in order to bolster self-identity, and thus to avoid inner emptiness and isolation", observes Elliott (2002, p. 49). Reciprocal relationship requires attitudes of care, responsiveness, respect (seeing the other without the distortion of my own fears or desires), and knowledge—all notably being eroded in our narcissistic and instrumentalising, indeed exploitative culture. Among the depressed clients mentioned in Chapter Seven (James, Shelly, and Isolde), all three have problems with relationship and love.
>
> (b) We are aware—in Heidegger's terms—of our "thrownness", without our knowledge or consent, into a world not of our making. We are thus driven to transcend our passivity and powerlessness by becoming creators—or destroyers. We may transcend our "thrownness" by creating—life, art, ideas, sowing seeds: "In man's need for transcendence lies one of the roots for love, as well as for art, religion and material production" (Fromm, 1990, p. 37). Plath's protagonist in *The Bell Jar* is creative, but as an emerging adult can see that this will be crushed as she is funnelled into acceptable female roles (Plath, 1999). Wurtzel (1996) wrote books as a young child, but this ended with her socialisation away from her own creativity between the ages of nine and thirteen; for her, creativity

and intellectual curiosity were interwoven, as we will see in section (e) below. If we cannot create, we can answer the need for transcendence by destroying. With females, this destructiveness is often turned inwards, as was the case for Esther Greenwood and Wurtzel, whose depression was linked with the stifling of their creativity.

James and Shelley are passive in the face of their "thrownness". They haven't (yet) acquired the sense of self that could produce the libido and power to create their own lives. However Shelley's anger at injustice suggests a potential—for creation or destructiveness, depending on how it is channelled.

(c) Mankind "can dispense with [his] *natural* roots only insofar as he finds new *human* roots" (Fromm, 1990, p. 38). Thus we have a need for the fraternity of the family, community, or nation state in which we can feel secure and at home.

Sally Brampton lacked a home in the sense of an extended family, community, or country in which she was embedded. Others may experience the feeling of rootedness in family or clan, but, perhaps because they are insecure in it, they cannot let go in order to move on and thereby block the development of their individuality, as was the case for James. His international way of life has ensured that his roots have never gone very deep. To compensate, he clings to his family, and therefore cannot move on into his own independent adult life. If we do move out to connect with new human roots, we may limit our identification to those of the same nationality, race, gender, sexual orientation, or other familiar subculture. Alternatively, in the most positive sense, we may experience ourselves as part of the human race where we accord the same rights to all others as to ourselves.

A large part of the reason for the current epidemic in depression is that we have lost our rootedness, not just in nature but also in the human community. We are trying to forge lives based largely on individual success and have lost a sense of being part of something bigger, as we saw in Chapter Nine. This generates profound isolation with ensuing anxiety and depression.

(d) Because human beings experience themselves as separate from nature and other people, they conceive of themselves as subjects. As such, I act upon nature and upon the other as that which is not me. This constellates a subject-object split. But, having lost our original unity, we have also lost our primordial, given identity and must construct one. Such a secondary identity can be understood as the inevitable consequence of the subject-object split, and as a *need* that must be actively fulfilled.

We have seen how a fragile sense of self predisposes the individual to depression (Chapter Eight). The question that arises now is whether self and identity amount to the same thing. I propose that they are related but not equivalent. Self is the outcome of the child's facilitating environment and is therefore never volitional. In contrast, identity, which is formed largely in adolescence and young adulthood, is the outcome of the interaction between this self and the culture and society into which it emerges; it is thus to some extent subject to the will. Self is who I am; identity is what I identify with. Both self and identity can vary in degrees of authenticity. The self can be "false" when our organismic truth has not been mirrored and we have been forced for our survival to over-adapt to the parental or social environment. In the absence of an authentic sense of self, our identity will necessarily be arbitrary and incongruent, because our choices have not been directed by an inner compass.

Unfortunately, we often substitute authentic identity with conforming to a herd mentality. The issues of rootedness and identity are intimately connected, and developing an authentic and individual identity is only possible if we have succeeded in psychologically separating ourselves from the group. At the same time, we need roots to provide a springboard from which we can jump into our own individual identities. It is clear this is what James has not yet succeeded in doing, while McEvoy (2011) has gone only part of the way in separating from her parents' demands and values. While Western culture provides considerable educational opportunity, and political and economic freedom, it is nevertheless the case that only a minority of people achieve individuation. Most either fail to emerge from the clan or, if they do, they simply move on to a new group-identity. Here they espouse the beliefs and values of their subculture, which may be defined by nation, class, religion, occupation, football team, music band, or computer game. However, in the absence of an authentic sense of identity we are living on the perilous edge of depression.

(e) Finally, we have a need to make sense of the world—that is, to orient ourselves intellectually—which results in the fashioning of a world view.

Just as we must learn the shape of the material world in our early years by sensual engagement and learning what things *do*, we must gradually learn to *make sense of* a mysterious world. "What makes lightning and rainbows and tsunami winds ...?", wondered the young Elizabeth Wurtzel (1996, p. 70). The avid curiosity we have as infants is for many of us stifled in older childhood: Wurtzel felt her spirit broke during five long summers of being forced to conform to the ethos of American summer camps. Her curiosity and exploration stopped as she was "expelled from that place where possibility still existed" (1996, p. 70).

It is necessary, for our sanity, to have some frame of orientation for understanding the world, even one that is false. We also have an additional, but secondary, need, which is to make sense of the world objectively, that is, in a way that is consistent with reality. Furthermore, because we are embodied beings, "any satisfying system of orientation contains not just intellectual elements but elements of feeling and sensing which are expressed in the relationship to an object of devotion" (Fromm, 1990, p. 65); this gives meaning to our existence, as we saw in Chapter Ten.

When our expectations are no longer met or when social change occurs so rapidly that we can no longer understand the world, we self-protectively withdraw and become depressed. Our capacity to make existential sense of the world is being eroded by the transfer of power (and therefore justice) out of human hands into abstract and uncontrollable forces, such as the market or mathematical algorithms, and the production of increasingly incomprehensible technology. Creswell et al. (2007) have shown that, following experimental activation, amygdala firing can be reduced simply by stating the name of the emotion that has been evoked. It appears that it is this "'cortical override' that enables awareness to modulate subcortical fear states" (Siegel, 2010, p. 230). If we can make sense of the nature of and reasons for even the worst misfortunes, we begin—however falsely—to feel in control and more accepting of them.

If part of our unreconstructed worldview is that hard work or good behaviour will be rewarded, the shattering of that illusion may lead to depression. Humans and other mammals have evolved for morality as well as self-interest and become depressed in the face of unfairness (Hodgson, 2013; de Waal, 2013; Wilkinson & Pickett, 2010).

Matrix of needs

Max-Neef (1992) argues, contrary to Maslow's concept of a hierarchy (1943) that we have a *matrix* of needs that must be constantly negotiated and balanced with each other. Extreme deprivation or excessive satisfaction (addiction) of one need drains the motivation or libido required to pursue other necessities, but not necessarily in a hierarchical way. A total lack of love (relationship) or home (rootedness) in one's life, the failure to form an authentic identity, the absence of imagination or spontaneity (creativity needs), or the inability to make sense of a rapidly changing world could all lead to depression and possibly suicide. This is an interdependent network where there has to be at least minimal satisfaction of every requirement to enable the individual to attend to other needs.

Often we sacrifice some essential needs on the altar of one that has come to dominate our lives, perhaps because of living out our parents' unmet ambitions, or because self-esteem in the family of origin was dependent on a very limited set of conditions. Keedwell (2008) cites the example of John Stuart Mill, who wrote *On Utilitarianism* at the age of nineteen and became depressed at twenty-one. He, like many of the memoir authors, learned through this experience that he should not have sacrificed his social and emotional development to his ambition.

Emotions have evolved precisely to motivate us to realise our needs: for example, it is sadness at separation that keeps us close to the people on whom we depend. As discussed in Chapter Five, moods are an integration of a variety of emotions; moods last longer than transient feelings and are less tied to specific triggers. When substantial needs remain frustrated, our mood plummets. Mild and transient low mood may be a way of dampening down these inner demands; but if deficits persist in the long term, a deeper depression may be a signal of crisis that requires that unrecognised needs must be given attention, whatever the cost to the fulfilment of other requirements that have hitherto been given precedence.

Threats to satisfaction of needs in twenty-first-century society

Frustration of our fundamental needs makes us vulnerable to low mood. We saw in the last three chapters how our current social climate is detrimental to the formation of a strong sense of self, the capacity to form intimate relationships or participate in social networks, and the ability to connect and find meaning in life. In writing about the philosophy of Giorgio Agamben, Jessica Whyte summarises what we are up against: "We are living through a period in which everything has been expropriated and offered up for consumption, in which all that was once directly lived is now instead represented, in which there is nothing authentic or natural, and no spaces, political or otherwise, that have not been thoroughly commodified" (2013, p. 129). The socio-cultural conditions of advanced, technologised, and globalised neo-liberal capitalism are particularly detrimental to the fulfilment of needs for relationship, rootedness, identity, understanding, and devotion in ways that generate vulnerability to depression and anxiety. Since these needs are interdependent, compromising one has further effects on the others. The ability to transcend our powerlessness is secondarily threatened, as it is not possible to be creative in the absence of authentic identity.

In the contemporary world, we relate to ourselves and each other in a more instrumental way, where self and other are valued not for who they are but what they can do. In Buber's terms, I-it relating dominates when we relate to others, and, indeed, the environment, primarily as objects to be used for our benefit (Buber, 2013). Our relating is becoming autistic in its nature: speedy, superficial, and performative rather than emotionally infused, contactful, and interactive. What is lost is true reciprocity and the whole realm of the implicit and of first-hand experience.

The sense of rootedness is most obviously devastated for the thirteen million refugees worldwide, many of whose homes and homelands have been destroyed. Likewise for migrants, whether forced out of their home countries through conflict, infringement of human rights, poverty, or lack of opportunity. But for the more privileged amongst us, our rootedness is compromised by social atomisation and globalisation as well as by the pace of change in our home environments.

The absence of rootedness and both the superficiality and the I-it nature of relating have catastrophic consequences for developing and maintaining a sense of authentic identity. We compensate by clinging on to temporary and false identities through acquiring the values or mimicking the style of transient cultural groupings. Writing about adolescents, Siegel observes that the more they "experience their roles as 'false' and not 'authentic', the more turmoil they feel. Social contexts that force individuals to adapt via self-states that are not reflective of their own experiences, mental states and needs may place these persons at higher risk of developing emotional disorders—of being vulnerable to 'disintegration'" (2012, p. 354). Authenticity and autonomy are interdependent. Without an authentic self for direction there can be no genuine autonomy: action is merely compliant, oppositional, or acting out. Without autonomy the self crumbles (Bettelheim, 1979).

In our new century we find ourselves in an unprecedented situation: what Bauman (2008) describes as a shift from solid to liquid modernity. This step change has overwhelmed our orienting sense and leaves us "uncertain both of our whereabouts, and of our heading" (Boxall, 2013, p. 19). Change is happening so fast that, paradoxically, nothing seems to be happening at all, because we have no stable reference point from which to observe the change. Allied to this is an inability to envisage a future, because of so many overwhelming and intractable problems but also because we can't imagine what shape the future might take when the present is so unstable and the past has been forgotten.

Top–down vs. bottom–up satisfaction of needs

This review of some of the major problems facing the developed world may lead us to believe that we might as well give up. However, there is some reason to believe that—as complexity theory holds—small changes can have large and unanticipated consequences. Max-Neef (1992) has shown how the "satisfier" of one need can have complex effects on the fulfilment of other necessities. He has identified five categories of satisfier according to their effects on needs other than the main target. There are singular satisfiers that answer only a single demand, and violator (e.g., bureaucracy), pseudo (e.g., mechanistic medicine), and inhibiting (e.g., overprotective parenting) satisfiers that are actively destructive in meeting a range of needs. But synergic satisfiers, by the way in which they fulfil a given requirement, also contribute to meeting other needs. Breast-feeding obviously provides subsistence, but also protection (via antibodies), affection, and identity through the development of the mother–infant bond. Other examples of synergic satisfiers are barefoot medicine and banking, direct democracy, preventative medicine, and meditation. Thus an individual may be drawn to meditation to achieve mental health (subsistence) or relaxation (leisure) but may also gain understanding, creativity, identity, or transcendence.

The first four categories of satisfiers (singular, violator, pseudo, and inhibiting) are top–down attempts to meet needs by authority systems such as governments, parents, or powerful professional classes. Because of this, they are contaminated by power and control motivations, so that their actual, though possibly unconscious, intention may differ from the stated one. Frequently this involves being driven by the demands of the economy rather than the needs of human beings. The fifth class has a bottom–up or grass-roots origin and is process-oriented instead of goal-directed. Top–down, goal-directed satisfiers are generated by the left hemisphere of the brain, which is conscious, abstract, linear, narrowly focused, and lacks a capacity for context or relationship. The bottom–up, process-oriented way of thinking emerges from the right hemisphere and is unconscious, holistic, contextual, broadly-focused, relational, and systemic (McGilchrist, 2010; Schore, 2010). It is no accident that synergic satisfiers are the only ones whose positive impact spreads in unanticipated ways and that meet the various needs of human potential. Because process-oriented thinking holds the goal lightly, it allows something else, indeed something new and unprecedented, to emerge.

The synergic, bottom–up satisfaction of needs provides social support, which is a potent protection against depression. Grass-roots developments, such as the Slow movement, and small-scale phenomena such as community placemaking (where people who use the space drive the agenda of urban design), support groups (e.g., for single or stay-at-home parents), community gardens, organic farms, artisanal businesses, book clubs, or meditation groups all counter isolation and community fragmentation. They build relationship and fraternity as well as slowing us down and facilitating first-hand experiencing of our lives in a wider context. Key concepts here are love rather than power values: slow, intimate, community, embodied, and real rather than virtual experience.

The personal and the political

> "No man hath affliction enough, that is not matured and ripened by it, and made fit for God by that affliction."
>
> —John Donne, *Devotions upon Emergent Occasions*, Meditation 17

Stemming the tide of depression requires action at both individual and societal levels. With respect to the former, psychotherapeutic treatment requires more than a CBT approach, which simply ignores the lesson that depression is trying to teach and whose effects are short term. Depth psychotherapy is essential to build and repair the self, and, unlike CBT, the gains of psychoanalytic psychotherapy were found to last for at least two years post-treatment (Fonagy et al., 2015). Taking personal responsibility and trusting their process is easier for those who can revision and hold the depression in a more expansive, quasi-spiritual framework, though this need not always involve a formal spiritual practice. Exemplars of such trust are to be found in the contributors to *Darkness Before Dawn*: a collection of short personal accounts, often with a Jungian colouring, by spiritually aware people who have suffered from depression (edited by Simon, 2015). One saw that despair cracked open her heart (Pipher); some understood that depression was a friend (Palmer), or "a pain that's a solution to a deeper pain" (Masters); others experienced it as "ingenious stagnation" (McLaren), "initiation" (Roberts, Ingerman), or "a wake-up call" (Foster). As Michael Beckwith observes in the same volume: "*Every moment of seeming self-disintegration is, in truth, a reintegration of the self with the Self*", which captures the reparative movement beyond identification with the ego and into expansion (2015, p. 73).

Some ideas for improving the psychosocial environment were suggested in the previous section; but if our current society is indeed a breeding-ground for depression, the personal and the societal must not remain separate. No individual can, on her own, resist the immense forces that confront us. If the project of psychotherapy is to take a political stance, it must do so from the perspective of creating a society that is more attuned to human needs. Freedom must be balanced by equality and fraternity, and by an awareness that humans are part of the natural world. We already have models for this in feminist therapy, ecotherapy, or in social therapy groups where "growth comes from participating in the process of building the groups in which one functions" (Holzman, 2013, p. 39).

As a final word, I want to emphasise, at the end of this long and complex investigation, that we should *pay attention* to depression. By this I do not simply mean that we should take it seriously as a debilitating condition that is affecting more and more people around the globe. Rather that we should listen to what it is telling us about the world we have created, our whole way of life, our priorities, beliefs, and values: telling us, by implication, what a fulfilled and humane life might look like.

REFERENCES

Abram, D. (1997). *The Spell of the Sensuous: Perception and Language in a More-Than-Human World*. New York: Vintage.

Allen, B., & Gilbert, P. (2000). Social intelligence, deception and psychopathology. In: P. Gilbert & K. Bailey (Eds.), *Genes on the Couch: Explorations in Evolutionary Psychotherapy* (pp. 151–175). Hove, UK: Brunner-Routledge.

Alloy, L., & Abramson, L. (1979). Judgment of contingency in depressed and non-depressed students: sadder but wiser? *Journal of Experimental Psychology: General, 108*: 441–485.

Alloy, L., Kelly, K., Mineka, S., & Clements, C. (1990). Comorbidity in anxiety and depressive disorders: a helplessness-hopelessness perspective. In: J. Maser & C. Cloninger (Eds.), *Comorbidity in Anxiety and Mood Disorders* (pp. 499–543). Washington, DC: American Psychiatric Press.

Almaas, A. H. (2001). *The Point of Existence: Transformations of Narcissism in Self-Realization*. Boston, MA: Shambhala.

Andersen, R., Curtis, J., & Grabb, E. (2006). Trends in civic association activity in four democracies: the special case of women in the United States. *American Sociological Review, 71*: 376–400.

Arumugam, M., Raes, J., Pelletier, E., Le Paslier, D., Yamada, T., Mende, D., Fernandes, G., Tap, J., Bruls, T. Batto, J-M., et al. (2011). Enterotypes of the human gut microbiome. *Nature, 473*: 174–180.

Baldwin, C. (2015). A spiritual response to our times. In: T. Simon (Ed.) *Darkness Before Dawn: Redefining the Journey Through Depression* (pp. 141–150). Boulder, CO: Sounds True.

Barreau, F., Cartier, C., & Leveque, M., Ferrier, L., Moriez, R., Laroute, V., Rosztoczy, A., Fioramonti, J., & Bueno, L. (2007). Pathways involved in gut mucosal barrier dysfunction induced in adult rats by maternal deprivation: corticotrophin-releasing factor and nerve growth factor interplay. *Journal of Physiology, 580*: 347–356.

Barrows, A. (1995). The ecopsychology of child development. In: T. Roszak, M. Gomes, & A. Kanner (Eds.), *Ecopsychology: Restoring the Earth, Healing the Mind* (pp. 101–110). San Francisco: Sierra Club Books.

Bate, J. (2001). *The Song of the Earth*. London: Picador.

Bauman, Z. (2008). *The Art of Life*. Cambridge, UK: Polity Press.

Beauvoir, S. de (1972). *The Second Sex* (Trans. H. M. Parshley). Harmondsworth, UK: Penguin.

Becker, E. (1985). Depression: a comprehensive theory. In: J. Coyne (Ed.), *Essential Papers on Depression* (pp. 366–389). New York: New York University Press.

Beebe, B., Jaffe, J., & Lachmann, F. (2005). A dyadic systems view of communication. In: J. Auerbach, K. Levy, & C. Schaffer (Eds.), *Relatedness, Self-definition and Mental Representations* (pp. 23–42). New York: Routledge.

Beevers, C., & Miller, I. (2004). Depression-related negative cognition: mood-state and trait dependent properties. *Cognitive Therapy and Research, 28*: 293–307.

Berger, R., & McLeod, J. (2006). Incorporating nature into therapy. *Journal of Systemic Therapies, 25*: 80–94.

Bergh, B. van den (2015). Late modernity and its discontented. In: F. Martinez & P. Runnel (Eds.), *Hopeless Youth!* (pp. 349–376). Tartu: Estonian National Museum.

Berman, M. (2000). *Wandering God: A Study in Nomadic Spirituality*. Albany, NY: SUNY.

Bettelheim, B. (1979). *Surviving and Other Essays*. London: Thames & Hudson.

Billings, A., & Moos, R. (1985). Psychosocial theory and research on depression: an integrative framework and review. In: J. Coyne (Ed.), *Essential Papers on Depression* (pp. 331–365). New York: New York University Press.

Blazer, D. (2005). *The Age of Melancholy: Major Depression and its Social Origins*. New York: Routledge.

Bolger, N., DeLongis, A., Kessler, R., & Schilling, E. (1989). Effects of daily stress on negative mood. *Journal of Personality and Social Psychology, 57*: 808–818.

Bollas, C. (1987). *The Shadow of the Object*. London: Free Association.
Boorstein, S. (1997). *Clinical Studies in Transpersonal Psychotherapy*. Albany, NY: SUNY.
Bowen, M. (1978). *Family Therapy in Clinical Practice*. New York: Jason Aronson.
Boxall, P. (2013). *Twenty-First Century Fiction*. Cambridge, UK: CUP.
Brampton, S. (2008). *Shoot the Damn Dog: A Memoir of Depression*. London: Bloomsbury.
Brefczynski-Lewis, J., Lutz, A., Schaeffer, H., Levinson, D., & Davidson, R. (2007). Neural correlates of attentional expertise in long-term meditation practitioners. *Proceedings of the National Academy of Sciences USA, 104*: 11483–11488.
Breggin, P. (2014). *Guilt, Shame and Anxiety: Understanding and Overcoming Negative Emotions*. Amherst, NY: Prometheus.
Britton, P., & Fuendeling, J. (2005). The relations among varieties of adult attachment and the components of empathy. *The Journal of Social Psychology, 145*: 519–530.
Brookner, A. (1989). *Latecomers*. London: Grafton.
Brown, G. (1985). A three-factor causal model for depression. In: J. Coyne (Ed.), *Essential Papers on Depression* (pp. 390–402). New York: New York University Press.
Brown, G., & Harris, T. (1978). *Social Origins of Depression*. London: Tavistock.
Buber, M. (2013). *I and Thou*. London: Bloomsbury.
Buddelmeyer, H., Hamermesh, D., & Wooden, M. (2015). The stress cost of children. NBER Working Paper No. 21223, May 2015.
Cacioppo, J., & Hawkley, L. (2003). Social isolation and health, with an emphasis on underlying mechanisms. *Perspectives in Biology and Medicine, 46*: S39–S52.
Cacioppo, J., Hughes, M., Waite, L., Hawkley, L., & Thisted, R. (2006). Loneliness as a specific risk factor for depressive symptoms: cross-sectional and longitudinal analyses. *Psychology and Aging, 21*: 140–151.
Cain, S. (2013). *Quiet: The Power of Introverts in a World That Can't Stop Talking*. London: Penguin.
Cain, S., Mone, G., & Moroz, E. (2016). *Quiet Power: The Secret Strengths of Introverts*. New York: Penguin.
Carter, R. (2009). *The Brain Book: An Illustrated Guide to its Structure, Function and Disorders*. London: Dorling Kindersley.
Caspi, A., Sugden, K., Moffitt, T., Taylor, A., Craig, I., Harrington, H., McClay, J., Mill, J., Martin, J., Braithwaite, A., & Poulton, R. (2003). Influence of life stress on depression: moderation by a polymorphism in the 5-HTT gene. *Science, 301*: 386–389.

Chiasson, A. M. (2015). Practices to reconnect, retrieve , revivify. In: T. Simon (Ed.), *Darkness Before Dawn: Redefining the Journey through Depression* (pp. 99–112). Boulder, CO: Sounds True.

Chourbaji, S., & Gass, P. (2009). Modelling depression by GR mutant animals. In: C. Pariante, R. Nesse, D. Nutt, & L. Wolpert (Eds.), *Understanding Depression: A Translational Approach* (pp. 111–122). Oxford, UK: OUP.

Claes, S., Binder, E., & Nemeroff, C. (2009). Genetic factors in stress and depression. In: C. Pariante, R. Nesse, D. Nutt, & L. Wolpert (Eds.), *Understanding Depression: A Translational Approach* (pp. 55–66). Oxford, UK: OUP.

Cleare, A. (2009). Does depression induce pain and fatigue? In: C. Pariante, R. Nesse, D. Nutt, & L. Wolpert (Eds.), *Understanding Depression: A Translational Approach* (pp. 249–260). Oxford, UK: OUP.

Clemente, J., Ursell, L., Parfrey, L., & Knight, R. (2012). The impact of gut microbiota on human health: an integrative view. *Cell, 148*: 1258–1270.

Clézio, J. M. G. Le (2011). *Desert* (Trans. C. Dickson). London: Atlantic.

Coan, J., Schaefer, H., & Davidson, R. (2006). Lending a hand: social regulation of the neural response to threat. *Psychological Science, 17*: 1032–1039.

Cohen, J. (2013). *The Private Life: Why We Remain in the Dark*. London: Granta.

Cooper, A. (1986). Narcissism. In: A. Morrison (Ed.), *Essential Papers on Narcissism* (pp. 112–143). New York: New York University Press.

Cortright, B. (1997). *Psychotherapy and Spirit*. Albany, NY: SUNY.

Cortright, B. (2007). *Integral Psychology*. Albany, NY: SUNY.

Cottingham, J. (2003). *On the Meaning of Life*. London: Routledge.

Cottingham, J. (2015). *How to Believe*. London: Bloomsbury.

Cowen P., & Harmer, C. (2009). Is it all monoamines? In: C. Pariante, R. Nesse, D. Nutt and L. Wolpert (Eds.), *Understanding Depression: A Translational Approach* (pp. 171–180). Oxford, UK: OUP.

Coyne, J. (1985). Towards an interactional description of depression. In: J. Coyne (Ed.), *Essential Papers on Depression* (pp. 311–330). New York: New York University Press.

Cozolino, L. (2010). *The Neuroscience of Psychotherapy: Healing the Social Brain* (2nd edn). New York: Norton.

Creswell, J., Way, B., Eisenberger, N. & Lieberman, M. (2007). Neural correlates of dispositional mindfulness during affect labeling. *Psychosomatic Medicine, 69*: 560–565.

Cruwys, T., Haslam, A., Dingle, G., Haslam, C., & Jetten, J. (2014). Depression and social identity: an integrative review. *Personality and Social Psychology Review, 18*: 215–238.

Cryan, J., & Dynan, T. (2014). Psychobiotics: the profound influence of the stomach over the mind. *New Scientist, 221*: 28–29.

Cusk, R. (2002). *A Life's Work*. London: Fourth Estate.

Cusk, R. (2015). *Outline*. London: Vintage.

Dantzer, R., O'Connor, J., Castanon, N., Lestage, J., & Kelly, K. (2009). Cytokines and depression: experimental evidence and intermediate mechanisms. In: C. Pariante, R. Nesse, D. Nutt, & L. Wolpert (Eds.), *Understanding Depression: A Translational Approach* (pp. 123–137). Oxford, UK: OUP.

Darrieussecq, M. (2004). *A Brief Stay with the Living* (Trans. I. Monk). London: Faber & Faber.

Dash, S., Berk, M., & Jacka, F. (2015). The gut microbiome and diet in psychiatry: focus on depression. *Current Opinion in Psychiatry, 28*: 1–6.

Davison, G., Neale, J., & Kring, A. (2004). *Abnormal Psychology* (9th edn). Hoboken, NJ: Wiley.

Deife, J. (2004). Sitting down with Catherine Ingram. *LA Yoga Magazine* Vol. 3, No. 2.

Deurzen-Smith, E. van (1997). *Everyday Mysteries: Existential Dimensions of Psychotherapy*. London: Routledge.

Diamond, J. (2012). *The World Until Yesterday*. London: Penguin.

Diehl, M., Elnick, A., Bourbeau, L., & Labouvie-Vief, G. (1998). Adult attachment styles: their relations to family context and personality. *Journal of Personality and Social Psychology, 74*: 1656–1669.

Dinan, T., & Fitzgerald, P. (2009) Neuroendocrine and immune crosstalk in major depression. In: C. Pariante, R. Nesse, D. Nutt, & L. Wolpert (Eds.), *Understanding Depression: A Translational Approach* (pp. 213–222). Oxford, UK: OUP.

Dowds, B. (2008). The chameleon self: over-adaptation and the death of feeling. *Eisteach, 8 (4)*: 9–14.

Dowds, B. (2010). The evolution of human consciousness and spirituality. *Inside Out, 61*: 20–29.

Dowds, B. (2014). *Beyond the Frustrated Self: Overcoming Avoidant Patterns and Opening to Life*. London: Karnac.

Dowds, B. (2016). Is life a bitch? The need to contextualise depression and realism. *Self and Society, 44*: 123–133.

Dowds, B. (2017). Going beyond sucking stones: connection and emergent meaning in life and in therapy. In: R. Tweedy (Ed.), *The Divided Therapist: Hemispheric Difference and Contemporary Psychotherapy*, in press. London: Karnac.

Drabble, M. (1996). Umbrella of darkness. In: S. Dunn, B. Morrison, & M. Roberts (Eds.), *Mind Readings: Writers Journeys through Mental States* (pp. 91-95). London: Minerva.

Eagleton, T. (2015). *Hope Without Optimism*. New Haven, CT: Yale University Press.

Edinger, E. (1992). *Ego and Archetype: Individuation and the Religious Function of the Psyche*. Boston, USA: Shambhala.

Ehrenberg, A. (2009). *The Weariness of the Self: Diagnosing the History of Depression in the Contemporary Age* (Transl. E. Caouette, J. Homel, D. Homel, & D. Winkler). Montreal, Canada: McGill-Queen's University Press.

Eiland, H., & Jennings, M. (2014). *Walter Benjamin: A Critical Life*. Cambridge, MA: Belknap.

Elliott, A, (2002). *Psychoanalytic Theory: An Introduction* (2nd edn). Durham, NC: Duke University Press.

Emanuel, R. (2002). Anxiety. In: I. Ward (Ed.), *On a Darkling Plain: Journeys into the Unconscious* (pp. 39–70). Cambridge, UK: Icon.

Eshun, S., & Gurung, R. (Eds.) (2009). *Culture and Mental Health: Sociocultural Influences, Theory and Practice*. Malden, MA: Wiley-Blackwell.

Eutamene, H., Lamine, F., Chabo, C., Theodorou, V., Rochat, F., Bergonzelli, G., Corthésy-Theulaz, I., Fioramonti, J., & Bueno, L. (2007) Synergy between *Lactobacillus paracasei* and its bacterial products to counteract stress-induced gut permeability and sensitivity increase in rats. *Journal of Nutrition, 137*: 1901–1907.

Feltham, C. (2016). *Depressive Realism: Interdisciplinary Perspectives*. London: Routledge.

Fisher, A. (2013). *Radical Ecopsychology* (2nd edn). Albany, NY: SUNY.

Flint, J., Greenspan, R., & Kendler, K. (2010). *How Genes Influence Behavior*. Oxford: OUP.

Fonagy, P. (2006). The mentalization-focused approach to social development. In: J. Allen & P. Fonagy (Eds.), *Handbook of Mentalization-Based Treatment* (pp. 53–100). Chichester, UK: Wiley.

Fonagy, P., Rost, F., Carlyle, J., McPherson, S., Thomas, R., Pasco Fearon, R., Goldberg, D., & Taylor, D. (2015). Pragmatic randomized controlled trial of long-term psychoanalytic psychotherapy for treatment-resistant depression: the Tavistock Adult Depression Study (TADS). *World Psychiatry, 14*: 312–321.

Ford, R. (2006). *Independence Day*. London: Bloomsbury.

Ford, R. (2016). Anatomy of Trump: a personal essay. *Times Literary Supplement*, 15 July. Available at: www.the-tls.co.uk.

Foster, C. (2016). *Being a Beast*. London: Profile.

Foster, J. (2015). Depression as a wake-up call. In: T. Simon (Ed.), *Darkness Before Dawn: Redefining the Journey through Depression* (pp. 199–210). Boulder, CO: Sounds True.

Foster, J., & Neufeld, K. (2013) Gut-brain axis: how the microbiome influences anxiety and depression. *Trends in Neurosciences, 36*: 305–312.

Frankl, V. (1985). *The Unheard Cry for Meaning: Psychotherapy and Humanism*. New York: Washington Square Press.

Frankl, V. (1988). *Will to Meaning: Foundations and Applications of Logotherapy*. New York: Meridian.

Franklin, T., Russig, H., Weiss, I., Graff, J., Linder, N., Michalon, A., Vizi, S., & Mansuy, I. (2010). Epigenetic transmission of the impact of early stress across generations. *Biological Psychiatry, 68*: 408–415.

Fredrickson, B (2001). The role of positive emotions in positive psychology: the broaden-and-build theory of positive emotions. *American Psychologist, 56*: 218–226.

Freud, S. (1917e). Mourning and melancholia. *S. E., 14*: 237–258. London: Hogarth.

Freud, S. (1926d). *Inhibitions, Symptoms and Anxiety. S. E., 20*: 77–174. London: Hogarth.

Freud, S. (1960). Letter to Marie Bonaparte, 13 August 1937. In: E. L. Freud (Ed.), *Letters of Sigmund Freud 1873- 1939* (pp. 436–437). New York: Basic.

Fromm, E. (1990). *The Sane Society*. New York: Holt.

Fromm, E. (1995). *The Essential Fromm: Life between Having and Being*. London: Constable.

Frosh, S. (1991). *Identity Crisis: Modernity, Psychoanalysis and the Self*. Houndmills, UK: Macmillan.

Fumoto, M., Oshima, T., Kamiya, K., Kikuchi, H., Seki, Y., Nakatani, Y., Yu, X., Sekiyama, T., Sato-Suzuki, I., & Arita, H. (2010). Ventral prefrontal cortex and serotonergic system activation during pedalling exercise induces negative mood improvement and increased alpha band in EEG. *Behavioural Brain Research, 213*: 1–9.

Gask, L. (2015). *The Other Side of Silence: A Psychiatrist's Memoir of Depression*. Chichester, UK: Summersdale.

Gendlin, E. (1996). *Focusing-Oriented Psychotherapy*. New York: Guilford Press.

Gerhardt, S. (2011). *The Selfish Society: How We All Forgot to Love One Another and Made Money Instead*. London: Simon & Schuster.

Gerhardt, S. (2015). *Why Love Matters: How Affection Shapes a Baby's Brain* (2nd edn). London: Routledge.

Geschwind, N., van Os, J., Peeters, F., & Wichers, M. (2009). The role of affective processing in vulnerability to and resilience against depression. In: C. Pariante, R. Nesse, D. Nutt, & L. Wolpert (Eds.), *Understanding Depression: A Translational Approach* (pp. 181–192). Oxford, UK: OUP.

Gilbert, P. (2000). Social mentalities. In: P. Gilbert & K. Bailey (Eds.), *Genes on the Couch: Explorations in Evolutionary Psychotherapy* (pp. 118-150). Hove, UK: Brunner-Routledge.

Gilbert, P. (2007). *Psychotherapy and Counselling for Depression* (3rd edn). London: Sage.

Glaser, E. (2011). *Get Real: How to Tell it Like it is in a World of Illusions*. London: Fourth Estate.

Grant, B. (2015). Antidepressant microbes in soil: how dirt makes you happy. *Gardening Know How*. 20 July. Available at www.gardeningknowhow.com.

Gratten, J., Wray, N., Keller, M., & Visscher, P. (2014). Large-scale genomics unveils the genetic architecture of psychiatric disorders. *Nature Neuroscience, 17*: 782–790.

Greenfield, S. (2009). *ID: The Quest for Meaning in the 21st Century*. London: Hodder & Stoughton.

Greenspan, S., & Shanker, S. (2006). *The First Idea: How Symbols, Language, and Intelligence Evolved from Our Primate Ancestors to Modern Humans*. Cambridge, MA: Da Capo Press.

Grimmond, G. (2015). How having children robs parents of their happiness. *South China Morning Post: Post Magazine*, 16 September. Available at: www.scmp.com.

Guignon, C. (2004). *On Being Authentic*. London: Routledge.

Gullone, E. (2000). The biophilia hypothesis and life in the 21st century: increasing mental health or increasing pathology? *Journal of Happiness Studies, 1*: 293–321.

Haig, M. (2015). *Reasons to Stay Alive*. Edinburgh: Canongate.

Harding, M. (2013). *Staring at Lakes: A Memoir of Love, Melancholy and Magical Thinking*. Dublin: Hachette.

Harding, M. (2014). *Hanging with the Elephant: A Story of Love, Loss and Meditation*. Dublin: Hachette.

Hart, S. (2008). *Brain, Attachment, Personality: An Introduction to Neuroaffective Development*. London: Karnac.

Hay, D. (2006). *Something There: The Biology of the Human Spirit*. London: Darton, Longman & Todd.

Hedges, L. (1994). *Working the Organizing Experience: Transforming Psychotic, Schizoid, and Autistic States*. Northvale, NJ: Jason Aronson.

Heller, L., & LaPierre, A. (2012). *Healing Developmental Trauma: How Early Trauma Affects Self-Regulation, Self-Image, and the Capacity for Relationship*. Berkeley, CA: North Atlantic Books.

Heron. J. (1998). *Sacred Science: Person-Centred Inquiry into the Spiritual and the Subtle*. Ross-on-Wye, UK: PCCS Books.

Hirschfeld, R., Montgomery, S., Keller, M., Kasper, S., Schatzberg, A., Möller, H., Healy, D., Baldwin, D., Humble, M., Versiani, M., Montenegro, R., & Bourgeois, M. (2000). Social functioning in depression: a review. *Journal of Clinical Psychiatry, 61*: 268–275.

Hodgson, G. (2013). *From Pleasure Machines to Moral Communities: An Evolutionary Economics without Homo Economicus*. Chicago: University of Chicago Press.

Holford, P. (2010). *The Feel Good Factor: 10 Proven Ways to Boost Your Mood and Motivate Yourself*. London: Piatkus.

Holmes, J. (2010). *Exploring In Security: Towards an Attachment-informed Psychoanalytic Psychotherapy*. London: Routledge.

Holzman, L. (2013). The development community and its activist psychology. In: R. House, D. Kalish, & J. Maidman (Eds.), *The Future of Humanistic Psychology* (pp. 29–42). Ross-on-Wye, UK: PCCS Books

Horkheimer, M., & Adorno, T. (2007). *Dialectic of the Enlightenment* (Trans. E. Jephcott). Palo Alto, CA: Stanford University Press.

Hughes, K. (2016). Seven years' war. *Literary Review*, March, p. 1. Available at: www.literaryreview.co.uk.

Hyde, C., Nagle, M., Tian, C., Chen, X., Paciga, S., Wendland, J., Tung, J., Hinds, D., Perlis, R., & Winslow, A. (2016). Identification of 15 genetic loci associated with risk of major depression in individuals of European descent. *Nature Genetics, 48*: 1031–1036.

Ingram, D. (1990). *Critical Theory and Philosophy*. St. Paul, MN: Paragon House.

James, H. (1987). The art of fiction (1884). In: R. Gard (Ed.), *The Critical Muse: Selected Literary Criticism* (pp. 186–206). London: Penguin.

James, O. (2003). *They F*** You Up: How to Survive Family Life*. London: Bloomsbury.

James, O. (2007). *Affluenza—How to be Successful and Stay Sane*. London: Vermilion.

James, O. (2008). *The Selfish Capitalist*. London: Vermilion.

Jamison, K. R. (1997). *An Unquiet Mind: A Memoir of Moods and Madness*. London: Picador.

Jang, K. (2005). *The Behavioral Genetics of Psychopathology: A Clinical Guide*. Mahwah, NJ: Lawrence Erlbaum.

Joseph, J. (2003). *The Gene Illusion*. Ross-on-Wye, UK: PCCS Books.

Jung, C. G. (1934). The soul and death. In: *The Structure and Dynamics of the Psyche, C. W. 8*. London: Routledge & Kegan Paul.

Jung, C. G. (1983). *Memories, Dreams, Reflections*. London: Flamingo.

Kafka, F. (1971). In the penal colony (Trans. W. & E. Muir). In: N. Glatzer (Ed.), *The Complete Stories* (pp. 140–167). New York: Schocken Books.

Kahneman, D., & Krueger, A. (2006). Developments in the measurements of subjective well-being. *Journal of Economic Perspectives, 20:* 3–24.

Kasser, T. (2002). *The High Price of Materialism*. London: MIT Press.

Keedwell, P. (2008). *How Sadness Survived: The Evolutionary Basis of Depression*. Abingdon, UK: Radcliffe Publishing.

Keen, A. (2015). *The Internet is Not the Answer*. London: Atlantic.

Keller, M., & Nesse, R. (2005). Is low mood an adaptation? Evidence for subtypes with symptoms that match precipitants. *Journal of Affective Disorders, 86*: 27–35

Keller, M., & Nesse, R. (2006). The evolutionary significance of depressive symptoms: different adverse situations lead to different depressive symptoms. *Journal of Personality and Social Psychology, 91*: 316–330.

Keller, M., Neale, M., & Kendler, K. (2007). Association of different adverse life events with distinct patterns of depressive symptoms. *American Journal of Psychiatry, 164:* 1521–1529.

Kelly, R. (2014.) *Black Rainbow*. London: Yellow Kite.

Kendler, K., Kuhn, J., & Prescott, C. (2004). Childhood sexual abuse, stressful life events and risk for major depression in women. *Psychological Medicine, 34*: 1475–1482.

Kendler, K., Thornton, L., & Gardner, C. (2000). Stressful life events and previous episodes in the etiology of major depression in women: an evaluation of the "kindling" hypothesis. *American Journal of Psychiatry, 157*: 1243–1251.

Kendler, K. S., Kessler, R. C., Walters, E. E., MacLean, C., Neale, M. C., Heath, A. C., & Eaves, L. J. (1995). Stressful life events, genetic liability, and onset of an episode of major depression in women. *American Journal of Psychiatry, 152*: 833–842.

Kernberg, O. (1980). *Internal World and External Reality*. New York: Aronson.

Kim, D. Y., & Camilleri, M. (2000). Serotonin: a mediator of the brain-gut connection. *The American Journal of Gastroenterology, 95*: 2698–2709.

Kitanaka, J. (2011). *Depression in Japan: Psychiatric Cures for a Society in Distress*. Princeton, NJ: Princeton University Press.

Klein, N. (2008). *The Shock Doctrine: The Rise of Disaster Capitalism*. London: Allen Lane.

Kleinman, A. (2004). Culture and depression. *New England Journal of Medicine, 351*: 951–953.

Knight, S. (2015). *The Life-Changing Magic of Not Giving a F**k*. London: Quercus.

Knight, S. (2016). Drowning in commitments? It's time to stop giving a damn. *The Guardian*, 2 January, Weekend, pp. 33–37. Available at: www.theguardian.com.

Kohut, H., & Wolf, E. (1986). The disorders of the self and their treatment: an outline. In: A. Morrison (Ed.), *Essential Papers on Narcissism* (pp. 175–196). New York: New York University Press.

Konrath, S., Chopik, W., Hsing, C., & O'Brien, E. (2014). Changes in adult attachment styles in American college students over time: a meta-analysis. *Personality and Social Psychology Review, 18*: 326–348.

Konrath, S., O'Brien, E., & Hsing, C. (2011). Changes in dispositional empathy in American college students over time: a meta-analysis. *Personality and Social Psychology Review, 15*: 180–198.

Korb, A. (2015). *The Upward Spiral: Using Neuroscience to Reverse the Course of Depression, One Small Change at a Time*. Oakland, CA: New Harbinger.

Kovacs, M., & Beck, A. (1985). Maladaptive cognitive structures in depression. In: J. Coyne (Ed.), *Essential Papers on Depression* (pp. 240–258). New York: New York University Press.

Kovel, J. (1987). Schizophrenic being and technocratic society. In: D. M. Levin (Ed.), *Pathologies of the Modern Self: Postmodern Studies on Narcissism, Schizophrenia, and Depression* (pp. 330–348). New York: New York University Press.

Kunkel, B. (2014). *Utopia or Bust: A Guide to the Present Crisis*. London: Verso.

Labanyi, P. (1989). When wishing still helped: Peter Schneider's left-wing melancholy. In: K. Bullivant (Ed.), *After the Death of Literature: West German Writing of the 1970s* (pp. 313–339). Oxford, UK: Berg.

Labanyi, P. (2002). Therapy, culture and the real self. *Eisteach, 2 (22)*: 33–37.

Labanyi, P. (2008). The emotional costs of globalisation. *Eisteach, 8 (4)*: 26–29.

Labanyi, P. (2011). Paradise found: beauty, nature and the power of reverence. *Eisteach, 11 (1)*: 8–12.

Lasch, C. (1978). *The Culture of Narcissism: American Life in an Age of Diminishing Expectations*. New York: Norton.

Leader, D. (2009). *The New Black: Mourning, Melancholia and Depression*. London: Penguin.

Leahy, R., Tirch, D., & Napolitano, L. (2011). *Emotion Regulation in Psychotherapy: A Practitioner's Guide*. New York: Guilford Press.

Leavis, F. R. (1962). *The Great Tradition*. London: Penguin.

Lemann, N. (1996). Kicking in groups. *The Atlantic Online*, April. Available at: www.theatlantic.com.

Leppanen, J. (2006). Emotional processing in mood disorders: a review of behavioral and neuroimaging findings. *Current Opinion in Psychiatry, 19*: 34–39.

Lessem, P. (2005). *Self Psychology: An Introduction*. Lanham, MD: Jason Aronson.

Levin, D. M. (1987a). Psychopathology in the epoch of nihilism. In: D. M. Levin (Ed.), *Pathologies of the Modern Self: Postmodern Studies on Narcissism, Schizophrenia, and Depression* (pp. 21–83). New York: New York University Press.

Levin, D. M. (1987b). Clinical stories: a modern self in the fury of being. In: D. M. Levin (Ed.), *Pathologies of the Modern Self: Postmodern Studies on Narcissism, Schizophrenia, and Depression* (pp. 479–537). New York: New York University Press.

Levin, D. M. (1988). *The Opening of Vision: Nihilism and the Postmodern Situation*. London: Routledge.

Lewis, C. S. (2013). *A Grief Observed*. London: Faber & Faber.

Lewis, G. (2002). *Sunbathing in the Rain: A Cheerful Book about Depression*. London: Flamingo.

Liedloff, J. (2004). *The Continuum Concept: In Search of Happiness Lost.* London: Penguin.

Loudon, M. (1996). Blocking the writer. In: S. Dunn, B. Morrison, & M. Roberts (Eds.), *Mind Readings: Writers Journeys through Mental States* (pp. 65–73). London: Minerva.

Louis de Canonville, C. (2015). *The Three Faces of Evil: Unmasking the Full Spectrum of Narcissistic Abuse.* Stouffville, ON: Black Card.

Lowry, C., Hollis, J., de Vries, A., Pan, B., Brunet, L., Hunt, J. Paton, J., van Kampen, E., Knight, D., & Evans, A. (2007). Identification of an immune-responsive mesolimbocortical serotonergic system: potential role in regulation of emotional behaviour. *Neuroscience, 146*: 756–772.

Lucassen, P., Meerlo, P., Naylor, A. S., van Dam, A. M., Dayer, A. G., Czeh, B., & Oomen, C. (2009). Do depression, stress, sleep disruption, and inflammation alter hippocampal apoptosis and neurogenesis? In: C. Pariante, R. Nesse, D. Nutt, & L. Wolpert (Eds.), *Understanding Depression: A Translational Approach* (pp. 139–156). Oxford, UK: OUP.

Lyons-Ruth, K. (1992). Maternal depressive symptoms, disorganised infant–mother attachments and hostile-aggressive behaviour in the preschool classroom: a prospective longitudinal view from infancy to age five. *Rochester Symposium on Developmental Psychopathology, 4*: 131–171.

Mabey, R. (2006). *Nature Cure.* London: Pimlico.

Macfarlane, R. (2016). Generation Anthropocene: how humans have altered the planet forever. *The Guardian*, 1 April. Available at: www.theguardian.com.

MacLeod, S. (1996). The art of starvation. In: S. Dunn, B. Morrison, & M. Roberts (Eds.), *Mind Readings: Writers' Journeys Through Mental States* (pp. 74–90). London: Minerva.

MacPherson, H., Richmond, S., Bland, M., Brealey, S., Gabe, R., Hopton, A., Keding, A., Lansdown, H., Perren, S., Sculpher, M., Spackman, E., Torgerson, D., & Watt, I. (2013). Acupuncture and counselling for depression in primary care: a randomised controlled trial. *PLOS Medicine, 10*: e1001518.

Maier, S., Amat, J., Baratta, M., Bland, S., Christianson, J., Thompson, B., Rozeske, R., & Watkins, L. (2009). The role of the medial prefrontal cortex in mediating resistance and vulnerability to the impact of adverse events. In: C. Pariante, R. Nesse, D. Nutt, & L. Wolpert (Eds.), *Understanding Depression: A Translational Approach* (pp. 157–170). Oxford, UK: OUP.

Malkin, C. (2015). *Rethinking Narcissism: The Bad—and Surprisingly Good—About Feeling Special.* New York: HarperCollins.

Mangen, A., & Kuiken, D. (2014). Lost in an iPad: narrative engagement on paper and tablet. *Scientific Study of Literature, 4*: 150–177.

Manning, M. (1994). *Undercurrents: A Life Beneath the Surface*. New York: HarperCollins.
Martin, L. (2008). *Woman on the Verge of a Nervous Breakdown*. London: John Murray.
Martin, L., Neighbors, H., & Griffith, D. (2013). The experience of symptoms of depression in men vs women. *JAMA Psychiatry, 70*: 1100–1106.
Maslow, A. (1943). A theory of human motivation. *Psychological Review, 50*: 370–396.
Matthews, D., & Jenks, S. (2013). Ingestion of *Mycobacterium vaccae* decreases anxiety-related behaviour and improves learning in mice. *Behavioural Processes, 96*: 27–35.
Max-Neef, M. (1992). Development and human needs. In: P. Ekins & M. Max-Neef (Eds.), *Real-Life Economics: Understanding Wealth Creation* (pp. 197–213). London: Routledge.
McEvoy, M. (2011). *How the Light Gets In*. Dublin: Hachette.
McGilchrist, I. (1995). It's not so much thinking out what to do, it's the doing of it that sticks me. *London Review of Books, 17*: 28–31. Available at: www.lrb.co.uk.
McGilchrist, I. (2010). *The Master and His Emissary: the Divided Brain and the Making of the Western World*. New Haven, CT: Yale University Press.
McGowan, P., Sasaki, A., D'Alessio, A., Dymov, S., Labonté, B., Szyf, M., Turecki, G., & Meaney, M. (2009). Epigenetic regulation of the glucocorticoid receptor in human brain associates with childhood abuse. *Nature Neuroscience, 12*: 342–348.
McGowan, P., Suderman, M., Sasaki, A., Huang, T., Hallett, M., Meaney, M., & Szyf, M. (2011). Broad epigenetic signature of maternal care in the brain of adult rats. *PLoS One*, 6: e14739.
McKibbin, D. (2007). Ecopsychology and the greening of psychotherapy. *Eisteach, 7 (3)*: 9–13.
McLaren, K. (2015). Ingenious stagnation. In: T. Simon (Ed.), *Darkness Before Dawn: Redefining the Journey through Depression* (pp. 25–33). Boulder, CO: Sounds True.
Mearns, D., & Cooper, M. (2005). *Working at Relational Depth in Counselling and Psychotherapy*. London: Sage.
Mearns, D., & Thorne, B. (2000). *Person-Centred Therapy Today*. London: Sage.
Merkin, D. (2009). A journey through darkness. *New York Times*, 10 May. Available at: www.nytimes.com.
Merkin, D. (2010). My life in therapy. *New York Times*, 4 August. Available at: www.nytimes.com.
Merritt, S. (2009). *The Devil Within*. London: Vermilion.
Messud, C. (2006). *The Emperor's Children*. London: Picador.

Midgley, M. (2011). *The Myths We Live By*. London: Routledge Classics.
Miller, A. (1986). Depression and grandiosity as related forms of narcissistic disturbances. In: A. Morrison (Ed.), *Essential Papers on Narcissism* (pp. 323–347). New York: New York University Press.
Miller, A., Pace, T., & Raison, C. (2009). Neuropsychiatric effects of IFN-alpha: relevance to depression. In: C. Pariante, R. Nesse, D. Nutt, & L. Wolpert (Eds.), *Understanding Depression: A Translational Approach* (pp. 223–236). Oxford, UK: OUP.
Monbiot, G. (2016). *How Did We Get into This Mess?* London: Verso.
Monroe, S., & Harkness, K. (2005). Life stress, the "kindling" hypothesis, and the recurrence of depression: considerations from a life stress perspective. *Psychological Review, 112*: 417–445.
Moore, M., & Fresco, D. (2012). Depressive realism: a meta-analytic review. *Clinical Psychology Review, 32*: 497–509.
Moore, T. (1992). *Care of the Soul: How to Add Depth and Meaning to Your Everyday life*. London: Piatkus.
Murakami, H. (2008). *After Dark* (Trans. J. Rubin). London: Vintage.
Murdoch, I. (1997). *Existentialists and Mystics*. New York: Allen Lane.
Murphy, S. (2013). Mood swings: beyond the serotonin hypothesis of depression. *New Scientist, 219*: 34–37.
Myerson, G. (2003). Heidegger, Habermas and the mobile phone. In: R. Appignanesi (Ed.), *The End of Everything: Postmodernism and the Vanishing of the Human* (pp. 139–187). Duxford, UK: Icon.
Nesse, R. (2009). Explaining depression: neuroscience is not enough, evolution is essential. In: C. Pariante, R. Nesse, D. Nutt, & L. Wolpert (Eds.), *Understanding Depression: A Translational Approach* (pp. 17–35). Oxford, UK: OUP.
Nichols, M. (2013). *Family Therapy: Concepts and Methods* (10th edn). Boston, MA: Pearson.
O'Malley, S. (2015). *Cotton Wool Kids: What's Making Irish Parents Paranoid?* Cork, Ireland: Mercier Press.
Panksepp, J. (2010). Affective neuroscience of the emotional brainmind: evolutionary perspectives and implications for understanding depression. *Dialogues in Clinical Neuroscience, 12*: 533–545.
Panksepp, J. (2011). The basic emotional circuits of mammalian brains: do animals have affective lives? *Neuroscience and Biobehavioral Reviews, 35*: 1791–1804.
Pavlov, S., Korenyok, V., Reva, N., Tumyalis, A., Loktev, K., & Aftanas, L. (2014). Effects of long-term meditation practice on attentional biases towards emotional faces: an eye-tracking study. *Cognition and Emotion, 29*: 1–9.
Pearmain, R. (2001). *The Heart of Listening: Attentional Qualities in Psychotherapy*. London: Continuum.

Pearson, H. (2016). *The Life Project: the Extraordinary Story of our Ordinary Lives*. Berkeley, CA: Counterpoint.

Pedulla, T. (2016). Depression: finding a way in, finding a way out. In: C. Germer, R. Siegel, & P. Fulton (Eds.), *Mindfulness and Psychotherapy* (pp. 148–166). New York: Guilford Press.

Petherbridge, D. (2013). *The Critical Theory of Axel Honneth*. Lanham, MD: Lexington.

Phillips, A. (1988). *Winnicott*. London: Fontana.

Pick, A. (2015). Auschwitz, truth and memory. *The Guardian*, 27 June. Available at: www.theguardian.com.

Piet, J., & Hougaard, E. (2011). The effect of mindfulness-based cognitive therapy for prevention of relapse in recurrent major depressive disorder: a systematic review and meta-analysis. *Clinical Psychology Review, 31*: 1032–1040.

Pinniger, R., Brown, R., Thorsteinsson, E., & McKinley, P. (2012). Argentine tango dance compared to mindfulness meditation and a waiting-list control: a randomised trial for treating depression. *Complementary Therapies in Medicine, 20*: 377–384.

Pippin, R. (2001). *Henry James and Modern Moral Life*. Cambridge, UK: CUP.

Piver, S. (2015). The sadness in bliss. In: T. Simon (Ed.), *Darkness Before Dawn: Redefining the Journey Through Depression* (pp. 113–120). Boulder, CO: Sounds True.

Plath, S. (1999). *The Bell Jar*. London: Faber & Faber.

Plomin, R., DeFries, J., Knopik, V., & Neiderhiser, J. (2013.) *Behavioral Genetics* (6th edn). New York: Worth.

Pollard, J. (2005). The value of attachment theory in understanding how psychotherapy works. In: J. Ryan (Ed.), *How Does Psychotherapy Work?* (pp. 187–211). London: Karnac.

Proust, M. (1992). *In Search of Lost Time, Vol VI: Time Regained* (Trans. A. Mayor & T. Kilmartin, revised by D. J. Enright). London: Vintage.

Putnam, R. (2000). *Bowling Alone: the Collapse and Revival of America Community*. New York: Simon & Schuster.

Radloff (1985). Risk factors for depression: what do we learn from them? In: J. Coyne (Ed.), *Essential Papers on Depression* (pp. 403–420). New York: New York University Press.

Randolph, J., & Dykman, B. (1998). Perceptions of parenting and depression-proneness in the offspring: dysfunctional attitudes as a mediating mechanism. *Cognitive Therapy and Research, 22*: 377–400.

Rholes, W., Riskind, J., & Neville, B. (1985). The relationship of cognitions and hopelessness to depression and anxiety. *Social Cognition, 3*: 36–50.

Rice-Oxley, M. (2012). *Underneath the Lemon Tree: A Memoir of Depression and Recovery*. London: Little, Brown.

Roemer, L., & Orsillo, S. (2016). Anxiety: accepting what comes and doing what matters. In: C. Germer, R. Siegel, & P. Fulton (Eds.), *Mindfulness and Psychotherapy* (pp. 167–183). New York: Guilford Press.

Rogers, C. (1967). *On Becoming a Person: A Therapist's View of Psychotherapy*. London: Constable.

Rosa, H. (2015). *Social Acceleration: A New Theory of Modernity* (Trans. J. Trejo-mathys). New York: Columbia University Press.

Roszak, T. (1993). *The Voice of the Earth: An Exploration of Ecopsychology*. New York: Touchstone.

Rothschild, B. (2000). *The Body Remembers: The Psychophysiology of Trauma and Trauma Interventions*. New York: W. W. Norton.

Rottenberg, J. (2014). *The Depths: The Evolutionary Origins of the Depression Epidemic*. New York: Basic.

Rowan, J. (1990). *Subpersonalities*. London: Routledge.

Rowe, D. (2003). *Depression: The Way Out of Your Prison* (3rd edn). Hove, UK: Brunner-Routledge.

Rowson, J., & McGilchrist, I. (2017). Divided brain, divided world. In: R. Tweedy (Ed.), *The Political Self: Understanding the Social Context for Mental Illness* (pp. 87–113). London: Karnac.

Runciman, D. (2016). Review of *Homo Deus: A Brief History of Tomorrow* by Yuval Noah Harari. *The Guardian*, 27 August. Available at: www.theguardian.com.

Rustin, M., & Rustin, M. (2009). States of narcissism. In: E. McGinley & A. Varchevker (Eds.), *Enduring Loss: Mourning, Depression and Narcissism Through the Life Cycle* (pp. 209–234). London: Karnac.

Sakamoto, S. (1999). A longitudinal study of the relationship of self-preoccupation with depression. *Journal of Clinical Psychology*, *55*: 109–116.

Salecl, R. (2004). *On Anxiety*. London: Routledge.

Salecl, R. (2010). *Choice*. London: Profile.

Salter, J. (2008). *Solo Faces*. London: Penguin.

Sass, L. (1992). *Madness and Modernism: Insanity in the Light of Modern Art, Literature and Thought*. Cambridge, MA: Harvard University Press.

Schor, J. (2004). *Born to Buy: The Commercialised Child and the New Consumer Culture*. New York: Scribner.

Schore, A. (1996). *Affect Regulation and the Origins of Self: The Neurobiology of Emotional Development*. New Jersey: Lawrence Erlbaum.

Schore, A. (2003a). *Affect Regulation and the Repair of the Self*. New York: W. W. Norton.

Schore, A. (2003b). *Affect Dysregulation and Disorders of the Self*. New York: W. W. Norton.

Schore, A. (2010). The right brain implicit self: a central mechanism of the psychotherapy change process. In: J. Petrucelli (Ed.), *Knowing,*

Not-Knowing and Sort-of-Knowing: Psychoanalysis and the Experience of Uncertainty (pp. 177–202). London: Karnac.
Scott, L. (2015). *The Four-Dimensional Human: Ways of Being in the Digital World*. London: William Heinemann.
Scruton, R. (2011). *Beauty: A Very Short Introduction*. Oxford, UK: OUP.
Seigel, J. (2005). *The Idea of the Self: Thought and Experience in Western Europe Since the Seventeenth Century*. Cambridge, UK: CUP.
Siegel, D. (2010). *The Mindful Therapist: A Clinician's Guide to Mindsight and Neural Integration*. New York: W. W. Norton.
Siegel, D. (2012). *The Developing Mind: How Relationships and the Brain Interact to Shape Who We Are* (2nd edn). New York: Guilford Press.
Simon, T. (Ed.) (2015). *Darkness Before Dawn: Redefining the Journey Through Depression*. Boulder, CO: Sounds True.
Skidelsky, R., & Skidelsky, E. (2012). *How Much is Enough?* London: Penguin.
Slater, L. (1999). *Prozac Diary*. New York: Penguin.
Smith, Z. (2013). *N.W.* London: Penguin.
Solms, M. (2012). Depression: a neuropsychoanalytic perspective. *International Forum of Psychoanalysis, 21*: 207–213.
Solms, M., & Panksepp, J. (2010). Why depression feels bad. In: E. Perry, D. Collerton, F. leBeau, & H. Ashton (Eds.), *New Horizons in the Neuroscience of Consciousness* (pp. 169–178). Amsterdam: John Benjamins.
Solomon, A. (2014). *The Noonday Demon: an Anatomy of Depression*. London: Vintage.
Spector, T. (2012). *Identically Different: Why You Can Change your Genes*. London: Weidenfeld & Nicolson.
Sroufe, A., Egeland, B., Carlson, E., & Collins, A. (2009). *The Development of the Person: The Minnesota Study of Risk and Adaptation from Birth to Adulthood*. New York: Guilford.
Staunton, T. (2008). Psychotherapy in a time of narcissism. *Eisteach*, 8(4): 15–18.
Stern, D. (2003). *The Interpersonal World of the Infant: A view from Psychoanalysis and Developmental Theory*. London: Karnac.
Stern, D. (2014). Vitality contours: the temporal contour of feelings as the basic unit for constructing the infant's social experience. In: P. Rochat (Ed.), *Early Social Cognition: Understanding Others in the First Months of Life* (pp. 67–80). Hove, UK: Psychology Press.
Stevens, A. (1997). *The Two Million-Year-Old Self*. New York: Fromm International Publishing Corporation.
Storr, A. (1989). *Solitude*. London: Flamingo.
Styron, W. (1992). *Darkness Visible*. London: Picador.
Sun, H., Kennedy, P., & Nestler, E. (2013). Epigenetics of the depressed brain: role of histone acetylation and methylation. *Neuropsychopharmacology, 38*: 124–137.

Taylor, C. (1989). *Sources of the Self: The Making of the Modern Identity*. Cambridge, UK: CUP.
Thompson, T. (1995). *The Beast: A Reckoning with Depression*. New York: G.P. Putnam's Sons.
Totton, N. (2005). Embodied-relational therapy. In: N. Totton (Ed.), *New Dimensions in Body Psychotherapy* (pp. 168–181). Maidenhead, UK: OUP.
Trivedi, M., Morris, D., Pan, J., Grannemann, B., & Rush, A. (2005). What moderator characteristics are associated with better prognosis for depression? *Neuropsychiatric Disease and Treatment, 1*: 51–57.
Tronick, E., Als, H., Adamson, L., Wise, S., & Brazelton, T. (1978). The infant's response to entrapment between contradictory messages in face-to-face interaction. *Journal of the American Academy of Child and Adolescent Psychiatry, 17*: 1–13.
Tronick, E. & Beeghly, M. (2011). Infants' meaning-making and the development of mental health problems. *American Psychologist, 66*: 107–119.
Tronick, E., Bruschweiler-Stern, N., Harrison, A., Lyons-Ruth, K., Morgan, A., Nahum, J., Sander, L., & Stern, D. (1998). Dyadically expanded states of consciousness and the process of therapeutic change. *Infant Mental Health Journal, 19*: 290–299.
Tucker, E. (2016). Tea and apathy. *The Guardian*, 27 February, Weekend, pp. 43–45. Available at: www.theguradian.com.
Turkle, S. (2011). *Alone Together: Why We Expect More from Technology and Less from Each Other*. New York: Basic.
Tweedy, R. (Ed.) (2017). *The Political Self: Understanding the Social Context for Mental Illness*. London: Karnac.
Twenge, J. (1997). Changes in masculine and feminine traits over time: a meta-analysis. *Sex Roles, 36*: 305–325.
Twenge, J. (2000). The age of anxiety? The birth cohort change in anxiety and neuroticism, 1952–1993. *Journal of Personality and Social Psychology, 79*: 1007–1021.
Twenge, J. (2014). *Generation Me: Why Today's Young Americans are More Confident, Assertive, Entitled – and More Miserable Than Ever Before* (revised and updated edn). New York: Atria.
Twenge, J., & Campbell, W. (2001). Age and birth cohort differences in self-esteem: a cross-temporal meta-analysis. *Personality and Social Psychology Review, 5*: 321–344.
Twenge, J., & Campbell, W. (2008). Increases in positive self-views among high school students: birth cohort changes in anticipated performance, self-satisfaction, self-liking, and self-competence. *Psychological Science, 19*: 1082–1086.
Twenge, J., & Campbell, W. (2009). *The Narcissism Epidemic: Living in an Age of Entitlement*. New York: Free Press.

Twenge, J., & Foster, J. (2008). Mapping the scale of the narcissism epidemic: increases in narcissism 2002-2007 within ethnic groups. *Journal of Research in Personality, 42*: 1619–1622.

Twenge, J., & Foster, J. (2010). Birth cohort increases in narcissistic personality traits among American college students 1982–2009. *Social Psychological and Personality Science, 1*: 99–106.

Twenge, J., Gentile, B., DeWall, C., Ma, D., Lacefield, K., & Schurtz, D. (2010). Birth cohort increases in psychopathology among young Americans, 1938–2007: A cross-temporal meta-analysis of the MMPI. *Clinical Psychology Review, 30*: 145–154.

Twenge, J., Konrath, S., Foster, J., Campbell, W., & Bushman, B. (2008). Egos inflating over time: a cross-temporal meta-analysis of the Narcissistic Personality Inventory. *Journal of Personality, 76*: 875–902; discussion, 903–918.

Vargas Llosa, M. (2015). *Notes on the Death of Culture* (Trans. J. King). London: Faber & Faber.

Verhaeghe, P. (2008). A combination that has to fail: new patients, old therapists. *Eisteach, 8 (4)*: 4–8.

Verhaeghe, P. (2014). *What About Me? The Struggle for Identity in a Market-based Society* (Trans. J. Hedley-Prôle). Melbourne: Scribe.

Waal, F. de (2013). *The Bonobo and the Atheist: In Search of Humanism Among the Primates*. New York: W. W. Norton.

Wade, T., & Kendler, K. (2000). The relationship between social support and major depression: cross-sectional, longitudinal and genetic perspectives. *The Journal of Nervous and Mental Disease, 188*: 251–258.

Walch, J., Rabin, B., Day, R., Williams, J., Choi, K., & Kang, J. (2005). The effect of sunlight on post-operative analgesic medication use: a prospective study of patients undergoing spinal surgery. *Psychosomatic Medicine, 67*: 156–163.

Waldinger, R., Cohen, S., Schulz, M., & Crowell, J. (2015). Security of attachment to spouses in late life: concurrent and prospective links with cognitive and emotional well-being. *Clinical Psychological Science, 3*: 516–529.

Ward, G. (2014). *Unbelievable: Why We Believe and Why We Don't*. London: I. B. Tauris.

Watt, D., & Panksepp, J. (2009). Depression: an evolutionarily conserved mechanism to terminate separation distress? A review of aminergic, peptidergic, and neural network perspectives. *Neuropsychoanalysis, 11*: 7–51.

Watters, E. (2006). DNA is not destiny: the new science of epigenetics. *Discover Magazine, Vol. 27*, 22 November. Available at: www.discovermagazine.com.

Wax, R. (2014). *Sane New World: Taming the Mind*. London: Hodder & Stoughton.

Weaver, I., Cervoni, N., Champagne, F., D'Alessio, A., Sharma, S., Seckl, J., Dymov, S., Szyf, M., & Meaney, M. (2004). Epigenetic programming by maternal behaviour. *Nature Neuroscience, 7*: 847–854.

Weiss, R. (1982). Attachment in adult life. In: C. M. Parkes & J. Stevenson-Hinde (Eds.), *The Place of Attachment in Human Behavior* (pp. 171–194). New York: Basic.

Werner, E. (1993). Risk, resilience, and recovery: perspectives from the Kauai longitudinal study. *Development and Psychopathology, 5*: 503–515.

West, M. (2016). *Into the Darkest Places: Early Relational Trauma and Borderline States of Mind*. London: Karnac.

Whippman, R. (2016). *The Pursuit of Happiness and Why It's Making Us Anxious*. London: Hutchinson.

Whyte, J. (2013). *Catastrophe and Redemption: The Political Thought of Giorgio Agamben*. New York: SUNY Press.

Wiebking, C., Bauer, A., de Greck, M., Duncan, N., Tempelmann, C., & Northoff, G. (2010). Abnormal body perception and neural activity in the insula in depression: an fMRI study of the depressed "material me". *World Journal of Biological Psychiatry, 11*: 538–549.

Wiech, K., & Tracey, I. (2009). The influence of negative emotions on pain: behavioral effects and neural mechanisms. *Neuroimage, 47*: 987–994.

Wilber, K. (2000). *Integral Psychology: Consciousness, Spirit, Psychology, Therapy*. Boston: Shambhala.

Wilkinson, R. (2005). *The Impact of Inequality: How to Make Sick Societies Healthier*. London: Routledge.

Wilkinson, R., & Pickett, K. (2010). *The Spirit Level: Why Equality is Better for Everyone*. London: Penguin.

Williams, Z. (2015). A force to be reckoned with. *The Guardian*, Review, p. 11, 19 December. Available at: www.theguardian.com.

Wilson, E. O. (1984). *Biophilia*. Cambridge, MA: Harvard University Press.

Wilson, K. (2015). Sentimental nihilism and popular culture. *Standpoint Magazine*, July/August. Available at: www.standpointmag.co.uk.

Winnicott, D. W. (1989). *Playing and Reality*. New York: Routledge.

Winnicott, D. W. (1990). *The Maturational Processes and the Facilitating Environment*. London: Karnac.

Wolf, M. (1998). An interview with Catherine Ingram. *Koorddanser Journal* (Amsterdam), October. www.dialogueswithcatherine.com/amsterdam/.

Wolpert, L. (1999). *Malignant Sadness: the Anatomy of Depression*. London: Faber & Faber.

Wolpert, L. (2009). Experiencing depression. In: C. Pariante, R. Nesse, D. Nutt & L. Wolpert (Eds.), *Understanding Depression: A Translational Approach* (pp. 1–5). Oxford, UK: OUP.
Wurtzel, E. (1996). *Prozac Nation: Young and Depressed in America*. London: Quartet.
Yalom, I. (1980). *Existential Psychotherapy*. New York: Basic.
Yehuda, R., Daskalakis, N., Bierer, L., Bader, H., Klengel, T., Holsboer, F., & Binder, E. (2016). Holocaust exposure induced intergenerational effects on FKBP5 methylation. *Biological Psychiatry, 80*: 372–380.
Yehuda, R., Engel, S., Brand, S., Seckl, J., Marcus, S., & Berkowitz, G. (2005). Transgenerational effects of posttraumatic stress disorder in babies of mothers exposed to the World Trade Center attacks during pregnancy. *The Journal of Clinical Endocrinology and Metabolism, 90*: 4115–4118.
Yellin, J., & White, K. (2012). *Shattered States: Disorganized Attachment and its Repair*. London: Karnac.
Young, E. (2009). PTSD and HPA axis: same hormones, different disorders. In: C. Pariante, R. Nesse, D. Nutt & L. Wolpert (Eds.), *Understanding Depression: A Translational Approach* (pp. 193–212). Oxford, UK: OUP.
Young, S. (2007). How to increase serotonin in the human brain. *Review of Psychiatric Neuroscience, 32*: 394–396.
Zhang, T-Y., & Meaney, M. (2010). Epigenetics and the environmental regulation of the genome and its function. *Annual Review of Psychology, 61*: 439–466.
Zhang, T-Y., Bagot, R., Parent, C., Nesbitt, C., Bredy, T., Caldji, C., Fish, E., Anisman, H., Szyf, M., & Meaney, M. (2006). Maternal programming of defensive responses through sustained effects on gene expression. *Biological Psychiatry, 73*: 72–89.
Žižek, S. (2011). *Living in the End Times*. London: Verso.

Web Resources

http://www.alastairmcintosh.com/general/resources/2007-Max-Neef-Fundamental-Needs.pdf, last accessed 9 February 2017.
Everyday Health, 2013, www.everydayhealth.com, last accessed 11 February 2017.
www.healthline.com, last accessed 20 October 2016.
www.heavy.com/news, last accessed 22 October 2016.
www.ted.com, Robert Waldinger posted 23 December 2015.
World Health Organization (2012) *Mental Health: Depression*. Retrieved from http://www.who.int/topics/depression/en/.

INDEX

Dr Laurence Errington

Note: Names appearing in the index are of memoir writers and various other persons excluding academics, researchers and theorists with the exception of the historical figures of Freud, Klein and Jung.

For Product Safety Concerns and Information please contact our EU
representative GPSR@taylorandfrancis.com
Taylor & Francis Verlag GmbH, Kaufingerstraße 24, 80331 München, Germany

www.ingramcontent.com/pod-product-compliance
Ingram Content Group UK Ltd.
Pitfield, Milton Keynes, MK11 3LW, UK
UKHW022349190926
475702UK00015B/2187
* 9 7 8 1 7 8 2 2 0 5 9 0 6 *